HOSPITALITY BRAND MANAGEMENT

HOSPITALITY BRAND MANAGEMENT

Sanjeev Srivastava

ABD PUBLISHERS
Jaipur ■ New Delhi

ABD PUBLISHERS

Regd. Off. "Bony Residency", Gate No. 2
Opp. Tilak Public School, Vishweswariya Nagar,
Gopalpura Road, Jaipur - 302018, India
Ph: 0141 - 2761280, Telefax: 2761381
Email: abdpublishersjpr@gmail.com

Delhi Office: 102, 1st Floor, Satyam House,
4327/3, Ansari Road, Darya Ganj,
New Delhi - 110002, India
Ph: 011-45652440

visit us: www.oxfordbookcompany.com

Distributed By
KEYA INTERNATIONAL PRESS LLP
E-mail: keyainternationalpressllp@gmail.com

Published in India, 2023

ISBN: 9788183767255

Typeset by Shivangi Computer, Jaipur

Printed and bound in India by Thomson Press Ltd.,
New Delhi

Contents

Preface

Executives from fast moving consumer goods companies have been attracted to the hospitality and leisure industry by the opportunity to transform businesses perceived as lagging behind in terms of brand development and innovation. Despite similarities between the hospitality and consumer goods sectors, those we spoke to referred to a marked distinction between how the sectors currently operate and future opportunities for growth. Asia Pacific, especially China, is expected to produce massive growth, as is Europe – still a fragmented sector due to the proliferation of family owned companies. Executives warn that businesses will have to decide whether they are top or bottom end niche players, since the middle ground is becoming increasingly commoditised with less room for growth. The Internet has had a significant impact on what is otherwise still a fairly conservative industry, bringing more choice for consumers and affecting the marketing model. The sector currently tends to lack sophistication in consumer insight, innovation and marketing. More emphasis is needed on creating strategies based on consumer data and research to determine consumer needs and behaviour. With a shortage of talent in the sector, more resources need to be invested in developing existing people. Nevertheless, the industry will continue to bring in talent from outside and address the relatively low levels of compensation. As the sector matures, attracting great talent, particularly in marketing, should become easier. Over the past decade, the hotel industry has exploded with new brands and concepts; therefore, navigating the course of franchise affiliation demands effective choices and decisions.

In recent years, many hospitality, hotel and restaurant firms have realized the strategic importance of co-branding . Particularly, some hotels face with diminished marginal profit from F & B. International hotels have started to utilize co-branding applications and strategies, such as making alliance with a prominent restaurant chain, to decrease these problems. Strategic management of branding in the hospitality sector is very critical, given that firms in the hospitality sector are involved in a competitive tourism market and hence deals with strong rivals . Companies in the hospitality sector (hotels, restaurants, etc.) prioritize research based branding to a specific customer target group in order to consolidate an outstanding corporate identity and service quality. They aim to distinguish their brand image and differentiate their product or service among the competitors by adopting particular brand strategies since identifying a target customer base and understanding their needs and preferences are of primary significance for hospitality firms.

Customers of hospitality firms usually give importance to image, quality and prestige of the services or products in their decision making processes. The achievement of a distinguished designation necessitates utilizing research based and strategic branding techniques and suggestions. One major branding strategy particularly for international firms is co-branding .Nevertheless, there are scarce studies which examine the role of strategic co-brand management in the hospitality sector. This review paper aims to critically discuss the current position of strategic co-branding in the hospitality sector and possible problems involved in this issue. Recommendations for future research on co-branding of hospitality firms within the strategic management paradigm are provided. Furthermore, managers in the hospitality sector are given suggestions for enhancing strategic management of co-branding in hospitality and particularly in destination firms.

The primary aim of writing this book on this subject is to present the subject matter in a concise and an intelligible form, keeping in view the needs of the average student.

— Sanjeev Srivastava

1

Hospitality Management Systems

Hospitality and Tourism Management (HTM) is a multidisciplinary field of study with the purpose of preparing people with the expertise, commitment, and skills for management, marketing, and operations positions in the expanding industry that provides food, accommodations, and tourism services to people away from home. As a field of study, Hospitality and Tourism Management is interdisciplinary. It draws upon a wide range of basic disciplines to provide the fundamental knowledge and skills that are required to fulfill the diverse demands placed upon individuals in management positions within the hospitality industry.

Tourism and Hospitality

Tourism and Hospitality in India

As per the Travel and Tourism Competitiveness Report 2009 by the World Economic Forum, India is ranked 11th in the Asia Pacific region and 62nd overall, moving up three places on the list of the world's attractive destinations. It is ranked the 14th best tourist destination for its natural resources and 24th for its cultural resources, with many World Heritage sites, both natural and cultural, rich fauna, and strong creative industries in the country. India also bagged 37th rank for its air transport network. The India travel and tourism industry ranked 5th in the long-term (10-year) growth and is expected to be the second largest employer in the world by 2019.

India has been ranked the "best country brand for value-for-money" in the Country Brand Index (CBI) survey conducted by FutureBrand, a leading global brand consultancy.

India also claimed the second place in CBI's "best country brand for history", as well as appears among the top 5 in the best country brand for authenticity and art & culture, and the fourth best new country for business. India made it to the list of "rising stars" or the countries that are likely to become major tourist destinations in the next five years, led by the United Arab Emirates, China, and Vietnam.

Contribution to the Economy

According to the Travel & Tourism Competitiveness Report 2009 brought out by the World Economic Forum, the contribution of travel and tourism to gross domestic product (GDP) is expected to be at US$ 187.3 billion by 2019.

The report also states that real GDP growth for travel and tourism economy is expected to achieve an average of 7.7 per cent per annum over the next 10 years.

Export earnings from international visitors and tourism goods are expected to generate US$ 51.4 billion (nominal terms) by 2019. The travel and tourism sector which accounted for 6.4 per cent of total employment in 2009 is expected to generate 40,037,000 jobs i.e. 7.2 per cent of total employment by 2019.

Foreign Tourist Arrivals

Estimates of foreign tourist arrivals (FTAs) and foreign exchange earnings (FEE) are important indicators of the tourism sector. According to the latest data released by the Ministry of Tourism, FTAs during January 2010 were 491,000 as compared to 422,000 in January 2009, an increase of 16.4 per cent. FEE in US$ terms during January 2010 were US$ 1.21 billion as compared to US$ 941 million in January 2009, a growth of 29.1 per cent.

Moreover, to give a further boost to the tourist arrivals, the Indian Association of Tour Operators (IATO) has drawn up plans to hold roadshows in the US, UK, European Union nations and Australia in 2010 to hard sell India as a tourist hub.

Government Initiative

The campaign 'Visit India Year 2009' was launched at the International Tourism Exchange in Berlin, aimed to project India as an attractive destination for holidaymakers. The government joined hands with leading airlines, hoteliers, holiday resorts and tour operators, and offered them a wide range of incentives and bonuses during the period between April and December, 2009.

Euromonitor International's Travel And Tourism in India report states that the Government of India increased spend on advertising campaigns (including for the campaigns 'Incredible India' and 'Ahithi Devo Bhava'-Visitors are like God) to reinforce the rich variety of tourism in India.

The ministry promoted India as a safe tourist destination and undertook various measures, such as stepping up vigilance in key cities and at historically important tourist sites. It also deployed increased manpower and resources for improving security checks at key airports and railway stations.

Medical Tourism

Despite the economic slowdown, medical tourism in India is the fastest growing segment of tourism industry, according to the market research report "Booming Medical Tourism in India". The report adds that India offers a great potential in the medical tourism industry. Factors such as low cost, scale and range of treatments provided in the country add to its attractiveness as a medical tourism destination.

In addition to the existence of modern medicine, indigenous medical practitioners are providing their services across the country with more than 3,000 hospitals and 726,000 registered practitioners catering to the needs of traditional Indian healthcare. A number of Indian hotels will tie up with professional organisations in a range of wellness fields to enter the wellness services market.

According to a report by RNCOS, medical tourism will grow at a CAGR of over 27 per cent in the period 2009–12 to generate revenues worth US$ 2.1 billion by 2012. The number of medical tourists is anticipated to grow at a CAGR of over 19 per cent to reach 1.1 million by 2012. The report adds that India's share in the global medical tourism industry will climb to around 2.4 per cent by the end of 2012.

Hospitality

The Indian hotel industry is adding over 90,000 more rooms across the country in the next five years to meet the demand. The contribution of the hotel industry to the country's GDP was 6.1 per cent in 2008-09.

- Carlson Group, the global hospitality chain, is bringing its luxury hotel brand Regent to India and has signed an agreement with real estate firm, Pioneer Urban Land and Infrastructure, which will invest US$ 49.97 million for building the first Regent hotel in Gurgaon that will open in 2013.
- The Leela plans to open six more properties by 2013, taking the total number of hotels to 12.
- ITC Ltd expects to add 8-10 hotels in India in the next 3-5 years to the existing 110 that it currently operates.
- The Thailand-based hospitality major, Amari, plans to foray into the Indian market by setting up seven four-star hotels near major airports in the country.

The Road Ahead

According to the latest Tourism Satellite Accounting (TSA) research, released by the World Travel and Tourism Council (WTTC) and its strategic partner Oxford Economics in March 2009:

- The demand for travel and tourism in India is expected to grow by 8.2 per cent between 2010 and 2019 and will place India at the third position in the world.
- India's travel and tourism sector is expected to be the second largest employer in the world, employing 40,037,000 by 2019.
- Capital investment in India's travel and tourism sector is expected to grow at 8.8 per cent between 2010 and 2019.

- The report forecasts India to get capital investment worth US$ 94.5 billion in the travel and tourism sector in 2019.
- India is projected to become the fifth fastest growing business travel destination from 2010-2019 with an estimated real growth rate of 7.6 per cent.
- Preparing for the 2010 Commonwealth Games in Delhi, the Tourism Ministry is exploring the provision of tented accommodation to tourists in Faridabad and Surajkund in nearby Haryana.

According to *World Travel and Tourism Council,* India will be a tourism hotspot from 2009-2018, having the highest 10-year growth potential. The *Travel & Tourism Competitiveness Report 2007* ranked tourism in India 6th in terms of price competitiveness and 39th in terms of safety and security. Despite short-and medium-term setbacks, such as shortage of hotel rooms, tourism revenues are expected to surge by 42% from 2007 to 2017.

Tourism by State

Andhra Pradesh

Andhra Pradesh has a rich cultural heritage and a variety of tourist attractions. The state of Andhra Pradesh comprises scenic hills, forests, beaches and temples. Also known as *The City of Nizams* and *The City of Pearls,* Hyderabad is today one of the most developed cities in the country and a modern hub of information technology, ITES, and biotechnology. Hyderabad is known for its rich history, culture and architecture representing its unique character as a meeting point for North and South India, and also its multilingual culture, both geographically and culturally.

Andhra Pradesh is the home of many religious pilgrim centres. Tirupati, the abode of Lord Venkateswara, is the richest and most visited religious centre (of any faith) in the world. Srisailam, the abode of Sri Mallikarjuna, is one of twelve Jyothirlingalu in India, Amaravati's Siva temple is one of the Pancharamams, and Yadagirigutta, the abode of an avatara of Vishnu, Sri Lakshmi Narasimha. The Ramappa temple and

Thousand Pillars temple in Warangal are famous for some fine temple carvings. The state has numerous Buddhist centres at Amaravati, Nagarjuna Konda, Bhattiprolu, Ghantasala, Nelakondapalli, Dhulikatta, Bavikonda, Thotlakonda, Shalihundam, Pavuralakonda, Sankaram, Phanigiri and Kolanpaka.

The golden beaches at Visakhapatnam, the one-million-year old limestone caves at Borra, picturesque Araku Valley, hill resorts of Horsley Hills, river Godavari racing through a narrow gorge at Papi Kondalu, waterfalls at Ettipotala, Kuntala and rich biodiversity at Talakona, are some of the natural attractions of the state.

Visakhapatnam is home to many tourist attactions such as the INS Karasura Submarine museum (The only one of its kind in India), Yarada Beach, Araku Valley, VUDA Park, Indira Gandhi Zoological Gardens.

The weather in Andhra Pradesh is mostly tropical and the best time to visit is in November through to January. The monsoon season commences in June and ends in September, so travel would not be advisable during this period.

Assam

Assam is the central state in the North-East Region of India and serves as the gateway to the rest of the Seven Sister States. Assam boasts of famous wildlife preserves – the Kaziranga National Park and the Manas National Park, the largest river island Majuli, and tea-estates dating back to time of British Raj.

The weather is mostly sub-tropical. Assam experiences the Indian monsoon and has one of the highest forest densities in India. The winter months (October to April) are the best time to visit.

Assam has a rich cultural heritage going back to the Ahom Kingdom which governed the region for many centuries before the British occupation. Other notable features include the Brahmaputra River, the mystery of the bird suicides in Jatinga, numerous temples including Kamakhya of Tantric sect, ruins of palaces, etc. Guwahati, the capital city of Assam, boasts many bazaars, temples, and wildlife sanctuaries.

Bihar

Bihar is one of the oldest continuously inhabited places in the world with history of 3000 years. The rich culture and heritage of Bihar is evident from the innumerable ancient monuments that are dotted all over this state in eastern India. This is the Place of Aryabhatta, Great Ashoka, Chanakya and many more.

Bihar is one of the most sacred places of various religions such as Hinduism, Buddhism, Jainism, Sikhism & Islam. Famous Attraction includes Mahabodhi Temple, a Buddhist shrine and UNESCO World Heritage Site is also situated in Bihar, Barabar Caves the oldest rockcut caves in India, Khuda Bakhsh Oriental Library the Oldest Library of India.

Delhi

Delhi is the capital city of India. A fine blend of old and new, ancient and modern, Delhi is a melting pot of cultures, religions. Delhi has been the capital of numerous empires that ruled India, making it rich in history.

The rulers left behind their trademark architectural styles. Delhi currently has many renowned historic monuments and landmarks such as the Tughlaqabad fort, Qutub Minar, Purana Quila, Lodhi Gardens, Jama Masjid, Humayun's tomb, Red Fort, and Safdarjung's Tomb. Modern monuments include Jantar Mantar, India Gate, Rashtrapati Bhavan, Laxminarayan Temple, Lotus temple and Akshardham Temple.

New Delhi is famous for its British colonial architecture, wide roads, and tree-lined boulevards. Delhi is home to numerous political landmarks, national museums, Islamic shrines, Hindu temples, green parks, and trendy malls.

Goa

Goa is one of the most famous tourist destinations in India. A former colony of Portugal, Goa is famous for its excellent beaches, Portuguese churches, Hindu temples, and wildlife sanctuaries. The Basilica of Bom Jesus, Mangueshi Temple, Dudhsagar Falls, and Shantadurga are famous attractions in Goa. Recently a Wax Museum (Wax World) has also opened in

Old Goa housing a number of wax personalities of Indian history, culture and heritage.

The Goa Carnival is a world famous event, with colorful masks and floats, drums and reverberating music, and dance performances. The celebrations run three days culminating in a carnival parade on fat Tuesday.

Himachal Pradesh

Himachal Pradesh is famous for its Himalayan landscapes and popular hill-stations. Many outdoor activities such as rock climbing, mountain biking, paragliding, ice-skating, and heli-skiing are popular tourist attractions in Himachal Pradesh.

Shimla, the state capital, is very popular among tourists. The Kalka-Shimla Railway is a Mountain railway which is a UNESCO World Heritage Site. Shimla is also a famous skiing attraction in India. Other popular hill stations include Manali and Kasauli.

Dharamshala, home of the Dalai Lama, is known for its Tibetan monasteries and Buddhist temples. Many trekking expeditions also begin here.

Jammu and Kashmir

Jammu and Kashmir is the northernmost state of India. Jammu is noted for its scenic landscape, ancient temples, Hindu shrines, castles, gardens, and forts. The Hindu holy shrines of Amarnath and Vaishno Devi attract tens of thousands of Hindu devotees every year. Jammu's natural landscape has made it one of the popular destinations for adventure tourism in South Asia. Jammu's historic monuments feature a unique blend of Islamic and Hindu architecture styles.

Tourism forms an integral part of the Kashmiri economy. Often dubbed "Paradise on Earth", Kashmir's mountainous landscape has attracted tourists for centuries. Notable places are Dal Lake, Srinagar Phalagam, Gulmarg, Yeusmarg and Mughal Gardens etc. However, the tourism industry is severely affected by the insurgency.

In recent years, Ladakh has emerged as a major hub for adventure tourism. This part of Greater Himalaya called "moon on earth" comprising of naked peaks and deep gorges was once known for the silk route to High Asia from the subcontinent. Leh is also a growing tourist spot.

Karnataka

Karnataka has been ranked as fourth most popular destination for tourism among states of India. It has the second highest number of protected monuments in India, at 507.

Kannada dynasties like Kadambas, Western Gangas, Chalukyas, Rashtrakutas, Hoysalas and Vijayanagaras, ruled Karnataka particularly North Karnataka. They built great monuments to Buddhism, Jainism, Shaivism. The monuments are still present at Badami, Aihole, Pattadakal, Hampi, Lakshmeshwar, Sudi, Hooli, Mahadeva Temple (Itagi), Dambal, Lakkundi, Gadag, Hangal, Halasi, Galaganatha, Chaudayyadanapura, Banavasi, Belur, Halebidu, Shravanabelagola, Sannati and many more.

Notable Islamic monuments are present at Bijapur, Bidar, Gulbarga, Raichur and other part of the state. Gol Gumbaz at Bijapur, has the second largest pre-modern dome in the world after the Byzantine Hagia Sophia. Karnataka has two World heritage sites, at Hampi and Pattadakal, both are in North Karnataka.

Karnataka is famous for its waterfalls. Jog falls of Shimoga District is one of the highest waterfalls in Asia. This state has 21 wildlife sanctuaries and five National parks and is home to more than 500 species of birds. Karnataka has many beaches at Karwar, Gokarna, Murdeshwara, Surathkal. Karnataka is a rock climbers paradise. Yana in Uttara Kannada, Fort in Chitradurga, Ramnagara near Bangalore district, Shivagange in Tumkur district and tekal in Kolar district are a rock climbers heaven.

Kerala

Kerala is a state on the tropical Malabar Coast of southwestern India. Nicknamed as one of the *"10 paradises of the world"* by National Geographic, Kerala is famous especially for its ecotourism initiatives. Its unique culture and traditions, coupled with its varied demography, has made it one of the most popular tourist destinations in India. Growing at a rate of

13.31%, the tourism industry significantly contributes to the state's economy.

Kerala is known for its tropical backwaters and pristine beaches such as Kovalam.

Madhya Pradesh

Madhya Pradesh is called the *"Heart of India"* because of its location in the centre of the country. It has been home to the cultural heritage of Hinduism, Islam, Buddhism, Sikhism, Jainism. Innumerable monuments, exquisitely carved temples, stupas, forts and palaces are dotted all over the State.

The temples of Khajuraho are world-famous for their erotic sculptures, and are a UNESCO World Heritage Site. Gwalior is famous for its forts, the Tomb of Rani Lakshmibai, and the Palace of Tansen.

Madhya Pradesh is also known as *Tiger State* because of the tiger population. Famous national parks like Kanha, Bandhavgadh, Shivpuri, Sanjay, Pench are located in MP. Spectacular mountain ranges, meandering rivers and miles and miles of dense forests offering a unique and exciting panorama of wildlife in sylvan surroundings.

Maharashtra

Maharashtra is the second most visited state in India by foreign tourists, with more than 2 million foreign tourists arrivals annually. Maharashtra boasts of a large number of popular and revered religious venues that are heavily frequented by locals as well as out-of-state visitors.

Ajanta Caves, Ellora Caves and Victoria Terminus are the three UNESCO World Heritage sites in Maharashtra and are highly responsible for the development of Tourism in the state.

Mumbai is the most cosmopolitan city in India, and a great place to experience modern India. Mumbai famous for Bollywood, the world's largest film industry. In addition, Mumbai is famous for its clubs, shopping, and upscale gastronomy. The city is known for its architecture, from the ancient Elephanta Caves, to the Islamic Haji Ali Mosque, to the colonial architecture of Bombay High Court and Victoria Terminus.

Maharashtra also has numerous adventure tourism destinations, including paragliding, rock climbing, canoeing, kayaking, snorkelling, and scuba diving. Maharashtra also has several pristine national parks and reserves. The Bibi Ka Maqbara at Aurangabad the Mahalakshmi temple at Kolhapur, the cities of Nashik, Trimbak famous for religious importance and the city of Pune the seat of the Maratha Empire and the fantastic Ganesh Chaturthi celebrations together contribute for the Tourism sector of Mahrashtra.

Orissa

Orissa has been a preferred destination from ancient days for people who have an interest in spirituality, religion, culture, art and natural beauty. Ancient and medieval architecture, pristine sea beaches, the classical and ethnic dance forms and a variety of festivals. Orissa has kept the religion of Buddhism alive. Rock-edicts that have challenged time stand huge and over-powering by the banks of the river Daya. The torch of Buddhism is still ablaze in the sublime triangle at Udayagiri and Khandagiri Caves, on the banks of river Birupa. Precious fragments of a glorious past come alive in the shape of stupas, rock-cut caves, rock-edicts, excavated monasteries, viharas, chaityas and sacred relics in caskets and the Rock-edicts of Ashoka. Orissa is also famous for its well-preserved Hindu Temples, especially the Konark Sun Temple. Orissa is the home for various tribal communities who have contributed uniquely to the multicultural and multilingual character of the state. Their handicrafts, different dance forms, jungle products and their unique life style blended with their healing practices have got world wide attention.

Puducherry

The Union Territory of Puducherry comprises four coastal regions viz-Puducherry, Karaikal, Mahe and Yanam. Puducherry is the Capital of this Union Territory and one of the most popular tourist destinations in South India. Puducherry has been described by National Geographic as "a glowing highlight of subcontinental sojourn". The city has many beautiful colonial buildings, churches, temples, and statues, which, combined with the systematic town planning and the well planned French style avenues, still preserve much of the colonial ambience.

Punjab

Punjab is one of India's most beautiful states. The state of Punjab is renowned for its cuisine, culture and history. Punjab has a vast public transportation and communication network. Some of the main cities in Punjab are Amritsar, Chandigarh, and Ludhiana.

Punjab also has a rich religious history incorporating Sikhism and Hinduism. Tourism in Punjab is principally suited for the tourists interested in culture, ancient civilization, spirituality and epic history. Some of the villages in Punjab are also a must see for the person who wants to see the true Punjab, with their beautiful traditional Indian homes, farms and temples, this is a must see for any visitor that goes to Punjab.

Rajasthan

Rajasthan, literally meaning *"Land of the Kings"*, is one of the most attractive tourist destinations in Northern India. The vast sand dunes of the Thar Desert attract millions of tourists from around the globe every year.

Attractions:

- Jaipur-The capital of Rajasthan, famous for its rich history and royal architecture.
- Jodhpur-Fortress-city at the edge of the Thar Desert, famous for its blue homes and architecture.
- Udaipur-Known as the "Venice" of India.
- Jaisalmer-Famous for its golden fortress.
- Barmer-Barmer and surrounding areas offer perfect picture of typical Rajasthani villages.
- Bikaner-Famous for its medieval history as a trade route outpost.
- Mount Abu-Is the highest peak in the Aravalli Range of Rajasthan.
- Pushkar-It has the first and one of the very Brahma temples in the world.

- Nathdwara-This town near Udaipur hosts the famous temple of Shrinathji.
- Ranthambore-Situated near Sawai Madhopur, this town has one of the largest and most famous national parks in India.

Sikkim

Originally known as Suk-Heem, which in the local language means "peaceful home", Sikkim was an independent kingdom till the year 1974, when it became a part of the Republic of India. The capital of Sikkim is Gangtok, located approximately 185 kilometers from New Jalpaiguri, the nearest railway station to Sikkim. Although, an airport is under construction at Dekiling in East Sikkim, the nearest airport to Sikkim would be Bagdogra. Sikkim is considered as the land of Orchids and mystic cultures and colorful traditions. Sikkim is well known among trekkers and adventure lovers, as West Sikkim has a lot to give them.

Places near Sikkim include Darjeeling also known as the Queen of hills and Kalimpong. Darjeeling, other than its world famous "Darjeeling tea" is also famous for its refined "Prep schools" founded during the British Raj. Kalimpong is also famous for its flora cultivation and is home to many internationally known Nurseries.

Tamil Nadu

Tamil Nadu lies in the southern Indian peninsula, on the shores of the Bay of Bengal. Many great rulers including the Cholas, Pallavas, Pandyas and the Vijayanagara Empire ruled over parts of Tamil Nadu. The state is known for its cultural heritage and temple architecture.

Attractions include Mahabalipuram, famous for its Shore Temple, Kanyakumari, the southernmost tip of India, Auroville, an International Utopian city, Mudumalai Wildlife Sanctuary, Ooty and Kodaikanal, two famous hill stations. The Nilgiri Mountain Railway is a Unesco World Heritage Site

Uttarakhand

Uttaranchal is the 27th state of the Republic of India. It contains glaciers, snow-clad mountains, valley of flowers, skiing slopes and dense forests, and many shrines and places of pilgrimage. *Char-dhams*, the four most sacred and revered Hindu temples: Badrinath, Kedarnath, Gangotri and Yamunotri are nestled in the Himalayas. Haridwar which means *Gateway to God* is the only place on the plains.

It holds the watershed for Gangetic River System spanning 300 km from Satluj in the west to Kali river in the east. Nanda Devi (25640 Ft.) is the second highest peak in India after Kanchenjunga (28160 Ft.). Dunagiri, Neelkanth, Chaukhamba, Panchachuli, Trisul are other peaks above 23000 Ft. It is considered the abode of *Devtas, Yakashyas, Kinners*, Fairies and Sages. It boasts of some old hill-stations developed during British era like Mussoorie, Almora and Nainital.

Uttar Pradesh

Situated in the northern part of India, Uttar Pradesh is important with its wealth of monuments and religious fervour. Geographically, Uttar Pradesh is very diverse, with Himalayan foothills in the extreme north, the Gangetic Plain in the centre, and the Vindhya Mountain Range towards the South.

It is also home of India's most visited site, the Taj Mahal, and Hinduism's holiest city, Varanasi.

The most populous state of the Indian Union also has a rich cultural heritage, and at the heart of North India, Uttar Pradesh has much to offer. Places of interest include Varanasi, Agra, Mathura, Jhansi, Prayag, Sarnath, Ayodhya, Dudhwa National Park and Fatehpur Sikri.

West Bengal

Kolkata, one of the many cities in the state of West Bengal has been nicknamed the City of Palaces. This comes from the numerous palatial mansions built all over the city. Unlike many north Indian cities, whose construction stresses minimalism, the layout of much of the architectural variety in Kolkata owes its origins to European styles and tastes imported by the British and, to a much lesser extent, the Portuguese and French. The buildings were designed and inspired by the tastes of the English gentleman around and the aspiring Bengali Babu (literally, a *nouveau riche* Bengali who aspired to cultivation of English etiquette, manners and custom, as such practices were favourable to monetary gains from the British). Today, many of these structures are in various stages of decay. Some of the major buildings of this period are well maintained and several buildings have been declared as heritage structures.

From historical point of view, the story of West Bengal begins from Gour and Pandua situated close to the present district town of Malda. The twin medieval cities had been sacked at least once by changing powers in the 15th century. However, ruins from the period still remain, and several architectural specimens still retain the glory and shin of those times. The Hindu architecture of Bishnupur in terracotta and laterite sandstone are renowned world over. Towards the British colonial period came the architecture of Murshidabad and Coochbehar.

Historic Monuments

The Taj Mahal is one of India's best-known sites and one of the best architectural achievements in India. Located in Agra, it was built between 1631 and 1653 by Emperor Shah Jahan in honour of his wife, Arjumand Banu, more popularly known as Mumtaz Mahal. The Taj Mahal serves as her tomb.

The Golden Temple is one of the most respected temples in India and the most sacred place for Sikhs. The Golden Temple is located in Amritsar, Punjab, India.

The Bahai temple in Delhi, was completed in 1986 and serves as the Mother Temple of the Indian Subcontinent. It has won numerous architectural awards and been featured in hundreds of newspaper and magazine articles.

The Victoria Terminus in Mumbai was built by the British and is a UNESCO World Heritage Site.

The Taj Mahal Palace is an icon of Mumbai.

The Victoria Memorial in Kolkata.

Nature Tourism

India has geographical diversity, which resulted in varieties of nature tourism.

- Water falls in Western Ghats including Jog falls (highest in India).
- Western Ghats
- Kerala backwaters
- Hill Stations
- Wildlife reserves.

Wildlife in India

India is home to several well known large mammals including the Asian Elephant, Bengal Tiger, Asiatic Lion, Leopard and Indian Rhinoceros, often engrained culturally and religiously often being associated with deities. Other well known large Indian mammals include ungulates such as the domestic Asian Water buffalo, wild Asian Water buffalo, Nilgai, Gaur and several species of deer and antelope.

Some members of the dog family such as the Indian Wolf, Bengal Fox, Golden Jackal and the Dhole or Wild Dogs are also widely distributed. It is also home to the Striped Hyaena, Macaques, Langurs and Mongoose species. India also has a large variety of protected wildlife.

The country's protected wilderness consists of 75 National parks of India and 421 Sanctuaries, of which 19 fall under the purview of Project Tiger. Its climatic and geographic diversity makes it the home of over 350 mammals and 1200 bird species, many of which are unique to the subcontinent.

Some well known national wildlife sanctuaries include Bharatpur, Corbett, Kanha, Kaziranga, Periyar, Ranthambore and Sariska. The world's largest mangrove forest Sundarbans is located in southern West Bengal. The *Sundarbans* is UNESCO World Heritage Site.

Hill Stations

Several hill stations served as summer capitals of Indian provinces, princely states, or, in the case of Shimla, of British India itself. Since Indian Independence, the role of these hill stations as summer capitals has largely ended, but many hill stations remain popular summer resorts. Most famous hill stations are:

- Pachmarhi, Madhya Pradesh-It is also known as The Queen of Satpura. .
- Araku, Andhra Pradesh
- Gulmarg, Srinagar and Laddakh in Jammu and Kashmir
- Darjeeling in West Bengal
- Munnar in Kerala
- Ooty and Kodaikanal in Tamil Nadu
- Shillong in Meghalaya
- Shimla, Kullu in Himachal Pradesh
- Nainital in Uttarakhand
- Gangtok in Sikkim
- Mussoorie in Uttarakhand.

In addition to the bustling hill stations and summer capitals of yore, there are several serene and peaceful nature retreats and places of interest to visit for a nature lover. These range from the stunning moonscapes of Leh and Ladhak, to small, exclusive nature retreats such as Dunagiri, Binsar, Mukteshwar in the Himalayas, to rolling vistas of Western Ghats to numerous private retreats in the rolling hills of Kerala.

Beaches

Elephants and camels rides are common on Indian beaches. Shown here is Havelock Island, part of the Andaman and Nicobar Islands. India offers a wide range of tropical beaches with silver/golden sand to coral beaches of Lakshadweep. States like Kerala and Goa have exploited the potential of beaches to the fullest. However, there are a lot many unexploited beaches in the states of Andhra Pradesh, Gujarat, Maharastra, Tamil Nadu and Karnataka. These states have very high potential to be develop them as future destinations for prospective tourists. Some of the famous tourist beaches are:

- Beaches of Vizag, Andhra Pradesh
- Beaches of Puri, Orissa
- Beaches of Digha, West Bengal
- Beaches of Goa

- Kovalam Beach, Kerala
- Marina Beach, Chennai
- Beaches of Mahabalipuram
- Beaches in Mumbai
- Beaches of Diu
- Beaches of Midnapore, West Bengal
- Andaman and Nicobar Islands
- Lakshadweep Islands.
- Adventure Tourism
- River rafting and kayaking in Himalayas
- Mountain climbing in Himalayas
- Rock climbing in Madhya Pradesh
- Skiing in Gulmarg or Auli
- Boat racing in Bhopal
- Paragliding in Maharashtra.

The Indian Tourism and Hospitality Industry

Tourism and Hospitality Industry

- Hospitality, as an industry segment in itself, is a US$ 3.5 trillion service sector within the global economy.
- In India, the tourism and hospitality industries are witnessing a period of exponential growth; the world's leading travel and tourism journal, "Conde Nast Traveller", ranked India as the numero uno travel destination in the world for 2007, as against fourth position in 2006.
- The year 2007 also marked the fifth consecutive year during which India has witnessed double-digit growth in foreign tourist arrivals.
- Along with the rise in foreign tourist arrivals, foreign exchange earnings have shown a robust growth of 25.6% during January-October 2007 to touch US$ 6.32 billion as against US$ 5.03 billion during January-October 2006.

- Tourism has now become a significant industry in India, contributing around 5.9 per cent of the Gross Domestic Product (GDP) and providing employment to about 41.8 million people.
- As per the World Travel & Tourism Council, the tourism industry in India is likely to generate US$ 121.4 billion of economic activity by 2015 and Hospitality sector has the potential to earn US$ 24 billion in foreign exchange by 2015.
- Additionally, India is also likely to become a major hub for medical tourism, with revenues from the industry estimated to grow from US$ 333 million in 2007 to US$ 2.2 billion by 2012, says a study by the Confederation of Indian Industry (CII) and McKinsey.
- The booming tourism industry has had a cascading effect on the hospitality sector with an increase in the occupancy ratios and average room rates. While occupancy ratio is around 80-85 per cent – up nearly 10 percent from three years back, the average increase in room rates over the last one year has hovered around 22-25%.
- It is pertinent to mention in this context, that according to recent estimates, there are a total of 110,000 rooms in India, as against a total requirement of approximately 250,000 – demonstrating the untapped potential that continues to exist in this industry.
- With a view to stimulating domestic and international investments in this sector, the government has implemented the following initiatives:
    1. 100% FDI under the automatic route is now permitted in all construction development projects including construction of hotels and resorts, recreational facilities and city and regional level infrastructure.
    2. 100% FDI is now permitted in all airport development projects subject to the condition that FDI for upgradation of existing airports requires FIPB approval beyond 74%.

iii. A five year tax holiday has been extended to Companies that set up hotels, resorts and convention centres at specified destinations, subject to compliance with the prescribed conditions.

iv. Plans for substantial upgradation of 28 regional airports in smaller towns and the privatization and expansion of Delhi and Mumbai airports

- The aforementioned initiatives have resulted in increasing FDI inflows being witnessed by this industry. For the period April 2000 to November 2007, a total of US$ 636 million in foreign direct investments was channelised towards development of hotels and tourism.
- The hospitality industry has also been receiving increasing interest from the Private Equity Sector – investments have tripled from US$ 60 million in 2004-05 to over US$ 180 million in 2006-07.
- It is estimated that the hospitality sector is likely to see a further US$ 11.41 billion in inbound investments over the next two years.
- Several global hospitality majors such as Hilton, Accor, Marriott International, Berggruen Hotels, Cabana Hotels, Premier Travel Inn (PTI) and InterContinental Hotels group have already announced major investment plans in India in recent years.

Food and Tourism

The concept of 'ethnic food tourism" may have relevance in present days due to increase in tourist industry in the Himalayas. Movement and interaction of people, sense of respect to traditional value and culture will serve to intricately link the enjoyment of dinning to locale, making this the standard of food culture of the region. France attracts the greatest number of tourists worldwide as estimated in 1998 reaching 70 million, which even exceeds the existing population of 58 million. The secret to this appeal is nothing but the delicious food and wine of France, served in inexpensive traditional restaurants that offer the delicious agricultural produce of the region which allows one to experience enjoyment and friendship. Finding enjoyment in eating the produce of the region while in that region – herein lies the essence of a food culture that gives confidence in life, pride to the people of the region and ultimately, enjoyment and friendship. Further, it imparts meaning to the act of travel and bestows happiness upon the traveller. The promoters have to focus on the specific food culture of a region in a presentable form where tourists can find local cuisine in menu.

Ethnic food culture harnesses the cultural history of particular community, their indigenous knowledge of food production, vast nutritious qualities, microbial diversity associated with fermented foods as genetic resources, source of income generation related to tourism and enjoyment of dining.

- Food tourism includes all unique and memorable food experiences, not just four star or critically acclaimed restaurants. Price is not necessarily indicative of quality. According to industry research, true food tourists are perfectly happy at a roadside cafe in the middle of nowhere, as long as there is something memorable about their visit.
- Tourist consumers were asked to list aspects that make a place a good food destination.

Activities

In addition to sampling local food and dishes, food tourists are also likely to engage in the following activities during their holiday:

- Visit museums
- Go shopping
- Attend music and/or film festivals
- Participate in general outdoor recreation.

Accommodation Preferences

- In an in-depth survey of 11 consumers regarding their perception of restaurants and destination, 91% of respondents indicated they choose their accommodation based on the availability of restaurants in the area. One consumer revealed this was because it was less restrictive price-wise, (i.e. more choice), while others mentioned the benefits of proximity, and being able to walk to and from restaurants.

- One consumer did not consider the availability of restaurants to be an important factor in their accommodation decision. This was because they simply expected most city-located accommodation to be situated near restaurant facilities.

Travel Party

Of the total domestic visitors who ate out and/or visited restaurants during their overnight trip, 31% were travelling as part of an adult couple and 24% were travelling alone.

Family groups (ie, parents and children) and friends and/or relatives travelling together (without children) each accounted for a further 19%.

Information Sources

Travellers on holiday use the following sources of information when selecting a restaurant:

- Travel guides
- Brochures from travel agencies
- Newspaper articles
- Magazines
- TV programs
- Word of mouth
- The internet
- Consumer's own knowledge
- Menu shopping.

Length of Trip

Domestic visitors who engaged in the activity of eating out and/or dining at restaurants stayed for an average of 4.5 nights on their trip. By comparison, the average length of stay for all domestic visitors was 4.0 nights.

Barriers

- Many who attempt to define food and culinary tourism immediately think of wineries and fine restaurants. These are two components of the niche, but by no means a definitive list. Food tourism can occur at a farmers' market, or even in the home of a friend or relative.
- Travellers do not often choose their holiday destination based on the food tourism experiences they anticipate to encounter, but still end up remembering their holiday to a certain extent on the quality of the food they experienced at the destination. This creates a conundrum in that many tourists choose holiday destinations based on one perceived aspect (e.g. beaches, accommodation etc.), but their actual satisfaction will be based on aspects (ie, food) they did not consider in their original holiday choice.
- According to research conducted into what aspects of food tourism consumers find appealing, 73% said that a variety of eating options was an important consideration in their destination choice. This automatically biases tourist consumers towards more developed destinations that receive a sufficient volume of visitors to support a diverse food industry. Only 36% of respondents mentioned regional food as being important.

Opportunities

- The food tourism niche market presents a new aspect of destination marketing, which can enhance the attractiveness of a destination without necessarily involving extensive new product development. Food tourism can essentially be viewed as a subset of cultural tourism, with the local cuisine being a product of the local culture and the natural environment. Therefore, regions that possess unique dishes and food products as a result of their culture and environment may be transformed into food tourism destinations with minimum marketing and product development.

- In terms of regional aspects, food tourism can be divided into a rural and an urban/city experience. The urban/city experience usually presents travellers with a wide variety of food tourism products, and convenience in the form of restaurant precincts and culturally distinct cuisine. Rural food tourism on the other hand is not usually considered as a developed tourism product. Activities such as visits to farms and farmers' markets, fruit picking and agricultural farm accommodation may provide important supplemental activities to struggling rural areas.
- Research suggests that in many instances, consumers attribute their lack of satisfaction with food on their holiday to the reason their trip did not become an overall memorable holiday. Destinations could develop higher consumer satisfaction levels (and hence higher return and recommendation rates) if they could guide tourists to food products that provide memorable experiences (whether it is service, quality, value for money, or uniqueness). This may be achieved through either consumer marketing (e.g. a tourist restaurant/food tourism brochure) or through cooperative product development.
- No state or local food tourism associations currently exist in Queensland. The marketing and development of new food tourism products could be assisted and facilitated by the formation of such an organisation. Membership could also act as a strong indicator to consumers of quality tourism food product.

Marketing

- A large proportion of consumers emphasise a variety of food product as being important in their overall satisfaction with a destination. Therefore, promoting the variety of restaurants and food products available in a destination may enhance destination attractiveness.
- True food tourism visitors can be accessed via industry associations such as the International Culinary Tourism Association and consumer publications.

- It could be useful to include information relating to the following features in any materials prepared for marketing the food tourism product:
  - o the location (including proximity to other local attractions),
  - o access to the property (roads, signage),
  - o attractions on the property (gardens, views),
  - o leisure opportunities (games, crafts, recreational pursuits), and
  - o local area attractions (tourist drives, museums, events).

Culinary Tourism

Judging by the surge since 2001 in the number of times "culinary tourism" has appeared as a subject matter or in a session title in tourism industry conferences and programs, we can see that Culinary Tourism is valued by tourism industry professionals as one of the most popular niches in the world's tourism industry. This makes sense, given recent consumer focus on healthy and organic eating, culinary/food pedigrees, and the simple fact that all travellers must eat. Not every visitor goes shopping or visits museums, but all travellers eat. For anyone who doubts, look at the increase in cooking shows featured on The Travel Channel [Anthony Bourdain No Reservations] or travel shows featured on The Food Network [Rachel Ray's $40 a Day series], as examples.

Culinary Tourism is not just experiences of the highest caliber-that would be gourmet tourism. This is perhaps best illustrated by the notion that Culinary Tourism is about what is "unique and memorable, not what is necessarily pretentious and exclusive". Similarly, wine tourism, beer tourism and spa tourism are also regarded as subsets of culinary tourism.

Indian Food Tourism

The finest of *India's* cuisines is as rich and diverse as it's civilization. It is an art form that has been passed on through generations purely by word of mouth, from *guru* teacher) to *vidhyarthi* (pupil) or from mother to daughter.

The hospitality of the Indians is legendary. In *Sanskrit* literature the three famous words *'Atithi Devo Bhava'* or 'The guest is truly your god' are a dictum of hospitality in India. Indians believe that they are honoured if they share their mealtimes with guests. Even the poorest look forward to guests and are willing to share this meager food with guest.

Lassi-Punjab

Lassi, by far, is the most easiest Indian dish to prepare and is taken cold. It is a good way to beat the scorching heat and get refreshed.

It can prepared in two ways either sweet or salty.

Biryani-Hyderabad

Hyderabadi Biryani is a famous meat and rice dish of *Hyderabad,* India.

It is a traditional celebration meal made using goat meat and rice and is the staple of a die-hard Hyderabadi. The blending of *mughlai* and *Telangana* cuisines in the kitchens of the *Nizam* (ruler of the historic Hyderabad State), resulted in the creation of Hyderabadi Biryani.

Halwa-Tirunelveli

This sweet (pronounced locally as ulva) is made from wheat and sugar. *Halwa* is brown and semi-solid in texture and contains lots of *ghee/Vanaspati* which gives it the oily look. It tastes the best when fresh and hot. Tirunelveli Halwa is said to owe its peculiar taste due to the recipe of this region.

Two of the famous halwa stores are *Irutu Kadai halwa (Dark Store halwa),* situated near the *Nellayappar* temple and Shanthi Sweets. The name *Irutu Kadai* of the former store derives from the fact that the looks of the store had been kept unchanged from the date it was started. Till date, there is no bright electrical lamp or even a board display to show the shop name!

Pani Puri/Golgappa/Golgappe-Indian Street Snack

Panipuri or Gol Gappa or Gup chup is a popular street snack in the Indian sub-continent. It comprises a round, hollow *puri,* fried crisp and filled with a watery mixture of tamarind, chilli and potato. The name *panipuri* literally means "water in fried bread". The snack has three major ingredients-Puris, pani (water) and stuffing.

Pesarattu-Andhra Pradesh

Pesarattu is a thicker verison of *Dosa* made specifically in major towns of Andhra Pradesh.

Idly-Kancheepuram

The *idli* is a savory cake popular throughout South India. The cakes are usually two to three inches in diameter and are made by steaming a batter consisting of fermented black lentils (de-husked) and rice.

Kancheepuram Idli as the name goes is from Kancheepuram, a holy city in Tamil Nadu, India. History goes that Kancheepuram Idly is served as *prasadam* (offering) in *Varadharaja Perumal Temple,* a famous Hindu temple dedicated to Lord Vishnu, located in the Kancheepuram. It is a huge Idli (Steamed Rice Cake) which is added with spices.

Why Food Tourism is Becoming more Important?

Today's tourist is more cultured than visitors of 20 years ago, is well travelled, is searching for new experiences, is concerned about the environment, is interested in taking part in a health/well-being lifestyle and wants to experience the local culture when he goes on holiday.

Trend analyst, Ian Yeoman writes that food is a significant aspect of the tourist's experience of a destination, driven by the growing trends of authenticity and the need to have a high-quality experience. Food tourism shapes gastro destinations such as France, Italy and California whereas in emerging destinations such as Croatia, Vietnam and Mexico food plays an important part of the overall experience.

What are the Trends Shaping our Interest in Food Tourism?

Trend 1: Disposable Income and Spending Patterns

All across world, growing affluence of the populations has

a profound impact on consumer spending. Consumers spend a higher proportion of their income on prepared food, gourmet products, eating out and food items with some form of health or ethical benefits.

The key point is that according to Michael Silverstein writing in his book Trading Up: The New American Luxury the consumer has traded up where the product is aspiration or traded down when the product is only function. This is one reason why producers and retailers have focused on quality through products such as Tesco's finest range or ethical consumption, where the consumer will pay a premium for 'fair trade' product.

Trend 2: Demographics and Household Change

According to research by the Future Foundation families are also becoming increasingly democratic in food choice, as children get older they have more influence in what they eat and where the family eats. Children are also spending increasing amounts of time with their grandparents with over two-thirds of children born between 1978 and 1986 being looked after by their grandparents at least once a month, compared to one quarter of those born in 1937 or earlier.

This increase indicates a demand for venues offering facilities that appeal to differing age groups and generations. By 2015, those aged between 45 and 59 will be part of the most populous age group in the United Kingdom.

Households headed by those aged 50 plus will account for around 50% of all households, and this same age group will account for over 39% of all consumers spending on leisure goods and services. In 2004, the 50–64 age groups spent US $24.80 per household per week on restaurant meals, US $2.40 more than the national average — this will be a key market in the future.

Another consequence of longevity is 'lifestyle fragmentation', the idea that life is increasingly being experienced as a series of non-linear events with no set pattern. As characteristics of different age groups becomes blurred and diverse, more people will expect the places they visit to be adaptable to different aspects of their daily lives. In other words, eating out opportunities suitable for whatever the situations requires —

whether this is work, with children or simply eating alone. And finally, rising divorce rates are also good for food tourism, as Michael Silverstein observe that divorcees have to search for new partners and subsequently will take prospective partners out for dinner and away for romantic weekends.

Trend 3: Individualism

Individualism means uniqueness as tourists search out local, fresh and good quality cuisine that reflects the authenticity of the destination. The end of mass customisation has seen Starbucks fail in Australia as the brand is perceived as bland and lacking individuality. Gone are the days of the British tourist wanting 'egg and chips' in Ibiza or American's only eating Kentucky Fried Chicken when in Australia.

Trend 4: The Multi-Cultured Consumer

The whole process of globalization has significantly amplified the meaning of the term multi-culturalism within our social order. Access to an even wider range of ideas and interests has never been easier.

The Internet boom, the expansion in specialist and minority TV channels, the relentless growth in international tourism, etc., combine to stretch perceptions and eliminate that what we might call mono-culturalism; seeing the world through only one set of pre-ordained, inherited notions.

The consumer of today will watch the latest Bollywood film, consume a curry, purchase exotic spices for cooking and will read about Rajasthan in the latest edition of the Lonely Planet. Multiculturalism has now become an everyday concept in the daily life of the consumer; today curry is the United Kingdom's favourite dish.

Trend 5: The Role of the Celebrity Chef and Media

The media has substantial influence in determining food product selection. The influence of celebrity chefs is often referred to as the Delia effect' after the media chef Delia Smith, whose 1998 television programme 'How to Cook' resulted in an extra 1.3 million eggs being sold in Britain each day of the series. The phenomena of Gordon Ramsey with 'Hells Kitchen' and the 'F word' or Jamie Oliver campaign for good wholesome school dinners all drives our interest in good quality real food.

The emergence of the niche food programmes, TV channels and magazines means the food celebrity and expert has been created. Today, that celebrity chef shapes tourism products, whether it is a cookery course with Rick Stein in Padstow or Martin Yan's food cruises across China.

Trend 6: Well-Being and Food

Around 30% of adults say that they have been eating less fat and sugar compared to the previous year and 28% say they are eating less salt, whereas other food groups, notably vegetables, fruit and bread/cereal/pasta/potatoes are on the rise. These trends have transformed themselves into the food industry with Starbucks offering Soya milk, and McDonalds offering salads.

In New York, the city council has banned certain types of fats. The proportion of vegetarians has only increased slightly in the last 20 years, with just over 5% of UK adults reporting themselves to be vegetarian in 2004. However, the number of food venues offering vegetarian options due to its association with healthy eating has increased exponentially along with a perception that vegetarian food in restaurants is more than 'vegetable lasagne' or a 'cheese omelette'.

Restaurants are also aware of specialist diets, whether it is catering for gluten free or the Atkins diet. Consumers will even visit a food nutritionalist or advisor of seek opinion about 'food balance' or 'sensitivity towards certain foods'.

The specialist diet is becoming more mainstream with individuals avoiding certain foodstuffs like 'dairy products' or the promotion of detox diets to cleanse the body. Consumers are therefore becoming ever more demanding and cautious regarding the food they eat.

These concerns and fears can be exploited in order to maximise potential marketing of certain products. However, due to the volatile nature of demands and trends, these requirements are hard to predict. Food providers need to have 'quick response' mechanisms in place to enable them to keep up with dietary fads and health scares.

Trend 7: Food as an Oasis

When on holiday, food becomes the social occasion when busy people create a 'time oasis', but also to connect with family members and friends who may in general be less time-impoverished. Food becomes a human-space within frequently much harried lives; the notion of the meal as a 'time oasis' seems to be a very powerful theme. As the consumer desire for new experiences increases, the 'authentic' restaurant experience becomes more important. Authenticity is about food that is simple, rooted in the region, natural, ethical, beautiful and human — all of the making for a food tourism destination.

Trend 8: Internet Usage

The world is online whether through your computer or mobile phone. Online restaurant reviews are the norm and companies like www.5pm.co.uk use the easyJet principles of yield management allowing consumer's discounts, reviews, auctions for exclusive restaurants, reservations and for restaurants a distribution system for selling unused capacity.

Trend 9: The Desire for New Experiences and Cultural Capital

Food has an important position and role in the emerging experience economy whether in the preparation of it, knowledge of it or consuming it.

As British sociologist Gershuny notes when discussing the whole concept of cultural capital. We have various skills in different sorts of consumption and organisational participation — we play football, we organise social events for the synagogue or church or mosque, we cook food and give dinner parties, we listen to music.

All of these activities give us different sorts of satisfaction, and different degrees of social status, depending on how fully and effectively we are able to participate in them. So, the growing importance of cultural issues, as a leisure activity and as a point of differentiation, means it is an important trend in food tourism as it is the tourist's knowledge of food that distinguishes them.

This means the food tourist has a desire for new tastes, knowledge and concepts and therefore food creates its own cultural capital — which destinations need to capitalise on. As consumers become richer and more sophisticated, they are drawn to new tastes and more adventurous than previous generations.

Trend 10: The Science of Food

Food tourism is shaped by the geopolitical trends. Today, we have rejected science from the food chain resulting in falling yields per hectare as we have rejected GM foods. Food inflation is rising all over the world, for example milk has doubled in price in the last 12 months Farmers are planting crops for fuel rather than food in the rush for biofuels.

Climate change is more disruptive and unpredictable. Rising temperatures mean less water in parts of the world. Land is becoming more expensive due to the increase in urbanisation, therefore less land for food production.

Because of these reasons, will the world return to science in order to protect future food supplies and increase yields? Does this mean cuisine is going to return to Star trek pills and NASA vac packs? Who knows?

Trend 11: However, the Consumer is a Hypochondriac

Although there is evidence that healthy eating is on the rise, the importance of organic food and a desire to try local produce—the consumer can be viewed as a hypochondriac as what they say and actually do can be two different things.

For example, obesity levels have trebled in the USA since 1980 and the amount of vegetables that people consume has steadily dropped since the 1970s.

On one hand, the French campaign against the company, saying it is a symbol of American imperialism and aggression in the world; promotes an unhealthy lifestyle and there is nothing good about its cuisine, whereas on the other hand, the French love the Big Mac, eating three times as many per head of population compared to Spain, Germany and Italy.

Food Tourism Destinations

Some destinations have begun to realise that there is great potential for food tourism to offer a sustainable tourism product, whether it is the fine wines of California or the great cheeses of France. One of the best examples of food tourism has been the rise in prominence of Ludlow in the United Kingdom as a food tourism destination whether it is festivals, slow food or Michelin star restaurants.

Ludlow from the early beginning of a farmers market has prospered into a major food tourism destination with a density of high quality restaurants, an abundance of local food suppliers in the high street and food festivals and events to attract tourists. Ludlow as a food destination illustrates its success through:

- Using food as a means to create cultural capital and social cachet
- Creating a density of food and drink suppliers which results in a tourism eating and shopping experience
- Creating a local authentic promise based upon good quality and fair pricing
- Creating a unique product better than that found in other regional food destinations
- Producers seeing themselves as being involved in tourism
- Tourism providers focusing on food as a point of difference.

Conclusions

Today, the consumer is better educated, wealthy, has travelled more extensively, lives longer, and is concerned about his health and the environment. As a result food and drink has become more important and have a higher priority amongst certain social groupings.

Too the extent food is the new culture capital of a destination, as if culture has moved out of the museum to become a living experience of consumption. One thing is clear; food must be a quality product, whether it is slow food or fast food. Finally, if food is not for you, there is always the no-food movement which is all the rage in Japan where holiday-makers are flocking to the Arina Hotel in the idyllic Nagano Mountains for a fasting feast!

2

Service Quality Management in Hospitality

Service Quality in Hospitality

Delivering good service to customers is the main goal that every service business strives to accomplish from time to time. The ability for a service provider to deliver quality service is considered an essential strategy for success and survival in today's competition. In this case, service encounter is a critical part of the service delivery process because it gives impact to customer's evaluations of service consumption experiences.

Therefore, there have been several studies and researches focusing on service encounter as it is believed that there is a causal relationship between the customer perception of service quality and the service encounter. Service encounter is one of the factors influencing customer perceptions of service quality, satisfaction and value as shown in the Hospitality industry is one of the service sector, with relatively high level of customer contact. The higher the level of customer contact the more numerous and longer service encounters between customers and service employees.

It implies that more attention must be focused on how to manage all the possible service encounters which will much influence the service quality of the hospitality organization and in the end the profit. Many hospitality organizations have invested considerably to develop service-delivery system which will ensure that customers will receive consistently high-quality service in every service encounter. This makes service encounter or 'moment of truth' in hospitality industry become much more important to be taken care of in the future.

While considerable research has been conducted in the service sector in general focusing on service encounters specific concern in managing service encounters in hospitality industry has received very little attention. The objectives of this article are to explore from a theoretical perspective how to manage service quality through managing the service encounters that takes place in hospitality industry. It also aims to set a framework of investigation for future empirical research.

Service Quality

Service quality is determined by what customers perceive. It means that customers play an important part in judging service quality. Very often companies define service quality apart from what the customers perceive of the quality so that time and money are poorly invested to poor quality programs. Grönroos (2000) identified two dimensions in service quality as it is perceived by customers; they are technical quality and functional quality. The technical quality is the outcome or the end result of a service production process. The functional quality is how a customer receives the service and how he experiences the simultaneous production and consumption process. All the tangibles will create the technical quality but the intangibles will generate the functional quality. For example in a restaurant setting, the delicious food served to the guest is the technical quality of a service; while how the guest is treated and served by the waiter is the functional quality.

Both of them give influence to the customer in perceiving the service quality. Very often the service provider who performs better in functional quality will gain competitive advantage when most of service providers provide relatively the same technical quality.

Service Quality Dimensions

In evaluating service quality, consumers consider five dimensions:

1. Reliability: ability to perform the promised service dependably and accurately
2. Responsiveness: willingness to help customers and provide prompt service
3. Assurance: employee's knowledge and courtesy and their ability to inspire trust and confidence
4. Empathy: caring, individualized attention given to customers
5. Tangibles: appearance of physical facilities, equipment, personnel, and written materials.

These dimensions are generally considered by consumers when they want to procure a service or when they want to estimate service quality. In the same way, these dimensions are very much contemplated when consumers experience the 'moment of truth'.

Service Encounter or "Moment of Truth"

The term service encounter and 'moment of truth' are used interchangeably when discussing the period of time where customers interact directly with a service. As it is stated by Lovelock (2002) that 'moment of truth' is "a point in service delivery where customers interact with service employees or self-service equipment and the outcome may affect perceptions of service quality". In the 'moment of truth', a careless mistake by an employee, a rude behavior or an unanticipated request by a guest can result in a dissatisfied guest. It is the crucial moment for service provider to influence customer perception of service quality. For example, a hotel guest may experience several service encounters when booking a room, checking into the hotel, being escorted to a room by a bellman, having meals in the hotel restaurant, requesting a wake-up call, using in-house services, and checking out. In these encounters hotel guests receive a picture of the hotel's service quality and each encounter contributes to the hotel guest's overall satisfaction and willingness to do business with the hotel organization again. As for the hotel, each encounter is an opportunity to deliver quality service to guests.

Positive service encounters will add up to a shared image of high service quality, whereas the negative ones will give the opposite effect. Hence, a combination of positive and negative encounters will make the customer *"feel unsure of the organization's service quality, doubtful of its consistency in service delivery, and vulnerable to the appeals of competitors"*. Besides, each encounter with different people and departments in an organization will also add to or detract from the potential for a continuing relationship.

Types of Service Encounters

There are three general types of service encounters in the hospitality industry: *remote encounters, phone encounters, and face-to-face encounters*. Remote encounters can occur without any direct human contact, such as: booking a room via the Internet. In this case the technical quality is the only point to control as there is no direct interaction with the service provider. While the phone encounter is the type of encounter between an end customer and the organization which occurs over the telephone, such as: booking a room or a table via telephone. In this case, tone of voice, employee knowledge, and effectiveness/efficiency in handling customer issues become important criteria for judging service quality.

As for face-to-face encounters, there is a direct contact between an employee and a customer. Both verbal and nonverbal behaviours are important determinants of service quality as well as the tangible cues such as employee attire, equipment, physical setting and other tangible symbols.

Analysis of Problems and Challenges in Managing Service Encounters

In order to avoid negative service encounters but ensure positive service encounters are in place, it is necessary to find out what sort of things may bring customer satisfaction and what other sort of things may cause customer dissatisfaction in a service encounter.

First of all, there are four common themes identified as the sources of customer satisfaction/dissatisfaction in memorable service encounters:

1. Recovery: employee response to service delivery system failures
2. Adaptability: employee response to customer needs and requests
3. Spontaneity: unprompted and unsolicited employee action
4. Coping: employee response to problem customers Failure to respond to the four themes accordingly will result in customer dissatisfaction. Therefore, understanding general service behavior is important to anticipate as much as possible the positive service encounters instead of the negative ones.

Secondly, the intangibility characteristic of service becomes another problem because research has shown that customer expectations are higher for services that are more intangible than for services with more tangible features. It becomes a challenge for a hotel organization to add more tangibility in the service encounter that may lessen the chance of a larger gap between customer expectations and perceptions when a problem arises with that encounter. In this manner, the service provider can add more tangibility when delivering the service by showing directly the service process to the customer. For example: in a restaurant setting, the service provider can present directly the food preparation and cooking process to the guests so that they may experience the process by themselves and see how the food is prepared. By adding more tangibility to the service we provide, it is more unlikely for a customer to judge a service delivery quality. As a result, the service provider will be able to prevent customer dissatisfaction from occurring or at least minimize it so that service quality will be better accomplished.

Thirdly, another point of consideration should also be given to nonverbal communication when managing service encounters. It is commonly known that employee's display of affective characteristics such as *"friendliness, responsiveness, and enthusiasm positively influences customer's overall evaluation of service encounter and perceptions of service quality"*. Moreover, Sundaram and Webster add that both *"verbal and nonverbal elements of communication between the service provider and the customer influencecustomer's affect or subjective feelings, which in turn influence their evaluation of the service encounter".*

There are several nonverbal cues influencing service encounters, they are:

1. Kinesics – body movements such as eye contact, nodding, hand shaking, smiling and adopting a relaxed and open posture;
2. Paralanguage – vocal pitch, vocal loudness or amplitude, pitch variation, pauses and fluency;
3. Proxemics – the distance and relative postures of the service provider and customer, and particularly the use of touch; and
4. Physical appearance.

Customer Perception of Service Provider Nonverbal Cues

No Nonverbal Cues Customer Perception

1. Smiling, light laughter and frequent eye contact Friendliness and courtesy
2. Head nodding Empathy, courtesy and trust
3. Frequent eye contact Credibility
4. Hand shaking Friendliness and courtesy
5. A slower speech rate, lower pitch, moderate pauses and less inflection Friendliness and credibility
6. A faster speech rate, higher pitch, high vocal intensity, and higher inflection Competence but less friendliness
7. Touch Friendliness and empathy
8. Physical attractiveness Friendliness, credibility, competence, empathy and courtesy
9. Colour and intensity of clothes Friendliness, competence and credibility.

When service employees know exactly what are expected from them in terms of nonverbal behavior besides the verbal communication, they will be able to enhance their effective communication skill verbally and non-verbally. As the effective communication skill increases, the service encounter or 'moment of truth' will more positive and the perceived service quality will be enhanced as the five dimensions of service quality are met accordingly.

Nevertheless, it needs some endeavour from the hospitality managers to build the service employee awareness of the importance of nonverbal behavior besides verbal communication in attaining effective communication skill that will enhance service quality.

Sundaram and Webster (2000) suggest that in order to make service employee more sensitive to nonverbal cues, the managers can utilize *role-playing* and show *videotapes* of actual service delivery which demonstrate both the positive and negative nonverbal cues. Continuous feedback will also be useful to remind service employees of the importance of nonverbal communication. Periodic surveys, in addition, are important to assess customers' perceptions of service employees' nonverbal behavior.

Providing incentives can be desirable to encourage service employees to implement the recommended changes in nonverbal behavior.

Thirdly, culture and purchase motivation become two other points to consider when attempting to manage service encounters. The involvement of people in service delivery implies that cultural diversities and norms quickly come into play when customers evaluate service encounters. This is obviously relevant especially in the hospitality industry where there is so much cultural exposure either with the international guests or among the service employees themselves.

The Asians and the Westerners are two different groups of people who have very different cultural backgrounds. Mattila (1999) states that Western customers care more about efficiency and timesaving of a service whereas Asian customers emphasizes on the quality of interpersonal relationship between employee and customer. Therefore, service styles in Asia are more people-oriented than in the West, where the efficiency of the service delivery is highly valued. Another thing that differentiates the two groups in terms of service expectation is that the Asians tend to expect the service employees who are lower in social status to provide customers with high

levels of service because their culture is characterized by relatively large power distance that reflect social hierarchies. On the other hand, the Western customers tend to expect more classless or democratic service as their culture less accepts of status differences.

Nevertheless, when these two different groups of culture are opposed to purchase motivation, the expectation will be different. For business customers regardless of cultural background, they tend to focus on the output not the style of the service delivery.

They are more interested in efficiency (including the speed of service) than in the functional quality of the interaction. Business customers driven by the need for efficiency might focus on the *"service outcome"* rather than on the *"feelings"* generated by the service encounter. Leisure customers, in contrast, tend to be more heterogeneous in their expectations according to their cultural background. Asian leisure customers tend to prefer *"high-context communication"* in which nonverbal cues are more important than explicit expressions. Asian leisure customers expect to be treated as *"deserving of high-quality service"* (Mattila, 1999). Likewise, some nonverbal cues may vary from culture to culture. Eye contact, for example, is very much expected by the Americans whereas in many Oriental cultures it is not proper to look in the eye too often someone who is superior. In fact, a bowed head represents a signal of respect to an authority figure.

Consequently, it is essential for hospitality organizations to develop employee training programs for guest-contact employees, such as: the Front desk employees in the hotel industry, to ensure that they are able to deliver the service the 'right' way. As for the organizations that expect to cater International guests, they need to give the employees a multicultural training program which includes a language training program and cross-cultural understanding to meet the possible cultural expectations of their foreign guests. This idea is in line with a research finding signifying that Front desk employees' performance is critical to guests' baseline evaluation of a hotel's service quality (Michael, Wooldridge and Jones, 2003). As for the restaurant, the waiters or waitresses should be trained well so that they will be more aware of how to be able to serve better according to what is expected by the guests and to have more control over the 'moment of truth'.

Service Blueprint

Service blueprints are pictures or maps of service processes that permit the people involved in designing, providing, managing, and using the service to better understand them and deal with them objectively. A service blueprint simultaneously depicts the service process and the roles of consumers, service providers, and supporting services.

Blueprints are designed by identifying and mapping a process from the consumer's point of view, mapping employee actions and support activities, and adding visible evidence of service at each consumer action step. Key components of service blueprints are consumer actions, "onstage" and "backstage" employee actions, and support processes. Service blueprint accentuates the customer interactions in the service operations processes and, that the line of visibility separated activities of the front stage, where customers obtained tangible evidence of the service, from the back office processing, which was out of customer view (Tseng et al., 1999). Hence, the service blueprint can facilitate problem solving and create thinking by identifying potential points of failure and highlighting opportunities to enhance customers' perceptions of the service.

Analysis of the Service Encounters

There are basically nine kinds of service encounters that happen in the service blueprint above as there are interactions between the service employee and the guest. First of all, when the guest calls the restaurant and books a table, there is a telephone interaction between the guest and the service employee who picks up the telephone. This is the first encounter or 'moment of truth' in which the guest will judge the service quality by evaluating the words spoken by the restaurant employee as well as the tone of voice or the nonverbal cues, in this case, the "paralanguage". In this 'moment of truth', it is very important that the service employee speaks the 'right' words in the 'right' way so that the guest will a first good impression about the service quality of the restaurant in his mind and he would want to go on to the next service encounter.

In this encounter, the guest will judge the service quality whether it is courteous, friendly, credible, competent and empathetic or not at all. Very often restaurants fail to attend to this very first encounter in the 'right' way. They fail to instill a good impression or even an excellent one about the service quality in the first place. This can happen since there is a different perception between the guest and the restaurant employee as the service provider on the "point of activation" when the first action in the service encounter begins (Hubbert et al., 1995).

It often happens that the service provider perceives that the first action in the service encounter starts when the guest actually arrives and enters the restaurant whereas the guest evaluates the first service encounter at the very first moment he or she contacts the restaurant and has the conversation with a restaurant employee. This can be a critical point in the 'moment of truth' in which the service provider needs to take care.

Secondly, when the guest arrives at the restaurant and he is greeted by a greeter who then asks for the reservation. This leads to the second interaction between the guest and the service employee but this time, it is more than just verbal communication but also nonverbal communication as there is direct contact between the two. When greeting the guest, it is important for the service employee to also demonstrate the 'right' nonverbal cues besides the verbal and tangible cues since all those cues will compose the overall notion of the service quality. In this stage, the service encounter will confirm the previous telephone encounter when the guest evaluates the service quality. In this case the critical point will be the credibility and friendliness of the service employees in welcoming the guests.

Then for the next service encounters (number 3-5), the guest will experience the next interaction with the service employee when he or she is being escorted to the table and seated. In this case the body language matters most as there will be less verbal communication but more nonverbal communication. Brenner (1998) noted on the powerful influence of body language on giving impact on others. The impact someone makes on others depends on what he or she actually says (7%), how he or she says it (38%), and by his or her body language (55%).

Besides, 93% of someone's emotion is communicated non-verbally without actual words. That is why it is of vital importance to pay attention to the body language and to make sure that the 'right' body language is shown during the service delivery. The body language can demonstrate whether the service employee is friendly, courteous and credible. As mentioned in the previous part it appears that some nonverbal cues are different from culture to culture.

That is why it is imperative that the service employee is aware of multicultural cues and able to perform eventually the 'multicultural' body language depending on the situation. The 'right' body language will generate good service encounters. In the end, good service encounters accumulated over time maintain a long-term exchange relationship between customers and organization.

In the next service encounters (number 6-7), when the guest enjoys the meal, besides the tangible things like the meals served, decoration and atmosphere of the restaurant, the attentiveness and responsiveness of the service employees will be the important points the guest evaluates in judging the service encounter. The judgment of the service encounter will be positive when the guest's expectation is met or even exceeded.

In the last service encounters (number 8-9), even though it is the last 'moment of truth' but it is also a crucial moment to take care it will leave a 'good' or 'terrible' last impression about the overall restaurant service. When the service provider neglects this last crucial moment, it may happen that the last 'terrible' moment will distort the whole first 'good' impression.

Global Hotel Guest Privacy Policy

Our Commitment

As one of our valued guest (hereinafter "You"), it is always a pleasure to welcome You to one of our hotels. Our first priority is to offer You exceptional stays and experiences around the world. Your full satisfaction and faith in Accor is essential to us. We recognize that privacy is part of Your expectations as a guest. Therefore, we have designed and implemented this Hotel Guest Privacy Policy which describes how Accor uses Your Personal Information on the basis of Accor's "7 Privacy Principles" (hereinafter "Accor 7 Privacy Principles") which constitute core principles for Accor and which therefore apply throughout the Accor Group (Accor and its subsidiaries) worldwide.

Consent to this Hotel Guest Privacy Policy

You should read this Hotel Guest Privacy Policy carefully before providing us with any of Your "Personal Information" (hereinafter referred to as "PI"), i.e. any information collected and recorded in any format that identifies You personally, whether directly (e.g. name) or indirectly (e.g. phone number).

This Hotel Guest Privacy Policy is part of Accor's terms and conditions governing our hotel services. By accepting said terms and conditions, You expressly consent to this Hotel Guest Privacy Policy. Accor may use Your PI for marketing purposes. If required by applicable law, You will be requested to give Your prior express consent to receive such marketing materials.

Accor 7 Privacy Principles

The following constitute Accor 7 Privacy Principles, which apply throughout the Accor Group worldwide.

a. Transparency: when collecting and processing Your PI, we will provide You with relevant information and notice, for what purposes and who are the recipients.

b. Legitimacy: we will collect and process Your PI only for the purposes which are mentioned to You in this Hotel Guest Privacy Policy.

c. Relevance & Accuracy: we will only collect PI which is necessary for the purposes of the data processing as set out in this Hotel Guest Privacy Policy. We will take all reasonable measures to ensure You that the PI that we have stored is accurate and up to date.

d. Storage: we will keep Your PI for the period necessary for the purposes of the data processing as set out in this Hotel Guest Privacy Policy and in accordance with local law requirements.

e. Access & Rectification: we offer You ways to access, modify, correct or delete Your PI.

f. Confidentiality & Security: we will implement reasonable technical and organisational measures to protect Your PI against accidental or unlawful alteration or loss, or from unauthorized use, disclosure or access.

g. Sharing & International Transfer: we may share Your PI within the Accor Group or with third parties (such as commercial partners and service providers) for the purposes described in this Hotel Guest Privacy Policy. We will take appropriate measures to secure such sharing and transfer. If You have any questions about these Accor 7 Privacy Principles, please contact Accor Data Privacy Contact as described in section 13 of this Hotel Guest Privacy Policy.

Scope

This Hotel Guest Privacy Policy is applicable to:

a. Any data processing implemented by Accor owned and managed hotels, i.e. hotels which are part of the Accor Group, including managed hotels, e.g. hotels operating under the following brands Sofitel, Pullman, Novotel, Grand Mercure, Mercure, MGallery, Suitehotel, Ibis, all seasons, Etap Hotel, Hotel F1, Formule 1, Studio 6, Motel6. This list is regularly updated.

b. Any Accor booking web sites, i.e. existing Accor websites, e.g. accorhotels.com. and also brand website (www.sofitel.com, www.mercure.com,...).

c. Any Accor loyalty program websites (e.g. www.a-club.com).

Although this Hotel Guest Privacy Policy does not apply to franchised hotels, Accor will use reasonable efforts to promote and request that the Accor 7 Privacy Principles be implemented by the said franchisees and that the said franchisees comply with all applicable laws in processing Your PI.

What Personal Information?

- Contact information, e.g. name, telephone numbers, e-mail addresses, postal addresses, etc.;
- Other personal details: date of birth; nationality,
- Children Information: name, birth date and age;
- Credit card details (only in transactional related system)
- Membership card numbers of any Accor loyalty program or any membership number of frequent flyer or any of Accor's partners You are registered with;
- Your dates of arrival and departure/visit from our hotels;
- our preferences and interests, e.g. smoking or non-smoking room, preferred location of Your room (low floor, high floor, etc.), type of bed, preferred newspaper, sports and cultural interests;

Any questions/comments You may have during or after Your stay in one of our hotels.

We do not knowingly collect PI from children under the age of 18, except name, date of birth and nationality as provided directly by an adult on their behalf or with adult's permission. Please make sure that Your children do not provide us with any PI without Your permission, e.g. online. If You believe Your child has submitted PI to us, please contact us so that we can delete such PI. Generally, we do not knowingly collect sensitive information such as racial or ethnic origin, political opinions, religious or philosophical beliefs, trade union membership, health or sex life details.

In addition, depending on the applicable law, other data than those listed above may also be considered as sensitive data: credit card number, leisure habits, personal activities and hobbies, cultural habits, smoker/non-smoker status, etc. However, we may need to collect such data which may be considered as sensitive, to satisfy Your request or provide You with specific services such as specific diet or any disability access facilities. In such case, if required by applicable law, we will ask You to expressly consent that we collect and process such sensitive information.

When is My Personal Information Collected?

PI may be collected in certain circumstances including without limitation as follows:

a. Hospitality activities such as:
   - Booking of an hotel room;
   - Check in and check out;
   - Consumption during a stay in an hotel as tracked through room charges;
   - Claims, requests and/or disputes.

b. Participation in marketing programs:
   - Registering with Accor's loyalty programs;
   - Contribution to guests surveys and/or comments (e.g. "Guest Satisfaction Survey", "Contact us"; "Guests comments"; "Satisfait ou invite");
   - Contests;
   - Subscription to newsletters, to receive e-mail offers or promotions.

c. Provision of information by third party service providers:

d. Internet activities:
   - Connection to any Accor websites (IP address, session cookies);
   - Fill in of an online collection form (e.g. online bookings, questionnaire, etc.).

What are the Purposes?

We use Your PI for the following purposes:

a. To manage Your reservation and booking:
   - To book and reserve Accor hotel rooms and requested accommodation;
   - To establish and maintain business records and comply with accounting requirements;

- For back office processing; including managing a list of undesirable guests, further to a non-payment, or to improper behaviour, etc.

b. To manage Your stay at the hotel:
   - To track consumption (telephone, bar, Internet, pay TV...);
   - To access rooms.

c. To improve our hospitality services, including:
   - To process Your PI in Accor's Clients Relationship Management (CRM) program;
   - To better understand Your needs and requests;
   - To tailor our products and services to better suit Your desires.

d. To send You newsletters, promotions and marketing material about tourism, hospitality or services, hotel promotions, or about Accor partners. You can choose to unsubscribe from our Email Newsletters service by clicking a link in one of our email newsletters.

e. To improve our Accor services, including:
   - To conduct surveys and analyze guests' questionnaires and comments and activity patterns;
   - To manage guests' complaints;
   - To let you benefit from our loyalty program.

f. To secure and improve Your use of Accor Internet websites, including:
   - To improve website navigation;
   - To implement security and fraud prevention means.

g. To comply with local regulations (e.g. retention of business or accounting documents).

Sharing of Your Personal Information

As a global company, we strive to offer You the same level of service and hospitality all around the world. To this end, subject to Your rights set forth in section 13 below, we may have to share Your PI with internal or external recipients in the following ways:

a. The Accor Group: we may share Your PI with any Accor entity authorized individuals who need to access Your PI to provide You with the requested services or in the context of an action as a consequence of You providing such PI:
   - Hotel Staff;
   - Reservation Staff using Accor reservation tools;
   - Information Technology,
   - Commercial partnership and marketing departments;
   - Medical services, if any;
   - Legal Department, if necessary.

b. Any relevant individuals of the Accor Group entities for specific categories of data. External service providers and partners: we may share Your PI with third parties for providing You with the requested services and improving Your stay with us:
   - Third party service providers: IT subcontractors, international call centres, banks, credit card providers; outside counsels, mailing service providers, printing companies;
   - Commercial Partners.

c. Local authorities – internal investigations: we may also share information with local authorities if required by local law or as part of internal investigations within the Accor Group in compliance with local regulations.

International Transfers

We may transfer for the purposes set forth in Article 7 of this Hotel Guest Privacy Policy Your PI to recipients, internal or external, which may be located in countries with different levels of PI protection. Therefore, in addition to the implementation of the present Hotel Guest Privacy Policy, Accor implements,, appropriate measures, including contractual clauses, to secure transfer of Your PI to any Accor entity or external recipient located in a country with a level of protection different from the one existing in the country in which the PI is collected.

Data Security

Accor takes appropriate technical and organisational measures, in accordance with local law requirements, to protect Your PI against accidental or unlawful destruction or accidental loss, alteration, unauthorized disclosure or access. To this end, we have implemented technical measures such as firewalls and organisational measures such as a login/efficient password system, physical protection, etc.

You may have to enter Your credit card details to complete Your reservations; in such event, Accor uses Secure Socket Layer (SSL) technology to encrypt such PI.

Session Cookies/External Links

Accor uses persistent cookies to manage Your session on Accor's websites and to personalize Your online experience (automatic recognition, list of Your favourite hotels, etc.).

We also collect technical information on Your computer each time You open a page during Your visit to our sites. This information includes Your IP (Internet Protocol) address, the operating system used, the type of browser, the screen resolution and the origin website address, as needed. We collect this information to improve the quality of Your visit to our site and do not sell or transfer this information to third parties. These temporary cookies are a built-in feature of the technology used. Most browsers automatically accept these cookies, but You can delete them or have them automatically refused. As each browser is different, You should refer to the "Help" section on Your browser toolbar to find out how to set Your preferences regarding cookies. However, You may not be able to use certain features on our site if You choose not to accept cookies.

We may offer You advertising or links to third-parties' websites which may collect PI about You when You view or click on their advertising or content through the use of cookies. Accor cannot control this collection of information and accepts no responsibility for this collection, use or disclosure of Your PI by third-party companies. You should contact these advertisers or content providers if You have any questions about their use of the PI they collect. Your visit to these third-parties' websites is in no way subject to this Hotel Guest Privacy Policy. Accor takes no responsibility for any privacy policies or practices of any third-parties' web sites accessible from Accor's websites.

Data Storage

We will store Your PI only for the time necessary for the purposes stated in this Hotel Guest Privacy Policy, or as permitted by the applicable law.

Access and Modification

You have the right to access, modify or delete Your PI. You can also object to the processing of Your PI as described in this Hotel Guest Privacy Policy provided that You have legitimate reasons. However, please note that if You object, we may in certain circumstances be unable to provide You with the service requested.

Hotel Service for Overnight Rooms

Bed and Breakfast

A bed and breakfast (or B&B) is a small lodging establishment that offers overnight accommodation and breakfast, but usually does not offer other meals. Typically, bed and breakfasts are private homes with fewer than 10 bedrooms available for commercial use.

Overview

Generally, guests are accommodated in private bedrooms with private bathrooms, or in a suite of rooms including an en suite bathroom. Some homes have private bedrooms with a bathroom which is shared with other guests. Breakfast is served in the bedroom, a dining room, or the host's kitchen. B&Bs and guest houses may be operated either as a secondary source of income or a primary occupation.

Usually the owners themselves prepare the breakfast and clean the room etc., but some bed and breakfasts hire staff for cleaning or cooking. Although some bed and breakfast owners hire professional staff, a property which hires professional management is usually no longer considered a bed and breakfast, but enters the category of inn or hotel.

Some B&Bs operate in a niche market. Floating bed and breakfasts for example are a concept originating in Seattle in which a boat or houseboat offers B&B accommodation.

Regional Differences

Australia

Despite the cultural similarities and a population more than twenty times greater, there are far fewer B&Bs in the whole of Australia than there are in just the South Island of New Zealand.

Since the 1960s the average per capita disposable income of Australians has been greater than that of New Zealanders and this has mitigated the powerful incentive to let out rooms in their homes to travellers. Another factor may be that Australia has, apart from City States such as Singapore, the greatest concentration of city dwellers anywhere on the globe and these cities are amply supplied with budget hotels and motels.

British Isles

B&Bs, and frequently guest houses, are a budget option where owners often take pride in the high service levels, local knowledge and personal touch that they are able to offer.

There tend to be concentrations of B&Bs in seaside towns where, historically, the working classes holidayed such as County Down, Northern Ireland, and Blackpool, England, and isolated rural areas such as the Highlands of Scotland and Connemara where there is not the year-round concentration of travellers that would sustain an hotel. They are present in most towns and cities, and their numbers vary on trade such as for business travellers and tourists: York and Edinburgh for example both have several hundred establishments known as either B&Bs or guest houses. In very busy areas, B&Bs may display a sign saying "VACANCIES" (rooms available) or "NO VACANCIES", to save both the hosts and potential guests the trouble of them having to enquire within. Breakfast is usually cooked on demand for the guest and is usually some kind of full breakfast, but some offer a continental breakfast.

In recent years B&Bs in the UK have struggled against budget hotel chains such as Premier Travel Inn and Travelodge.

Traditionally, business travellers used B&Bs but many of these clients now tend to stay in budget hotel chains. However, in holiday areas the B&B and guest house still prevail. Unlike the hotel chains, they provide a more comprehensive service and breakfast is included in the price, and some who stay regularly may simply like knowing their hosts. B&Bs tend to place their bedrooms within three different categories:

- *Deluxe*: This standard of B&B accommodation in Ireland is considered to be very high and deluxe rooms would be available in high end B&Bs and guesthouse accommodation. Deluxe rooms would often have additional furniture or Jacuzzis in the bathroom. Check the description.
- *En-Suite*: There is a private bathroom within the bedroom. This will always contain a WC and washbasin, and a shower or bath or both.
- *Standard*: There is not a bathroom within the bedroom. In this case there will be shared bathroom facilities in another room on the corridor. Usually there will be a washbasin within the room.

Cuba

In Cuba, which opened up to tourism in the 1990s after the financial support of the Soviet Union ended, a form of B&B called *casa particular* ("private home") became the main form of accommodation outside the tourist resorts.

Israel

The Israeli B&B is known as a *zimmer* (German for *room*). All over the country, but especially in the north of the country and the Galilee, *zimmers* have become an alternative to hotels for romantic weekends or family vacations.

Italy

In Italy, regional law regulates B&Bs.

India

In India, the government is promoting the concept of bed & breakfast. The government is doing this to increase tourism, especially keeping in view the expected demand for hotels during the 2010 Commonwealth Games in Delhi. They have classified B&B in 2 categories-Gold & Silver B&B. All B&B will be approved by the Ministry of Tourism who will then categorize it as Gold or Silver based upon the pre-defined criteria.

Kyrgyzstan

The tourism industry in Kyrgyzstan includes some B&Bs. One group, called CBT, organises homestays with people who own homes and rent rooms by the night. They help tourists and travellers in Kyrgyzstan find places to stay.

New Zealand

As in the USA, bed and breakfasts in New Zealand tend to be more expensive than motels and often feature historic homes and furnished bedrooms at a commensurate price.

North America

Many B&Bs in North America try to create a historical ambiance, with old properties turned into guesthouses decorated with antique furniture. For example, the Holladay House in Orange, Virginia is an 1830s Federal-style brick building that has been converted into a bed and breakfast. In the last ten years, B&B and Inn owners have been launching upscale amenities to improve business and move "up-market." It is not uncommon now to find free wireless Internet access, free parking, spa services, or nightly wine and cheese hours. Due to the need to stay competitive with the rest of the lodging industry, larger bed and breakfast inns have expanded to offer wedding services, business conference facilities, and meeting spaces as well as many other services a large hotel might offer.

The custom of opening one's home to travellers dates back the earliest day of Colonial America. Lodging establishments were few and far between in the 1700s, and apart from a limited number of coaching inns (a few of which survive as inns today), wayfarers relied on the kindness of strangers to provide a bed for the night. Hotels became more common with the advent of the railroad, and later, the automobile, and most towns had at least one prominent hotel.

During the Great Depression, tourist homes provided an economic advantage to both the traveller and the host. Driving through town (no Interstates then), travellers stopped at houses with signs reading Tourists or Guests, indicating that travellers could rent a room for the night for about $2. The money generated needed income for the home owner and saved money for the traveller.

After World War II, middle-class Americans began travelling in Europe in large numbers, many experiencing the European-style B&Bs (Zimmer frei in Germany, chambres d'hotes in France) for the first time. Some were inspired to open B&Bs in the U.S.; tourist home owners updated their properties as B&Bs. The interest in B&Bs coincided with an increasing interest in historic preservation, spurred by the U.S. Bicentennial in 1976 and assisted by two crucial pieces of legislation: the National Historic Preservation Act of 1966, and the Tax Reform Act of 1976, which provided tax incentives for the restoration and reuse of historic structures.

Through the 1980s and 1990s, B&Bs increased rapidly in numbers and evolved from homestay B&Bs with shared baths and a simple furnishings to beautifully renovated historic mansions with luxurious decor and amenities. The next big change started in the mid 1990s when the Internet became a major marketing force, making it affordable for innkeepers to promote their properties worldwide. Email marketing, in particular, serves as a useful tool for the Bed & Breakfast industry, for it proactively builds relationships with the existing guests after their stay. This helps increase the likelihood for more repeat bookings and also guest referrals in the future. At present, travellers research and book B&B online, checking out detailed photos, videos, and reviews. B&Bs are found in all states, in major cities and remote rural areas, occupying everything from modest cottages to opulent mansions, and in restored structures from schools to cabooses to churches.

Spain

In Spain, B&Bs are often run by people who place personal or family needs ahead of wealth and profit maximization. The business attracts numerous entrepreneurs with predominantly lifestyle motives, yet challenges them in specific ways. Spain does not have a B&B culture like Great Britain. As anything "modern" rules, locals usually shake their head at tourists visiting B&Bs when they could stay at a "proper hotel" for the same money or less. A study of the years 1997–2000, using a sample of 1131 Spanish firms, suggests that marketing must be done over the medium to long term to be effective.

Regulations

Regulations and laws vary considerably between jurisdictions both in content and extent and in enforcement. The most common regulations B&Bs must follow pertain to safety. They are usually required by local and national ordinances to have fire resistance, a sufficient fire escape plan in place, and smoke detectors in each guest room. Kitchens and equipment used to serve meals are also often required to be monitored for hygienic operation, but there are significant national and local differences.

In Hawaii, it is illegal to open a new bed & breakfast on Oahu as of 1989. The reason for the moratorium is to force home owners with extra room to rent out their extra space to low income residents who otherwise cannot afford housing on crowded Oahu.

Professional and Trade Associations

Many inns and bed and breakfasts are members of professional associations. There are international, national, regional, and local associations, all of which provide services to both their members and the travelling public. Many require their members to meet specific standards of quality, while others simply require a lodging establishment to pay dues. These associations also facilitate marketing of the individual B&Bs and provide a stamp of approval that the business in question is reputable.

While various local governments have regulations and inspect lodging establishments for health and safety issues, membership in a state/provincial/national bed and breakfast association can indicate a higher standard of hospitality. Associations sometimes review their members' properties and tend to have additional standards of care. In the US for example, each state has an innkeeping association (usually non-profit) that exists to promote the industry and tourism. However, many state associations, have rigorous inspection criteria that often exceed government requirements for safety and cleanliness.

In Australia, the industry is represented by the Bed & Breakfast, Farmstay and Accommodation Australia Ltd (BBFAA).

Organizations such as the Automobile Association also provide periodical inspections of B&B inns.

In the British Isles the national approval boards set up by governments are far more stringent than others, while in Ireland there is an association that will only use the national tourist board's approved members (Almara Accommodations Dublin).

Studies

Tourism Queensland Study

In January 2003 Tourism Queensland conducted a review of current research to gain a better understanding of the Bed & Breakfast (B&B) market:

Key needs that must be met for people staying at bed and breakfast style accommodation include: pampering and personalised service in an attractive location in an attractive house, opposed to more 'standard' hotelrooms.

The following attributes are also appealing:

- Homely or wholesome atmosphere (older segments) or luxurious/heritage surrounds
- Home style meals
- Area for conversing with other guests
- Ability to tap into local knowledge of attractions and activities in local area.

Guests at B&Bs were asked to identify the features and factors which motivated them to choose the establishment they were staying at. The friendliness of the host was the most important factor, followed by easy access to other places, the site being the most appealing place in the region. Usually B & B′s are privately owned, and therefore very different from standard commercial hotels. Bed & Breakfasts provide mutual benefits for both the visitor and the operator. Visitors have the opportunity for a relaxing break in a homely environment. Operators have the opportunity to develop a profitable business, make new friends and contacts, understand the cultures andlifestyles of others, and to educate guests about their way of life.

Income and leisure time have changed so that shorter breaks with greater choice of leisure activities are sought. Changing work patterns have increased the popularity of shorter breaks that minimize the absence from work and the effect of absences on workflow and involvement.

Bed & Breakfast holidays tend to be short break holidays and could benefit from the increased popularity of short breaks, sought by people who aim for authenticity and personal service.

Motel

Entering dictionaries after World War II, the word motel, a portmanteau of *motor* and *hotel* or *motorists' hotel,* referred initially to a type of hotel consisting of a single building of connected rooms whose doors faced a parking lot and, in some circumstances, a common area; or a series of small cabins with common parking. As the United States highway system began to develop in the 1920s, long distance road journeys became more and the need for inexpensive, easily accessible overnight accommodation sited close to the main routes, led to the growth of the motel concept.

History

Auto camps predated motels by a few years. Unlike motels, auto camps and tourist courts typically provided bed and breakfast or hotel style service, usually with stand-alone cabins. After the invention of the motel, auto camps continued in popularity through the Depression years and after World War II, their popularity finally starting to diminish with the construction of freeways and changes in consumer demands. Examples include the Rising Sun Auto Camp in Glacier National Park and Blue Bonnet Court in Texas. Such facilities were "mom-and-pop" facilities on the outskirts of a town that were as quirky as their owners. They attracted the first "road warriors" as they crossed North America in their new automobiles. The 1935 City Directory for San Diego, CA lists "motel" type accommodations under Tourist Camps.

In contrast, though they remained "Mom and Pop" operations, motels quickly adopted a homogenized appearance and were designed from the start to cater purely for motorists. The motel concept originated with the Motel Inn of San Luis Obispo, constructed in 1925 by Arthur Heineman. In conceiving of a name for his hotel Heineman abbreviated *motor hotel* to *motel.*

Motels are typically constructed in an 'I'-or 'L'-or 'U'-shaped layout that includes guest rooms, an attached manager's office, a small reception and, in some cases, a small diner. Post-war motels sought more visual distinction, often featuring eye-catching neon signs which employed themes from popular culture, ranging from Western imagery of cowboys and Indians to contemporary images of spaceships and atomic era iconography.

Motels differ from hotels in their common location along highways, as opposed to the urban cores favoured by hotels, and their orientation to the outside (in contrast to hotels whose doors typically face an interior hallway). Motels almost by definition include a parking lot, while older hotels were not built with automobile parking in mind.

With the 1952 introduction of Kemmons Wilson's Holiday Inn, the mom-and-pop motels of that era went into decline. Eventually, the emergence of the interstate highway system, along with other factors, led to a blurring of the motel and the hotel, though family-owned motels with as few as five rooms may still be found, especially along older highways.

Long-term

Motels/hotels with low rates sometimes serve as housing for people who are not able to afford an apartment or have recently lost their home and need somewhere to stay until further arrangements are made. Motels catering to long-term stays often have kitchenettes.

Short-time

In most countries of Latin America and some countries of East Asia, motels are also known as short-time hotels, offering a short-time or "transit" stay with hourly rates, primarily intended for people having sexual liaisons and not requiring a full night's accommodation. In Mexico, love hotel equivalents are known as "Motel de paso" (Passing Motel), even if they are actually meant mostly access. In Argentina, these establishments are called *albergue transitorio* ("temporary lodging"), though known as *telo* in vesre-slang. In Panama, love hotels with individual garages are known as Push Buttons (referring to the button that you push to close the garage door and the other button that grants access to the room). In Paraguay, similarly to Brazil and Colombia, motels may charge only by the hour and are also popularly known as *reservados*. In Singapore, cheap hotels often offer a slightly more euphemistic "transit" stay for short-time visitors. In Manila, a campaign against the hotels, believed by religious conservatives to contribute to social decay in the predominantly Roman Catholic country, ended with the city banning hotels from offering stays of very short duration. As of December 2006, there are still many short time hotels in operation. In Belgium and France, these establishments are known as *hotels de passe*. In Chile, they are known as *motels parejeros* (coupling motels), and many of them offer hourly rates. In the United States and Canada, some ordinary motels in low income areas—often called *no-tell motels* or *hot sheet motels*—play a similar role to love hotels.

Sustainable Competitive Advantage

Sustainable competitive advantage is the focal point of your corporate strategy. It allows the maintenance and improvement of your enterprise's competitive position in the market. It is an advantage that enables business to survive against its competition over a long period of time.

Todays' Era of Hypercompetition

Hypercompetition is a key feature of the new economy. New customers want it quicker, cheaper, and they want it their way.

The fundamental quantitative and qualitative shift in competition requires organizational change on an unprecedented scale. Today, your sustainable competitive advantage should be built upon your corporate capabilities and must constantly be reinvented.

Distinctive Capabilities

Distinctive capabilities are the basis of your competitive advantage. According to the new resource-based view of the company, sustainable competitive advantage is achieved by continuously developing existing and creating new resources and capabilities in response to rapidly changing market conditions.

Among these resources and capabilities, in the new economy, knowledge represents the most important value-creating asset.

In the twenty-first-century landscape, firms must compete in a complex and challenging context that is being transformed by many factors, from globalization, technological development, and increasingly rapid diffusion of new technology, to the development and use of knowledge. This new landscape requires firms to do things differently in order to survive and prosper. Specifically, they must look to new sources of competitive advantage and engage in new forms of competition.

This, in turn, requires a clear understanding of the nature of competition and competitive dynamics.

One popular approach to understanding competitive dynamics is the resource-based view of the firm. According to this view, the explanation for why some firms ultimately succeed and others fail can be found in understanding their resources and capabilities.

A firm's resources and capabilities influence both the strategic choices that managers make and the implementation of those chosen strategies.

To understand why certain competitive strategies are more effective than others, one must consider the distribution of resources in competing firms. Although a given firm may possess more or less of any particular resource, only those resources that are rare, valuable, and difficult to imitate provide a sustainable competitive advantage. When the strategies employed are successful in leveraging the firm's rare, valuable, and difficult-to-imitate resources, that firm is likely to gain an advantage over its competitors in the marketplace and thus earn higher returns. Competitive advantages that are sustained over time lead to higher performance.

If a firm could modernize its plant, or develop a more efficient distribution process, or access cheaper credit, it could compete successfully and prosper. But firms employ both tangible and intangible resources in the development and implementation of strategies, and as the nature of work and competition changes, intangible resources are becoming more important.

Examples of intangible resources are reputation, brand equity, and—for our purposes the most important of these—human capital. In fact, in any competitive landscape it has been argued that intangible resources are more likely to produce a competitive advantage because they often are truly rare and can be more difficult for competitors to imitate.

Among a firm's intangible resources, human capital may be the most important and critical for competitive advantage because it is the most difficult to imitate.

Tourism Academics

Taking important lessons within the confines of a classroom is the first and foremost way of augmenting knowledge and it is altogether certain that knowledge can be gained by reading books, talking to people and also by opting for other means of communication. However, in the present times, apart from these popular methods of acquiring knowledge, traveling to foreign locations and enrolling in short term courses in those countries is getting popular as an effective method of gaining knowledge in a specific subject/field. What is interesting is that while visiting a foreign country on an educational trip, the visitor also gets to know the culture and history of its people, the tidbits on people's lifestyle and architecture.

This is exactly the educational tourism phenomenon that is attaining universal popularity and jumping on the bandwagon, people from far-flung corners of the world are especially considering India as an important destination for their educational tours. These tours are especially focused on having a share of the educational experiences available in the country and also to enhance knowledge on the rich Indian history and culture.

The various aspects of educational tourism include an educational program in which the participants chose to travel to a region or country in specific groups with the aim of learning something from the visited region. In specific terms, educational tourism is all about visiting and then staying in a foreign country for more than 24 hours and not more than one year in a row for the purpose of availing short term language classes, education in school/universities, vocational and other specialized courses.

Apart from being a mystic beauty India is also known for its strong educational system which offers broad range of educational scopes here. The striking fact associated with the ever-increasing popularity of educational tourism in India is that short term courses are available in Indian universities and other educational institutions at a very nominal fee compared to other universities and this is hugely attracting foreigners to partake in the Indian educational system.

One of the premier Indian universities, the Delhi University offers cheap courses lasting for a period of around 4 months in subject areas such as Introduction to Sanskrit Language, Indian Economy After Independence, Indian Music, Indian Philosophy and Culture et al and various other related topics.

Foreigners are hugely attracted by the cost-effectiveness of these courses and as these courses throw light on different aspects of Indian culture and history, the tourists studying them are introduced to the variegated facets of Indian cultural experience in an effective manner.

However, likewise to the University of Delhi, the University Of Madras also offers short term training/courses on subjects such as Folk Music of India, Folk Dances of India, Indian Music and Bharatanatyam, Women and Environment in India, Travel Medicine et al. The educational tourism sector is also mushrooming in the Indian subcontinent due to the use of highly standardized English in various educational institutions across the country, cost-effectiveness of courses available here and a higher degree of academic standards. a Moreover, a range of study tours and student exchange programs are also facilitated by Indian universities welcoming students from different parts of the world, this too has led to a tremendous growth in the educational tourism industry in India.

Most importantly, comprehensive educational tourism packages are offered by the Indian universities which are prepared in a way that it is possible for the tourist to gain a firm hold on the specific subject matter. Further, as the people visiting India in search of wholesome learning experience gain ample scope to educate themselves on the history and culture of the country, wildlife and ecology, flora and fauna of the nation in addition to gaining expertise in their own course material, the number of visitors looking for educational opportunities in India has increased tremendously making India the nerve centre of global educational tourism.

Visitors opting for Educational Tourism in India are entitled to the following services:

- Internationally approved courses at top-rated Indian universities/colleges/other educational institutions.
- Comprehensive educational packages at cheap rates
- Standardized fooding and lodging facility for all foreign students
- Flights and visa arrangement at the earliest.
- Special security cover is available for girl students at all universities and colleges.

3

Hotel Resource Management in Hospitality

Resource Management: An Introduction

Basic Idea

You have acquired a set of resources, but for you to be effective, you need you to come up with a scheme to use these resources. Remember that you may not have the resources "forever," as it the case with dynamic resources, so you are best advised to make the best of what you have for as long as you have them. Even if the resources are dedicated resources, you still would need a way to ensure high utilization. Resource managers are needed for you to achieve this goal. A typical resource manger uses some sort of a scheduler to ensure proper usage or resources by increasing their utilization. Scheduling is the concept of sharing a scarce resource amongst users without starving any of the users, and at best gives the impression that every user has access to all of what that resource has to offer. This poses a challenge when the numbers of users increase dramatically or the duration of the jobs varies greatly. What makes this challenge even greater is that scheduling problems are mostly NP-Complete, with a very limited number of scenarios that are considered to fall under the P-type problem domain.

Single criterion scheduling are problems where the user is interested in maximizing or minimizing only one thing or criterion (minimize the flow, time, or the completion time). Many scenarios, machine shop or otherwise, require more than criteria to be optimized. For example, on a multi-processing machine, you want to minimize startup time and at the same time minimize completion time of all the tasks.

There are times where these two criterions conflict; in other words, you might need to suspend a task, thus delaying its completion time, to start a newly arrived task. The point is that "sacrifices" must be made, and that is the point of heuristic-type algorithms; they aim to minimize the overall sacrifice one has to make to optimize everything near-perfectly. This does not always work, however, but considering the problem domain, it is a very good attempt at solving the unsolvable. As you might expect, scheduling shares a number of ideas from optimization theory.

Quality of Service (QoS) for Grid computing has a special meaning because it no longer applies only to network resources. Compute, data, and network resources together need to be managed and there needs to be a mechanism that provides a quantifiable way of dictating QoS across all three domains. Scheduling systems thus need to take QoS guarantees into account when scheduling tasks across resources and administrative domains. The concept of QoS and data scheduling is further complicated when talking about globally distributed and/or dense systems where scheduling becomes more difficult; therefore, meeting QoS guarantees becomes even more complex.

Think of an operating system and how it schedules various threads or processes on the CPU. As the number of CPUs increase, the problem becomes more difficult, but the concept is still the same. These are a number of different scheduling algorithms, but I will not cover them in this article. The main focus here is to break down a resource manager into its core components, and talk about how these components work together to achieve a single goal: high resource utilization.

Resource Manager Components

Conceptually speaking, the resource manager is very simple:

- Queue incoming tasks
- Keep a record of available resources

- Match resources with the incoming tasks (scheduler)
- Queue results.

I am not saying that it is easy to design or write a resource manager, however, but from a conceptual standpoint it is a simple enough design that you can relate to. There are a number of ways that this architecture can be realized, but the one thing you need to keep in mind here is that network queuing theory plays a major role here. If you have an influx of tasks that is greater than the speed that your processing engine is able to off-load, the client queue will get backed up and you will start to lose tasks. This is the same behavior if you were to talk about a router placed in a network with large amounts of data transfer. Congestion control is implicit in the case of a resource manager as the resources will only be ready and request to process the next task when the current task has already been completed. This makes our understanding of the environment a little easier as if we were seeing a backlog of tasks waiting to be processed, this is a clear indication that we need only to add more resources to assist with the heavy load of the incoming tasks.

Your goal in this article is not to build a resource manager, but rather have a clear and better understanding of how one actually works and what its main components are. Focus a bit on the overall flow. You will delve into the details in the subsequent sections.

The flow is something like the following:

1. Resources log on to the Grid resource manager.
2. Basic resource information is sent to the resource manager such as OS type, amount of free memory, number of CPUs, and a number of other parameters based on the Resource Manager involved.
3. Data and any updates as synchronized between the resource manager and the resource.
4. Resource goes in to a waiting queue ready to be assigned a task.
5. The resource manager updates the table of available resources with the new resource.

6. The scheduling engine assigns a task to the resource if and when a new task is available.
7. The resource gets the task and the data, loads the appropriate service, and executes the task.
8. The task result is sent back to the client.
9. The resource is ready for another task.

Changes in Asian HRM

Ten years ago, Human Resource Management was almost an unknown term in Asia. Training, selection, and performance appraisal were given very short shrift, and staff specialists, when they existed, were known as Personnel Managers, or had a dual role of Administration Manager with a "Personnel" tag thrown in for good measure.

Back in those days, Asian companies were not aware of how effective management of the human resource had a major bearing on the bottom line. The educational sector gave little support. Professional associations were fledgling to say the least. A "personnel" position was often something in which you ended up in after failing to make sales, and seen as a dead end position. The National University of Singapore, the government anointed showcase of an Asian university did not offer one unit in psychology. China funded anything to do with science and technology, but soft sciences such as management and HRM were ignored.

Part of this was due of course to the culture of staffing of Asian business. *Guanxi* reigned supreme in staffing decisions, with family controlled companies meaning promotion was often the sole pre-rogative of family members. Cash reigned supreme as a way of evaluating jobs, where opportunities for professional development, training, and knowledge acquirement played very much the second fiddle to the salary level and perks. Objective rating of performance in many companies was therefore irrelevant, even if there was the competence to perform it well.

The bubble economy decade, where for many companies profits and growth were assured despite the competence (or incompetence) of management, effectively masked the growing malaise of Asian organizations. The signs were there, as a review of the past items on the Chao Phraya River Rat would attest. Over five years, the Rat's column drew attention to monstrous staff turnover rates, which meant that any investment in development or training was to naught anyway, as staff were likely to leave any time for a job which paid a few dollars extra, and often in an industry or function totally unrelated. We referred to the unsustainability of professional and management salaries, and salary packages and perquisites so over valued and out-of-kilter with other economies that warning bells about an Asian crisis should have re sounded well before that fateful day in June.

In the meantime, interest in MBA and professional qualifications was increasing, and appealed to many for the prestige and authority they bestowed on the holder. However, these qualifications rarely integrated well with individual and organizational career and skills development, and were valued as status symbols rather than an experience that "added value" to the real worth of an individual to an organization. The race for the MBA merely added costs to a companies payroll (in having to pay extra for the perceived value of an MBA, or sponsoring studies) with limited real benefit to the bottom line.

This week's election of articles that focus on Human Resource Management however, demonstrate that things are indeed changing. Companies and researchers are looking seriously at how effective Human Resource Management and Human Resource Development can build more substantial organizations than those that stumbled badly during the Asian crisis, where poor attendance to training, staff development, selection, and performance appraisal finally wrought it's savage consequences.

Some of the best articles this week, focus on the difference between effective Human Resource Management in Asia compared to the West, where many of the principles were conceived and developed.

Causes of Organizational Change

This is a time of unprecedented change in our society. The changes one experiences are happening at faster and faster rates.

As examples, the telephone, radio, TV, and microwave weren't even in use decades ago, and today these gadgets are commonplace, along with the computer, Internet, and fax machine.

In just a few months, the technology that an organization uses on an everyday basis may be outdated and replaced. That means an organization needs to be responsive to advances in the technological environment; its employees' work skills must evolve as technology evolves. Organizations that refuse to adapt are likely to be the ones that won't be around in a few short years. If an organization wants to survive and prosper, its managers must continually innovate and adapt to new situations.

Every organization goes through periods of transformation that can cause stress and uncertainty. To be successful, organizations must embrace many types of change. Businesses must develop improved production technologies, create new products desired in the marketplace, implement new administrative systems, and upgrade employees' skills. Organizations that adapt successfully are both profitable and admired.

Managers must contend with all factors that affect their organizations. The following lists internal and external environmental factors that can encourage organizational changes:

- The external environment is affected by political, social, technological, and economic stimuli outside of the organization that cause changes.
- The internal environment is affected by the organization's management policies and styles, systems, and procedures, as well as employee attitudes.

Typically, the concept of organizational change is used to describe organization-wide change, as opposed to smaller changes such as adding a new person, modifying a program, and so on. Examples of organization-wide change might include a change in mission, restructuring operations (for example, restructuring to self-managed teams or due to layoffs), new technologies, mergers, or new programs such as Total Quality

Management, re-engineering, and so on. Managers should note that all changes should be implemented as part of a strategy to accomplish an overall goal; these transformations should not take place just for the sake of change.

Solving Operational Problems in Performance Management Schemes

This essay identifies some common difficulties in performance management schemes.

Firstly, we will analyse root cause of these problems so as to gain a deeper insight into its complexity. This is followed by some suggestions for solving these problems. The problems are selected from various stages of the performance management cycle so as to provide an overview of the functioning of the performance management scheme.

The six problems discussed are as follows:-

- The problem of employees' opposition and rejection to the performance management scheme.
- The problem of non-involvement of the CEO during implementation of the scheme.
- Difficulties caused by unstable strategic goals in employees' appraisal and reward determination.
- Difficulties in the operations of performance appraisal.
- Weakness in the feedback mechanism.
- Weaknesses in the performance-related pay scheme.

Various forms of performance management schemes are commonly prescribed for the modern organisation with the objective of effecting continuous performance improvement. However, the studies of Bevan and Thomson (1996) as well as Guest and Peccei (1994) have failed to show conclusive evidence that the use of performance management schemes have actually resulted in performance improvement. Granted it is difficult to demonstrate the cause-effect between performance management and performance improvement. Other factors, both intrinsic and extrinsic, exert their influences on the organisation's performance. However, the lack of verifiable results does cause one to question the theory. Another possibility for the lack of clear success could be the faulty or half-hearted implementation of the scheme in the work place.

A common difficulty encountered during the introduction of performance management scheme is the employees' opposition and rejection of the performance management scheme.

The introduction of performance management scheme represents a radical change to the organisation. Not only does it seek to change the organisational culture, it also alters the employee's psychological contract. In practice, performance management schemes which are hastily introduced often fail because of lack of cooperation from the employees.

Cummings and Worley (1993) tells us that generally most employees do not support change as it entails moving from the known to the unknown. However, the employees may support the change if they perceived there are good reasons for them to do so.

To ensure effective integration and acceptance of the performance management scheme into the organisation, there is a need to prepare the mindset of both management and employees before launching the scheme. Firstly, senior and middle management should invest sufficient time to research and understand the full intricacies of the scheme. A study on the potential effects of the scheme on the workforce and also operations would be useful for anticipating problems later. Ultimately, the management team, especially the CEO, must be truly converted to the benefits of the scheme, or else they would be unable to convince the rest of the organisation.

As the employee dislike moving into the unknown, providing them information on the scheme through training and seminars will allay their fears and doubts. The training for both management and employees should cover skills such as setting objectives, measuring performance, appraising performance, giving feedback, motivating, coaching and counseling.

Another difficulty faced by some organisations is the non-involvement of the CEO during traumatic period of implementation. As the performance management scheme changes the work culture and the psychological contract, the employees may feel disorientated and demoralized.

Studies conducted by Sparrow and Hiltrop (1994) showed that 90% of senior management have not received performance appraisals in the last two years. The non-participation of senior management in the process, which supposedly they endorsed, sends out the wrong signal to employees on the importance of the scheme.

In practice, the CEO may moot the idea of a performance management scheme. However, the personnel department (sometimes with the assistance of an external consultant), are often given the task of designing the scheme. Therefore, ownership of the performance management scheme remains solely with the personnel department. Implementation of the scheme is delegated to line managers, who lack the know-how, commitment, authority and enthusiasm to get the scheme to work.

The employee's perception of the CEO's commitment is vital for the acceptance of the scheme within the organisation. The CEO should be highly visible in his role as champion of the scheme. The emphasis on performance should continually be reiterated in the CEO's daily dealings with his employees. If the employees sense that their CEO is uncertain about the scheme, some of them will attempt to undermine its implementation.

Most employees are not naturally motivated toward high performance as it entails much effort. Therefore, if performance is to become ingrained into the work culture, the CEO must lead the rest of the organisation towards improvement.

The CEO, due to his privileged position at the top of the organisation hierarchy, can inspire, motivate, assure and move his followers to accept difficult changes. He is able to silence sceptics, promote speedy adoption of the scheme and instil the required discipline for the maintenance of the scheme.

The unstable nature of strategic goals can cause difficulties in employee's appraisal and reward determination

To ensure alignment of an individual's performance objectives with the overall organisation strategic plans, Beardwell and

Holden (2001) propose that performance objectives be cascaded from overall business strategy.

Stiles et al. (1997)'s research shows that linking performance objectives to strategic goals can result in performance objectives having a short-term focus. Strategic goals are becoming increasingly unstable as the organisation responds to the changes in the external environment. Therefore, performance targets or even the objectives themselves may be changed midpoint due to the change in business strategy.

Appraising the employee's performance and calculating the reward becomes complicated. The employee may have put in effort to achieve the obsolete performance objective. However, as the business strategy has changed, his effort did not contribute to organisational performance. In practice, many organisations will not pay out reward for the employee's effort.

I believe that fair play must always prevail, or the employees will be disillusioned and loose faith in the scheme. Before setting new performance objectives, the manager should make an assessment of the employee's achievement thus far in relations to the obsolete performance objective. A fair amount of incentive should be paid to the employee in recognition of his effort. The manager should then re-negotiate the new performance objectives, targets and expected rewards.

In my opinion, senior management should realize that there are costs incurred whenever the business strategy is changed midpoint. It would not be fair to ask the employee to bear even a small portion of this cost

There are difficulties in the operation of performance appraisal.

Lawler et al. (1984) described performance appraisal as an unpleasant activity, which is despised by managers and supervisor. While Napier and Latham (1986) suggested employees often see no value in the performance appraisal interview and feel that it does not have a significant influence on their performance or development.

I consider the above-mentioned perceptions to be overly severe. In contrary, performance appraisal continues to be the most popular method of assessing employee's performance. Most managers and employees approach it with a sense of anticipation and high expectation as it effects the pay packet.

However, due to a major flaw in its construct, many managers and employees alike may have some doubts about its effectiveness. The performance appraisal has two main objectives which are in conflict.

The performance appraisal's first objective is to assess the employee's past performance for the purpose of determining rewards or promotions, while the second objective is to plan for the development and improvement of the employee. McGregor (1957) rightfully pointed out that the appraiser is often unable to resolve the conflicting roles of "disciplinary judge" and "helpful counsellor".

It is difficult to perform the first role (disciplinary judge) well without affecting the other. In his first role, the appraiser may have to give a negative but fair assessment of the employee's performance. However, he risks ruining the good working relationship he has with the employee. A good working relationship build on trust is vital for the appraiser to be effective in his second role of "helpful counsellor". Additionally, most employees are reluctant to report serious problems at work during the appraisal. Understandably, there is genuine fear that the work problems may be construed as the employee's weaknesses or poor performance. In practice, appraisers often compromise on the evaluations in a futile attempt to fulfil both objectives.

I concur with Randell (1973) who argues that the reward review should be separated from the performance review in terms of operation and documentation. Therefore, the solution is a re-design of the performance appraisal. Two separate reviews with a different focus to resolve the appraiser's dilemma of conflicting roles.

The developmental review focuses on improving the work performance of the employee. It should be held regularly, at least once a month, between the employee and his direct manager. During the review, the manager will provide the necessary coaching and counselling to the employee.

Feedback on the work performance is both requested for and given to the employee. Training and developmental issues are discussed with the employee. The employee's performance targets and successes to date are reviewed. Notable accomplishment are recognized and recorded in the meeting. A small incentive payment can be made immediately to motivate the employee.

The reward review may be held less frequently or once a year. It is held to decide on the employee's annual increment, bonuses or promotion. I propose that the appraiser for the reward review be the manager's immediate superior.

The manager's presence in the reward review shall be to support the employee's case for the reward. He confirms the accomplishments of the employee during the previous year. The manager's new role placed him on the same side as the employee. This arrangement promotes openness, strengthens working relationship and increases mutual respect between employee and manager.

There is an inherent weakness in the feedback mechanism of a performance management scheme. Feedback is an indispensable control mechanism for performance management. In practice, Folger and Cropanzano (1998) pointed out that most managers dislike giving negative feedback during the performance appraisal interview and are not skilled in providing it.

The lack of skill in giving feedback causes the following problems in the workplace. Feedback is often too positively biased and therefore inaccurate. Work problems remain unsolved as managers avoid passing negative feedback to the employee. Consequently, the employee remains unaware of his own weaknesses and mistakes.

On the other hand, a poorly delivered criticism can cause the employee to be severely de-motivated. Disagreement over the feedback can result in tension or poor working relationship between the manager and the employee.

There are contradictory views on feedback and its effect on the motivation. Hackman and Oldham (1980) suggest that performance feedback increase job satisfaction and motivation.

However, Bratton and Gold (1999) disagree and state that feedback has a definite influence in the de-motivation of employees. In my opinion, both the perspectives can be correct depending on the circumstances. However, I am an optimist leaning more towards Hackman and Oldham's perspective.

My suggestions for improving the feedback mechanism are as follows. Training in effective communications, motivation and human relation skills should be given to all managers.

Additionally, there should be two separate reviews, which is the reward review and developmental review. Feedbacks given during developmental reviews are more likely to be received positively, as the manager is playing the role of "helpful counsellor".

Lastly, I wish to suggest a few practical methods on giving feedback. One way is to re-phrase the feedback as suggestions for improvement. Another method is to guide the employee using non-threatening questions to discover the problem by himself. However, if the manager's relationship with the employee is excellent, the direct approach would always be preferred.

Performance-related pay scheme in its most common form has the following weaknesses: long time delay between performance and reward, unable to reinforce positive behaviour patterns and non-sustainable use of pay rise as reward.

Performance-related pay seems to be the most common remuneration scheme for an organisation implementing performance management. In performance-related pay the employee's financial rewards are link to the achievement of performance targets. In the ensuing paragraphs I will suggest some practical improvement to this remuneration scheme.

In practice, most organisations mete out rewards (such as promotions, salary increase or bonus payment) or punishment (such as demotion, salary freeze, no bonus or reprimand) after the annual performance appraisal.

Although significant accomplishments and critical failures are recorded throughout the year, reward and punishment are delayed until the end of the year. My criticism is that this delay weakens the employee's perception of a link between measured performance and reward. According to Mabey and Salaman (1995), the employee's perception of the link between measured performance and reward are crucial to the success of the performance management system.

The reward or punishment meted out reinforces the overall contribution of the employee, which is an aggregation of both accomplishments and failures for the year. My criticism is that this arrangement is unable to provide the direct link between positive behaviour patterns to the reward.

According to Torrington and Hall (1998), an organisation using pay rise to motivate employee may be facing an escalating financial burden. The organisation faces the danger of an "inflationary spiral" as it takes an ever-increasing quantum of pay increase to maintain the same level of high performance.

My criticism is that the use of pay rise as reward is not sustainable in the long term. An organisation cannot afford to pay high staff overheads in a sluggish economy.

In most schemes, even poor performers will get a pay adjustment to counter inflation. The employee is often not told the percentage of the pay rise, which is inflation related. My criticism is that the link between performance and pay rise (reward) becomes obscured. The problem is compounded by the fact that each employee's pay and quantum of pay rise are considered private and confidential information. Therefore an employee is unable to justify or compare his reward against that of his colleague.

I would like to suggest some changes to the performance-related pay scheme. In the re-designed scheme, the manager is allocated an annual budget for his department's reward payments. The manager and his superior shall negotiate the amount of the reward budget during the setting of the department's performance objectives. The manager shall be given the authority to disburse the budget amount with the intention of motivating performance in his department.

However, the amount that is eventually utilized for the year must correlate to department's success in meeting its performance objective. If the department is deemed to have achieve 50% of the set target, then 50% of the budget can be disburse as rewards to the employees. Amount not used at the end of the year may be distributed as bonus payments to deserving employees.

When an employee accomplishes significant success, the manager shall record the accomplishment in the developmental review and immediately reward the employee with an incentive payment. Applying Thorndike's Law of Effect, the immediate reward will reinforce the employee's positive behaviour pattern.

The re-designed performance-related pay scheme offers the following advantages.

Firstly, since reward is given immediately upon recording performance, a clear link between performance and its corresponding reward is established.

Secondly, correct behavior patterns that lead to success are positively reinforced.

Thirdly, the financial costs for the reward scheme are pre-determined and non-escalating.

Fourthly, it can be assumed that the manager will ensure effective distribution of the incentives so as to achieve the best possible performance.

Fifth, the autonomy given to the manager to reward will increase the manager's authority and control over his department.

However, the re-designed scheme is not able to remove the subjectivity that is inherent in performance-related pay schemes. The manager's decision on the distribution of reward can be subjective.

Therefore, some employees may complaint of favouritism and unfairness. A possible solution is to have the manager's superior verify any reward decision. Ultimately, the manager is forced to demonstrate fairness, as a demoralized department will not meet its performance targets.

From our analysis above, we have learnt the following.

Firstly, the employees' rejection and opposition to the introduction of a performance management scheme can be reduced by providing training and seminar before the launch of the scheme. Secondly, the CEO plays an important role during the implementation of the scheme.

Thirdly, the employee should be rewarded for his effort should the performance objectives be changed midpoint.

Fourthly, the effectiveness of the performance appraisal can be improved by having separate reviews for reward and employee development.

Fifthly, training in effective communications, motivation and human relation skills can improve the effectiveness of the feedback mechanism.

Lastly, the performance-related pay scheme can be improved by paying immediate reward when achievement is recorded. Cash incentives are more viable as reward compared to pay rise which is not sustainable over the long term.

HR Professionals in Managing Performance of Hotel

The management of people is the most critical component of an organisation's ability to implement its strategy effectively and compete in an increasingly complex and dynamic global economy.

For organisations, and HR departments in particular, understanding the international context in which you and your company operate is more important now than ever before with reorganisation demands driven by the marketplace. HR must ensure they are in a position to manage a more globally dispersed workforce and support international business growth within their organisation.

To succeed in the global marketplace, HR must act at a strategic business partner with a thorough understanding of the organisation's big picture and be able to influence key decisions and policies. Recruiting in different talent markets; implementing a global reward strategy; and ensuring effective talent and performance management are just some of the challenges facing HR, not to mention complying with local employment law and practice.

The lodging industry, routinely dealing with employee turnover rates as high as nearly 160 percent for some employees, has also had to deal with the downturn in revenues attributed to the economy's sluggishness and the terrorist attacks. As a result, hotel companies across the spectrum—from resort complexes to moderately priced facilities-have to work harder to win travellers' business.

Booking beds comes down to quality of service, according to HR professionals in the hotel industry. "We're only as good as our staff," says Nicola Thomson, director of management, recruiting and selection for Toronto-based Four Seasons Hotels & Resorts. "If we don't have people who want to serve and are good at it, we are not successful."

To foster a service orientation in lower-paid employees—and to keep the best people and reduce costly turnover—hotel companies are adopting incentives that range from bonuses, recognition and transportation assistance to programs that offer training and advancement.

The First Steps

Retaining good employees, industry observers say, depends on recruiting and hiring the most suitable job candidates. Although the applicant pool has expanded during the current economic slowdown, it's still not necessarily easy to find the right people for the jobs, particularly for low-skill, entry-level spots such as housekeeping. In the hospitality industry, unlike other businesses, job competency isn't enough. Hotels require employees to be, well, hospitable. Expressing an opinion shared by many HR professionals for hotel companies, Welzel says: "You can teach skills—how to make a bed, how to answer the phone—but you can't teach people to smile. The single best indicator of whether someone will work here is: Are they friendly? If so, we hire them and will work with them to attain specific skills."

A proven approach in recruiting is a referral program. Under a program that Welzel introduced at Classic Hospitality, an employee who refers someone who is hired and stays on the job for six months gets an extra week's salary.

Another way to attract job candidates is to highlight a hotel's attributes. For example, at the new Washington Terrace

Hotel, a downtown property that used to be a Doubletree and that underwent a $14-million renovation, General Manager Peter Carroll has hired many of the former Doubletree employees. He increased service demands but didn't have to increase pay. "It's a matter of pride for the employees" to be able to say they work at the Washington Terrace, he says.

In Denver, one of the hospitality industry's fastest-growing markets, strong competition for workers prompted the Denver Marriott to get creative in its recruiting.

The hotel started "partnering with local schools for interns and trainees, doing alternative advertising [such as on buses that serve low-income neighborhoods] and recruiting people with disabilities," a traditionally underemployed segment of the population, says Rebecca Peralta, PHR, director of human resources.

Although hotels in more remote locations usually don't have those kinds of community resources to tap, they can take advantage of their strengths.

The Woolverton Inn, a small, upscale property near Stockton, N.J., and not far from Pennsylvania s Bucks County attractions, highlights its pastoral setting as a pleasant place to work. "We are not near a big city, so we can't attract a big number of people" says coowner Matthew Lovette, who handles HR for the business.

"We make it a point to do public relations in the community. We run local ads and get the local papers to do articles on us so we get out in front of potential employees. Our strategy has worked. We literally have people walking up the hill and asking for jobs because they've heard about us'

Although a remote location can he a headache for attracting job candidates, devising a solution for the problem can prove to be a plus for retaining good employees. When the Four Seasons organization opened its Scottsdale, Ariz., resort three years ago, inadequate public transportation virtually ruled out workers who didn't have cars.

"The bus from Phoenix took 45 minutes and dropped people off about two miles from the hotel," explains corporate recruiting director Thomson, who helped open the property. "What we wound up doing is arranging our own bus service to pick up employees in Phoenix and take them to our door," she says.

That solution not only filled jobs but also launched new Four Seasons careers. "Many people who came to work with us were Croatian refugees, who have stayed and worked their way up to supervisory positions," Thomson says.

Keeping the Best

Four Seasons promotes internally when possible, Thomson notes, and that's believed to be a major reason that the company has some of the industry's lowest turnover rates—25 percent for all Four Seasons employees, 19 percent for managers. Turnover rates throughout the industry, according to the American Hotel & Motel Association, are 158 percent for front-line employees and 129 percent for managers.

Carol Etheridge, HR director for Bermuda-based Orient-Express Hotels Ltd., which owns or runs 41 leisure properties in 16 countries, and who currently serves as acting HR director of Charleston Place in Charleston, S.C., says, "When we find great employees and we find out they want to stay, well, we do everything we can to make that happen."

A retention program at Charleston Place, called Trading Places, enables employees to train in other departments at full pay for three weeks. Delores Collins, who started as a housekeeper at the hotel in 1993, expressed interest in working at the front desk and entered the program. Six months after completing her training, she was hired for ajob in reservations.

For Orient-Express, anecdotal evidence—stories such as Collins' and those of other employees—has added up. Etheridge now travels to all Orient-Express locations in North America to ensure that each property has strong retention programs in place. "Every property is different, so we don't expect them to duplicate what we did at Charleston Place;' she says. "But we do expect every property to have a component like it."

It's Not Always About Salary

With lodging industry revenues under pressure, many hotel

companies say they can't afford to use salary increases as a retention tool. "We can only go so high in terms of what we pay housekeepers," says the Woolverton Inn's Lovette. "We've come up with other ideas of ways to recognize people, like our Room Check program."

At Charleston Place, Etheridge established the WOW! Program, which encourages co-workers to recognize outstanding service. Employees give one another WOW! certificates, which ultimately add up to companywide recognition, a gala and travel prizes.

Informal recognition is important, too. "I'm a big believer in empowerment," says Etheridge. "I always tell employees, 'I'm the HR expert; you're the expert at what you do.' I put the power in their hands and say 'I trust you.

That pays off." Etheridge cites an instance in which a housekeeper overheard two guests talking about how they were celebrating their anniversary at the hotel. The housekeeper had a complimentary bottle of champagne sent to their room as a congratulatory gesture on behalf of the hotel. "It cost that housekeeper nothing," Etheridge says. "She made a $50 tip, and she made the hotel look great."

Classic Hospitality throws an annual holiday party for employees. "It's important to us that spouses and children come too, so that everyone feels included in this hotel family," says HR director Welzel. She believes that the company's emphasis on a personal connection between employees and the hotels is the prime reason retention rates are so strong. Forty-three percent of employees have been with the organization for three or more years, for example. "We have several housekeepers, beverage servers and engineers who have worked for us for over 20 years," she adds.

Bringing employees together also goes a long way in keeping them with the hotel. "Every year we do something special to show them and their families how much we appreciate their work," says the Woolverton Inn's Lovette. Recently the company took its staff to New York for dinner and a Broadway show. Overall, the Woolverton's multiple retention efforts have paid off: The inn has had no employee turnover in the past 12 months.

"Treat people the way you expect hotel guests to be treated," says Thomson. "Do that and you will attract great employees and keep most of them."

Hotel and Restaurant Law

The hospitality industry is affected by the law in a multitude of ways, whether one operates a restaurant, hotel, resort, or hotel and restaurant destinations. To be successful in the hospitality industry, business managers must make informed decisions, engaging in preventative management by knowing how to avoid legal problems in carrying out their duties.

4

Tourism Research, Education and Training

Tourism and Hospitality SME Training needs and Provision: A Sub-Regional Analysis

There is now a significant and growing body of knowledge concerning small business and entrepreneurship in tourism and hospitality. It is often emphasised that this focus is justified by the fact that, in many areas, particularly resort and rural or peripheral areas, small, often family owned and operated firms, provide most of the services and attractions and are the foundation of destination competitiveness (Getz *et al.*, 2004).

The requirement for tourism destinations to deliver high-quality service and products, coupled with the labour intensive nature of the industry, results in a need for the tourism sector to recruit and retain well-educated and well-trained professionals. Indeed, as Government's have increasingly come to recognise the economic significance of tourism and hospitality there has emerged a growing emphasis on the need for workforce development and the provision of business support services (Thomas *et al.*, 2000). Within the UK, the Department for Culture Media and Sport (DCMS, 2004: 22) has stated thatIf the [tourism] industry is to deliver a truly high quality product, it must become the career of choice for more of our brightest and most ambitious people. If that is to happen, high quality training and development strategies are needed, covering the entire range of activities from 'hands on' skills to management, and addressing the needs of both the industry and individuals. Yet in spite of the strategic priority being afforded to training and development initiatives, as manifested in the activities of agencies such as People 1st, Learndirect and Business Link, there has been little direct research into the precise nature of the skills development and workforce training needs of SMEs operating in the different subsectors of the visitor economy. The work that does exist, has only rarely considered the skills and training issues associated with SMEs operating in particular sub-regions or within specific localities. This represents a potential difficulty for those seeking to provide small business support services as an insight into the influence of such factors as geographic location and local economic conditions, business size and ownership profiles is likely to be crucial if local and regional development agencies are to intervene effectively to support the development of the industry.

This paper utilises some of the findings gathered for a research project that was completed in 2002 for the Telford and Shropshire Marketing Partnership (TSMP). The purpose of the research was to identify the recruitment, training and skills issues pertinent to Shropshire's tourism industry in order that this insight could then be used to inform training policy in the county. As such, the research was not intentionally small firm specific but, in common with many predominantly rural destinations, Shropshire's tourism industry is dominated by small firms and 95 percent of the final sample was comprised of small (20 percent) or micro (75 percent) firms as defined by the European Union (European Commission, 1996). The data gathered for the research is used in this paper to provide a case study insight into a range of small firm attitudes to training and training supply in the sub-region. First, a review of the literature that informed the empirical study is presented.

Training Needs and Provision: A Literature Review

Industry-specific analyses have concluded that recruitment difficulties and skills shortages are affecting the UK tourism and hospitality industry to a greater extent than in other industrial sectors (Hospitality Training Foundation. Some attribute the industry's skills shortages to recruitment difficulties associated with the industry's poor reputation as an employer. There is also evidence that the reported link between a lack of skills/experience and recruitment difficulties is specific to certain sectors of the industry, in particular to hotels, restaurants and travel agents and to certain operative level occupations, in particular chefs/cooks and waiters/waitresses. Regional imbalances are also apparent with Thomas *et al.* (2000) and more recently Impact Research (2003), highlighting the West Midlands as a region reporting significant skills shortages.

The size of an organisation is also likely to play a part in determining an employer's perception of skills shortages and recruitment difficulties. Small tourism and hospitality firms in particular have been found to be less likely to perceive recruitment difficulties than larger firms (Thomas and Long, 2001) and this has been linked to a lower perceived level of need for skilled staff and to the lower level of labour turnover in such firms. It is more likely that in small firms, skill needs will be firm specific and multi-skilled employees will be in higher demand (Curran *et al.*, 1997).

It is important at this juncture to explore what is meant by 'skills'. First, there are a number of broad skills categories. These are generally accepted to include generic transferable skills, vocational/sector transferable skills and organisation/job-specific skills. Generic skills are widely recognised as those that can be used across all occupations, for example, communication, problem solving, IT skills, numeracy, team working and work planning, as well as personal values and attitudes. Vocational skills in contrast are those needed in specific occupations, such as those described in national Occupational Standards. Some of them are transferable from job to job, for example language skills, while others are job specific.

Research in the hospitality industry suggests that the most valued skills are generic, such as the ability to follow instructions, the willingness to learn, the ability to be flexible and adaptive and show initiative, as well as personal presentation and appearance. This is closely followed by a need for vocational/sector transferable skills such as customer care skills. This research also suggests that the importance of these skills is likely to increase in the future. This confirms the importance of personal, 'softer' skills that have been identified as important to UK industry in general across other research projects. Other authors identify a wide range of desirable skills including diversity management, managing skills shortages, negotiation, political and commercial awareness. Interestingly, contemporary skills, such as IT skills, are least likely to be considered important by employers, in both general studies and tourism sector-specific studies (HtF, 2001a, 2001b). Also less important, according to surveys of hospitality employers, are a need for skills in people management, literacy and numeracy (HtF, 1999a).

Evidence is conflicting as to which skills are considered by employers to be deficient among their workforce and the extent to which this is considered problematic. The HtF (1995) has condemned the hospitality industry as 'one of the most under qualified in the UK' and numerous surveys have indicated that large percentages of small tourism and hospitality firm employers believe that their employees could improve their skills. A more detailed analysis of these findings reveals that the percentage of businesses reporting skills deficiencies varies by subsector, with Thomas *et al.* (2000) noting that tour operators and hotels were the most likely to identify skills gaps.

Hospitality employers' surveys have found that the top five skills that employers perceived employees to lack were communication skills, job-specific skills, initiative, customer service and willingness to learn. This, the HtF (2001a, 2001b) argue, highlights a paradox in expectation: organisations want people who are good at following instructions while also being capable of exercising their initiative. Surveys of the tourism and leisure sectors have also found skills gaps in customer care to be a key area of concern. These surveys, however, also identified IT/ computing as a key area of concern. This points to an interesting difference between the skills felt to be most important and those that are considered deficient. It would seem that while customer service and IT skills are considered less important than some other softer skills, their lack is felt when they are not evident.

It is at this point that the findings of different surveys conflict. Keep and Mayhew (1999) found additional skills gaps in entrepeneurial and management skills, and in the training of volunteers, while employers surveyed by Thomas *et al.* (2000) identified commercial awareness as a further area of concern. Beaver and Lashley (1998) have suggested the existence of a number of perceived managerial skill deficiencies across hospitality SMEs. These include financial, market, communications, people management, legal responsibility, quality, computer skills, maintenance and general management. Once again, sectoral differences and firm size issues are also apparent. The CBI (1995) and Thomas *et al.* (2000) found that language skills are seen as the most significant skills gap by tourism firms, in particular tour operators, while higher proportions of hotels, public houses and restaurants noted a deficiency of customer care skills. Meanwhile, research undertaken for a recent DCMS (2005) report suggests that smaller businesses in hospitality, leisure and tourism are less likely to perceive skills gaps.

Training in Tourism: A Demand Side Perspective

Where skills gaps are identified, the main remedy is still training. While there are a variety of perspectives on the relative value of different forms of training intervention, it is widely accepted that training is beneficial to business performance. Despite this, the tourism industry has a reputation as being a poor trainer. Indeed, Keep and Mayhew (1999) argue that much of the training that does take place is driven by legislative requirement. Surveys of the industry have revealed that up to 75 percent of employees have received no job-related training since leaving full-time education (DNH, 1996a), although, again, survey findings vary. For example, Thomas *et al.* (2000) found that just under 50 percent of the small firms surveyed were engaging in training (Thomas *et al.*, 2000), while the HtF (1999b) found that 85 percent of hospitality employers surveyed provided some training for some employees. It is likely that these headline figures vary so dramatically because they conceal a wide and complex variety of practice and attitudes to training (Lynch, 1994).

Once again, sectoral variations can be considered but survey findings are not consistent. The HtF (1999b) identified that restaurants and hotels provided lower levels of post-induction training than other sectors, while Thomas *et al*. (2000) found that this was the case for B&B/guesthouses and self-catering operators. When the formality of training provision was considered, travel agents and visitor attractions were, however, most likely to make use of external training provision. This distinction between formal and informal training provision is an important one, especially when considered alongside the size of the organisation. As Kitching and Blackburn (2002: viii) note,' there is considerable evidence that small employers provide less formal training than larger companies and are less likely to participate in government training schemes'.

Evidence from the tourism and hospitality industry appears to confirm this conclusion. The HtF (1999b) noted that training activity among smaller employers was significantly lower than among medium and large employers, while Thomas *et al.* (2000) found that the use of external training provision increases with firm size and identified a particularly low participation of tourism employers in accredited training schemes, such as S/NVQs and Modern Apprenticeships. There is evidence that SMEs are 'unconvinced of the value of outside assistance' in skills development (Smith *et al*., 2002: 4) and that they are constrained by the higher average cost of training provision (Lange *et al*., 2000). It would seem that the majority of training that does occur in tourism firms is informal and undertaken on the job.

This, in itself, is not necessarily negative. As Kitching and Blackburn (2002) note, in-house training can be perceived as relevant and convenient and also brings the benefit of being low cost, advantages that are likely to be particularly attractive to small firms. The nature and quality of this kind of training may, however, vary significantly. As Westwood (2001) argues 'sitting next to Nellie' is neither cost effective, creative, nor taken seriously by staff.

Kitching and Blackburn (2002) suggest that 15 percent of small firms are 'low trainers' training as a last resort, if at all. Fifty-five percent are 'tactical trainers' training as and when necessary, 30 percent are 'strategic trainers', with a positive and systematic approach. Their research suggests that small firms are more likely to be strategic trainers if they are larger, younger, innovative and exhibiting fast growth. The propensity to hire other managers/professionals also has an impact here. They go on to suggest a focus on initial training as the only training especially in small hotel and catering firms (Kitching and Blackburn, 2002). This seems disturbing, although research by the HtF shows an increasingly positive picture. For instance, the incidence of post-induction training in small firms increased from 40 percent in 1995 to 53 percent in 1999.

The concept of training is taken on board by most managers, but often does not become a reality (Wilson *et al.*, 1998). Kitching and Blackburns survey (2002) suggests that, despite identifying a lack of skills, and with 77 percent of respondents agreeing that training leads to better business performance, 52 percent of small firms feel that there is no need to provide more training while the other 48 percent suggest genuine supply-side reasons for not training further. Lange *et al.* (2000) categorise these barriers as being cultural, financial, access/provision and awareness related. The HtF (2001b) suggests that barriers to training tend to come from the employer rather than the employee side, and many authors concur that these barriers include lack of time, cost, lack of staff, difficulty in providing cover, staff not staying long enough to be trained and the perceived unsuitability of training courses.

The explicit impact on the 'bottom line' is considered by Clements and Josiam (1995) who state that 'while the costs of training are up front and obvious, the benefits are frequently unmeasurable'. Others suggest that previous negative experiences of training can act as a barrier. While Boella (1996), for example, argues that 'many proprietors and managers have no formal training themselves and are unaware of the benefits of training', adding that 'many employers are concerned with immediate operational problems and, as such, do not have time to plan ahead'. Others may worry that training staff makes them more attractive to competitors and thus, in a high turnover industry, represents a waste of time and money (HtF, 2001b). Wilson *et al.* (1998) add that employers feel that potential employees should already be skilled, and that it is 'the responsibility of others, such as colleges, to provide them with trained staff'.

Given this context, it is not surprising to note that research has found that few tourism and hospitality organisations make financial provision for training. HtF research (1996) suggested that only 19 percent of hospitality firms had a training budget, while Jameson (2000) suggests that as little as 12 percent of small tourism and hospitality firms have training budgets. Yet, while these figures are disappointingly low, they are in line with data for SMEs in other industries.

There is a general consensus that this lack of an emphasis on training reflects a general 'unsophisticated' style of management, which is also frequently reflected in informal methods of recruitment. Szivas and Riley (1999) and the HtF (2001a, 2001b) argue that the core of the issue is the extent to which tourism is a professional career. Szivas and Riley (1999: 770) state that:' The reality in many countries is, for better or worse, a persistently 'contingent' workforce, employed under very flexible conditions, on non-standard terms and on a part-time and seasonal basis.... a refuge when job opportunities in other sectors are scarce.'

Training in Tourism: A Supply-side Perspective

There is a widespread lack of knowledge and confusion about the nature of training provision in the industry (Thomas *et al.* 2000). While government initiatives receive some research attention, there is less written about the effectiveness of existing programmes. National Vocational Qualifications (NVQs), Modern Apprenticeships and other qualifications have both their champions and their detractors. Experience suggests that the most popular programmes are those that are short, inexpensive, easily applied and with visible personal and business benefits. Perhaps the best example of this is the Welcome family of qualifications, with Welcome Host being completed by 115,000 people between 1992 and 1999.

It is, however, not just the relevance and accessibility of programmes that is of concern. Beeton and Graetz (2001), writing from an Australian perspective argue that the scattered urban/

rural, small firm-dominated nature of the industry makes it difficult for training providers to assess the industry and provide specific training.

What emerges from the literature is that larger providers are more visible and more active than independent providers. Thomas *et al.* (2000) found that most tourism firms surveyed approach Tourist Boards, Trade Associations and colleges for training provision.

Sector-specific training-related organisations such as the Training and Enterprise Councils (TECs) seem to have been ineffective in establishing themselves as intermediary agencies for skills development among small tourism and hospitality firms. This is a key issue for their successors, the Learning and Skills Councils (LSCs) and for the Sector Skills Councils (SSCs) who seek to promote education and training and ensure investment in skills and innovation (HTF, 2002).

The literature presents a complex picture of skills and training in the UK tourism and hospitality industry. Despite variations in perceptions of skills deficiencies across sectors and regions and by organisational size, there do, however, appear to be some common issues.

Generic skills are perceived to be lacking, with an emphasis on softer skills and customer service. The general response to skills issues is still training, but training is often patchy, informal and reactive rather than proactive.

The issue of regional complexity is reflected by Thomas and Long (2001: 231), who contest that the industry as a whole has to want to train 'from a local policy making perspective'. They argue that 'a key challenge is to understand the extent to which organisations within particular localities demand and utilise appropriate skills and the extent to which the local skills infrastructure is geared to their provision'.

Small businesses, particularly, need easily accessible training provision that understands their particular needs. In addition, regional and sub-regional differences in tourism consumption mean that different skills are required. This leads us into a consideration of the findings of this sub-regional research.

Methodological Approach

The primary research investigation on which this paper is based was carried out between March and July 2002 and comprised a business questionnaire survey and a telephone survey of training providers. The business questionnaire survey sought to establish tourism organisations' perceptions of their own skills, training and recruitment needs and to identify reasons for participation and non-participation in training. The survey comprised of 30 closed format questions, developed to mirror the themes that had emerged from the secondary research.

A sample of 1,319 Telford and Shropshire-based businesses was identified, which collectively reflected the sub-region's broad range of tourism and hospitality business activities. The business questionnaire was mailed out and responses encouraged with covering letters from key local industry organisations likely to be familiar to most respondents. Despite this, the response was still disappointing even for a mail survey with a final response rate of 10.5 percent (141 usable responses). It should be noted, however, that this was, at the time, the second biggest survey of this type administered in the UK.

The training providers' survey sought to identify the nature of the training available, the training providers' level of involvement in the tourism industry, together with the providers' understanding of the tourism industry's view on training. Thirty-seven training providers were identified within the Shropshire survey area and 21 (57 percent) completed a telephone interview. The quantitative data generated from both surveys were analysed using the SPSS package to detect associations and patterns between the variables, while the more limited qualitative data were analysed thematically.

The Field Area

Shropshire, together with Telford and Wrekin, is defined as a rural area by the regional tourist board and is situated in the west of the West Midlands bordering Cheshire to the north, Staffordshire to the east, Herefordshire and Worcestershire to the south and Wales in the west. Together Telford and Shropshire have a population of 435,900 (Shropshire County Council (SCC),

2002), of which 45 percent live in Shrewsbury and Telford (SCC, 2002).

The county is visited by around 9 million visitors per annum, spending a total of around £254m (Heart of England Tourist Board (HETB), 2002). Approximately 60 percent of these visitors come on a holiday or irregular long leisure trips away from home and around 1 million of the total stay overnight. Around 14 percent are overseas visitors and although figures for the county do not show the country of origin of these visitors, for the tourist board region as a whole the key markets are USA (15 percent), Germany (12 percent) and France (12 percent).

The tourism industry directly supports approximately 6,630 jobs and an additional 2,120 non-tourism jobs in the area (HETB, 2002). Of the directly supported jobs, around 22 percent are in the accommodation sector, 35 percent in catering, 25 percent in retailing, 14 percent in leisure/attractions/entertainment and 4 percent in transport services (HETB, 2002). The importance of the tourism industry and the need for investment have been acknowledged in the Shropshire and Telford and Wrekin Joint Structure Plan 1996–2011 (SCC, 2000). Furthermore, the latest strategic review of tourism in Shropshire (Stevens and Associates, 2004) recognises the need for a robust framework for business development if the area is to achieve its potential as a visitor destination.

Although little information about the nature of firms in the area is available, the picture in Shropshire suggests a widely dispersed industry with some dependence on tourism, which supports approximately 4 percent of the economically active workforce. Unemployment in the area is broadly commensurate with national figures, although geographic and economic factors could make it difficult to match vacancies to potential recruits.

Findings

The Tourism Business Survey

The tourism industry in Shropshire was, as expected, predominantly made up of well-established, independent, rural micro-businesses. The survey included representation across most tourism subsectors, with the majority being accommodation or food and beverage providers. The vast majority of respondents recognised themselves to be either the owner or owner-manager of their business, with over half stating that they had worked in the same capacity for more than five years. Few had seen their performance decrease over the past 12 months and most were optimistic about future business levels.

There was evidence of labour turnover in the region, although there were some sector variations here. The problem was, unsurprisingly, less pronounced in micro-businesses, many of which employed few or no staff. Recruitment problems were broadly in line with national findings and the main reason was cited as a failure to attract applicants, although the reasons for this varied across sectors. Rural firms were the most likely to have unfilled vacancies, and operative staff were identified as the hardest to find. Larger firms were more likely to have difficulties filling vacancies and tended to look for more qualified/experienced staff than smaller firms. Local channels, especially word of mouth, were the most popular method of trying to fill vacancies.

The majority of employers stated that they were convinced about the benefits of training, especially its impact on customer satisfaction. Despite this awareness and despite seeing skills gaps in their workforce, most were, however, happy with the level of training they provided.

Their analysis of needs reflected their generally informal approach, emerging predominantly from observation and employee feedback. Furthermore, while employers were concerned about some skills among employees, they did not appear concerned about their own development. Some suggested that, as small businesses, they did not need training and that they knew their business better than anyone else. Others recognised very specific gaps in their own knowledge (for example, general maintenance, web design, advertising). On the whole, though, the perception was that skills gaps rest with their employees, rather than with themselves. The literature bears this out to an extent. While some authors see definite gaps in management skills and business awareness, the generally *ad hoc* approach to management and the lifestyle nature of many of these organisations often means that self-development is undervalued.

Training levels, at first glance, appeared to be higher than the national picture but much of this training was informal, on-the-job training. The key barriers to further engagement in formal training were time and cost related, with low levels of agreement concerning willingness to fund skills development. In fact, the only training that employers agreed they would fund was customer care/service. Where formal training did take place, there was a propensity to access programmes provided by tourist boards and trade association/industry bodies. To be acceptable to employers, respondents agreed that training needed to be short, inexpensive, convenient (location/time) and relevant.

The Training Providers' Survey

The profile of the training providers was very similar to that of the tourism organisations surveyed, being predominantly independent organisations (86 percent) and micro-businesses (95 percent). Most had a bank of freelance trainers available, or worked closely with associates in order to widen their provision as necessary. Providers offered training across a range of enterprises in a variety of industries but this was not often accessed by tourism organisations. Many of the smaller training providers surveyed were passionate about their services and showed a degree of insight into the tourism industry. They were often willing to tailor their programmes and delivery to clients' specific needs and work closely with them to analyse their training needs. Most were keen to provide training for tourism-related organisations, but had found demand for their services was low. The predominant method of attracting new business was word of mouth referral, yet many of the providers were simply not coming into contact with tourism networks. In short, the region has a valuable source of both industry specific and generic expertise available to tourism organisations but this was largely untapped.

The sub-regional picture of small tourism and hospitality firm attitudes to training and training provision that is presented in this paper, in many ways mirrors what is known at a national level. In terms of training supply, a wide range of generally appropriate provision is available but this is often poorly understood and rarely accessed by employers. Trade organisations and bodies, especially the RTBs, are most likely to be perceived as the most suitable source of training provision by small firms. Essentially, there is evidence of a great deal of untapped potential among Shropshire training providers, both the larger public organisations and the smaller independents. Often this is down to a lack of awareness of the available products, especially the opportunities for flexible, tailored programmes. This leads directly to the first recommendation that work needs to be undertaken not only into the content of training programmes, but also the format, modes of delivery and the associated logistics, in order to establish what offering is likely to prove most attractive to small business operators. Of course, the ideal programme of training provision is likely to vary from business to business, but this should not detract from an investigation into which approaches to training are likely to prove most successful in engaging specific sub-categories of small firm.

The key finding of this paper is, however, not related to training provision, but rather the fact that it is on the demand side that most workforce development problems exist. This in itself should not be surprising. It has now been repeatedly demonstrated that tourism and hospitality attracts many business owners for reasons that may collectively be termed as 'lifestyle oriented' (Dewhurst and Horobin, 1998). Such orientations tend to emphasise a focus on personal and social goals with fewer focusing exclusively upon the more commercially oriented goals such as business growth that are more commonly associated with classical interpretations of entrepreneurship. The extent to which such businesses are likely to engage in business development measures such as training will perhaps always be questionable.

There is therefore a need to focus on developing and shaping the demand for training from a lifestyle-dominated industry. As we (Dewhurst and Horobin, 1998) and others (eg Brownlie, 1994) have previously argued this will require a better understanding of the owner-managers' goals for success and associated business strategies and a tailoring of training provision to match such priorities. This is, however, not in itself enough, as there is also a need to work with small firms to achieve a broader realisation among small business owner-managers that a better business organisation can also assist in the attainment of lifestyle-oriented goals (Wanhill, 2004). Subsequent to the primary research investigation profiled in this paper, funding was secured for a two-year training project aimed specifically at small firms in Shropshire. This sought to engage firms over the period, to reduce or eliminate some of the key identified barriers to training — cost, location and time — and work with the recognised public sector organisations to deliver a suite of tailored training programmes. It will be the focus of a future paper to report the findings of this project and to reflect upon the extent to which the perceived barriers to engagement in training identified in this paper, are more or less real than those created by a focus on lifestyle-oriented goals.

Sustainable Development of Tourism, CSR and Innovation

The concept of sustainable development was introduced in 1987 by the World Conference on Environment and Development (known as the 'Brundtland Commission', whose report defined sustainable development as development meeting the needs of the present without compromising the ability of future generations to meet their own needs; (WCED, 1987). Tourism was not specifically addressed either by the Brundtland report or by the 'Agenda 21', the outcome action programme that emerged from the 'Earth Summit' held in Rio de Janeiro in 1992 (UNCED, 2000). Only in 1997 did the travel and tourism sector issue its first programmatic affirmation to the sustainable development principles in the document *Agenda 21 for the Travel and Tourism Industry,* jointly elaborated by the World Tourism Organization, the World Travel and Tourism Council and the Earth Council.

Some of the reasons for the difficulties on sustainability research in tourism refer to the multidisciplinary nature of the sector (WTO, 2001) and a general conceptual 'fuzziness' of the area.

For a long period, the sustainable tourism investigations have been focusing on identifying and documenting social, ecological, cultural and economic impacts of tourism, etc. In recent years, however, concerns related to tourism development expanded beyond the issue of impacts, and are increasingly explored in the context of globalization. Implementation of neo-liberal development policies also raised the issue of responsibility of the business sector for promoting sustainable development, leading to the emergence of CSR and business ethics as new business studies areas.

In its generic use, the term CSR is understood as the explicit adoption and implementation of environmentally conscious, ethical and socially responsible standards of conduct in and by the business, on a voluntary basis and going beyond the minimum legal requirements. In recent years, the concept has been institutionalised politically in the international context both by the European Union and by the UN. Under the definition of the European Commission (2001), CSR is 'a concept whereby companies integrate social and environmental concerns in their business operations and in their interaction with their stakeholders on a voluntary basis' (European Commission, 2001).

The Commission further emphasises four relevant aspects: first, that CSR covers *both* social and environmental issues, in spite of the English term CSR; secondly, that CSR is not or should not be separate from business strategy and operations; thirdly, that CSR is voluntary; and fourthly, that interaction with internal and external stakeholders is an important aspect of CSR. The United Nations is also playing an important role in promoting the CSR agenda through the Global Compact (UN Global Compact, 2007), a framework for businesses to align their operations and strategies within ten universally accepted principles of human rights, labour, environment and anti-corruption.

Tourism adoption of CSR practices is still in its infancy. Of all the industrial sectors that the World Bank Group CSR Practice reviewed in 2003, tourism was the 'least developed' in terms of codes of conduct and CSR initiatives. With regards to the content of existing initiatives, Epler-Wood and Leray (2005) point out that existing voluntary schemes, guidelines and codes of conduct have predominantly addressed questions of environmental management, with little or no focus on issues of human rights and labour.

In his *Tourism Ethics,* Fennell (2006) sees the research concentration on tourism environmental impacts as excessive and limiting for the field, noting the 'absence of an underlying ethical basis for critical thought in tourism'. Fennell argues that it may be the recognition of the 'immense void in ethics' that determined tourism being pulled behind other disciplines that progressed both conceptually and theoretically. Fennel further suggests that tourism ethics 'has the potential to emerge as the next main research platform' (2006: 358) in this field.

Ethics and CSR are also promising operating frameworks for the private sector. Among the first industry publications specifically addressing CSR was a World Travel and Tourism Council report from 2002, which reviews selected examples of social leadership by top companies of the sector (WTTC, 2002). In WTTC's view, the business case for CSR by tourism companies results from: favouring of responsible companies by governments and communities prioritising sustainability; building brand value and the market share of socially conscious travellers; attracting socially conscious investors; enhancing businesses' ability for recruitment of highly skilled workforce; improved risk assessment and response capacity.

Despite the reasons given by the industry, a study by Dodds and Joppe (2005) found that there is little overt demand for sustainable tourism, and both the consumer and the industry are still overwhelmingly driven by price. The same was noted when the Organization for Economic Co-operation and Development (OECD) organised an 'Innovation and Growth in Tourism' conference in 2003. In this context, private sector representatives noted that 'price competition and its consequences of productivity improvement, and not product innovation, has occupied the minds of senior managers in this [tourism] sector over the past ten years' (Brackenbury, 2003). Weiermair (2005) also points out that innovation is undertaken in the tourism value chain only in the areas where there is sufficiently high information dividend paying for the added cost and risk.

Price-driven improvements have been well studied in other industries. The discourse in the field of industrial innovation, however, rarely addresses the service sectors and is particularly silent in what concerns tourism. The research focusing on tourism innovation is limited, and as a field still sparse and fragmented. Hjalager (2002) builds on the model of Abernathy and Clark (1985), who describe the tourism innovation process in terms of: production, process, management, logistics and institutional improvements.

In further work, Hjalager connects the low occurrence of innovation with deficiencies of knowledge transfer, suggesting that in tourism, the central elements of innovativeness are generally human resources, competence, knowledge and access to networks.

While most traditional views of innovation in tourism, starting with Schumpeter's work (1934), concern technical and resource exploitation processes, researchers increasingly point to the need of a behavioural interpretation of innovation incorporating the social capital within the scope of innovations. In this direction, Macbeth *et al.* (2004) use the concept of social, political and cultural capital, arguing that The use of the concepts of SPCC in regional tourism development needs to have a broader agenda than pointing the finger at communities and telling them to take responsibility.

There is also a need for corporations and government to accept the need to contribute to building social capital, and to do so equitably across gender, age, ethnicity and socio-economic level. […] if tourism development is to be sustainable, it must ensure its development efforts accept corporate civic responsibility.

These comments point to a link between CSR and innovation, calling for tourism managers to see themselves and also to act as social entrepreneurs. On a more general basis, it appears that there is a need for innovation to be understood in a broader sense, as having a relationship with CSR in supporting the fulfilment of the 'social contract' of tourism.

Trafficking and Child Sex Tourism

Easily negotiated international borders and increased demand for cheap labour sustain a global slave industry worth approximately $9bn in annual profits, for which 600,000–800,000 immigrants are trafficked across international borders every year (Glover, 2006). The main premise of human trafficking is that increased poverty leads hopeless immigrants to seek opportunities beyond the borders of their homelands (Coonan and Thompson, 2005).

Trafficking and child sex tourism are among what Payne and Dimanche (1996) consider the myriad of issues and problems in the tourism industry tied to ethics, or lack of thereof. While sex tourism is better known in the tourism academic research circles, trafficking has been only recently associated to tourism. Child Sex Tourism (CST) is a narrow topic within the wider issue of sex tourism, which was developed as a legitimate area of tourism studies from the 1970s.

Tourism researchers have reported extensively on sex tourism over the last two decades, significant exploratory work being carried out by Carter and Clift (2000), Garrick (2005), Hall (1996), Jeffreys (1999), O'Connell Davidson (2000), Oppermann (1999), Rao (1999), Ryan and Hall (2001), Seabrook (2000), Truong (1990), Ryan and Kinder (1996), and others. Important field research was carried out in the 1990s in Thailand, Goa, Venezuela, Dominican Republic, South Africa, Cuba, and Costa Rica, by O'Connell Davidson and Sanchez Taylor (1995).

Their reports were commissioned by ECPAT International and used in preparation for the 1996 1st World Congress against the Commercial Sexual Exploitation of Children (reports available from ECPAT International (End Child Prostitution, Child Pornography and Trafficking of Children for Sexual Purposes) website www.ecpat.net).

Moving beyond merely observing CST as a component of tourism and sexuality, recent works progressed toward more sophisticated aspects of CST, such as those including commonalities with sex tourism in general (O'Connell Davidson, 2004), tourists' rationalisations (Garrick, 2005), sex tourism and citizenship (Cabezas, 2004).

CST is distinguished from the wider topic of sex tourism studies by its classification as a national or international crime. As adult prostitution is legal in some countries, adult sex tourism, while controversial, is not a crime under certain national jurisdictions. Tourism, however, for the purpose of sexual relation with a minor is a crime and a clear and unambiguous violation of human rights (UNWTO, 2004) under the international legislation. A tourist who engages in sex with a minor commits a violation of the UN Convention of the Rights of the Child, and of the Optional Protocol on the Sale of Children, Child Prostitution and Child Pornography. Children's fundamental right to be protected against commercial sexual exploitation is addressed in the UN Convention on the Rights of the Child (CRC), whose Article 34 recognises the cross-border aspects that are typical of the phenomenon.

More recently, new information increasingly links CST with trafficking in human beings, a phenomenon considered by the UN Office on Drugs and Crime to be the 21st century form of the old worldwide slave trade (UNODC, 2006). UNODC defines trafficking in the context of the UN Convention against Transnational Organized Crime, and of two of its supplementing protocols: the Protocol to Prevent, Suppress and Punish Trafficking in Persons, Especially Women and Children, and the Protocol against the Smuggling of Migrants by Land, Sea and Air, both adopted by the UN General Assembly in 2000. Trafficking is defined as the recruitment, transportation, transfer, harbouring or receipt of persons, by means of the threat or use of force or tougher forms of coercion, of abduction, of fraud, or deception, or the abuse of power or of a position of vulnerability or of the giving or receiving of payments or benefits to achieve the consent of a person having control over another person, for the purpose of exploitation. Exploitation includes, at a minimum, the exploitation of the prostitution of others or other forms of sexual exploitation, forced labour or services, slavery or practices similar to slavery, servitude or the removal of organs. (UNODC, 2006: 7)

The links between trafficking and child sex tourism are also noted by the US Department of State Office to Monitor and

Combat Trafficking in Persons (TIP Office), which issues an annual Trafficking in Persons Report (TIP Report). The Protection Project at John Hopkins University (Protection Project, 2007) reviewed the 2006 edition of the TIP report, finding that 29 countries were referenced as either origin or destination countries. These references point out the fact that the TIP Office lists other governments' efforts to combat CST among the measures to eliminate trafficking in persons. The aspects of 'transportation, transfer, harbouring or receipt of persons' in the trafficking definition make it possible for tourism businesses to be used, voluntarily or involuntarily, in relation to the trafficking phenomenon. In what concerns adult victims, there is often confusion between trafficking and smuggling of migrants. The differentiating aspects concern the nature of consent (coercive, deceptive or abusive in the case of trafficking), and the aspect of continuous exploitation and coercion for illegal profits which characterise trafficking. Also, unlike smuggling, which is always transnational, trafficking can be both internal and trans-boundary (UNODC, 2007).

In regard to minor victims of CST and trafficking, the legal determination is clear. According to the existing international legal framework, children under 18 cannot give valid consent, and any recruitment, transportation, transfer, harbouring or receipt of children for the purpose of exploitation is a form of trafficking regardless of the means used (UNODC, 2007). A common misconception is that sex tourists are primarily paedophiles. According to Glover (2006), however, the majority of perpetrators are primarily prostitute users in general. UNICEF quotes surveys indicating that 30–35 percent of all sex workers in the Mekong sub-region of south-east Asia are between 12 and 17 years of age (UNICEF, 2007a), 2 million children are believed to be exploited through prostitution and pornography, and 1.2 million children are trafficked every year (UNICEF, 2007b). While child sex tourism is booming worldwide, according to Glover (2006) Asia is at the centre of child prostitution, with 60,000 child prostitutes in the Philippines, 400,000 in India, 800,000 in Thailand. Most of them are girls under the age of 16, or boys in the case of Sri Lanka's 20,000 child prostitutes. Child prostitution and sex tourism, however, cannot be blamed on tourists alone, as they seem to be thriving in places where a culture of prostitution is connected to the local customs or historical circumstances. In Sachs (1994), Hnin Hnin Pyne estimates that 75 percent of Thai men have had sex with a prostitute. With such a demand, children are sought in the most impoverished areas to be brought to developed entertainment destinations, often tourism destinations, to serve the red light districts.

Models of Tourism Innovations Preventing Trafficking and Sex Tourism

The existing body of knowledge on child sex tourism and trafficking in the context of sustainability and CSR is thin. Furthermore, the theoretical contextualisation on CST and trafficking phenomena turns obsolete quickly, due to the volatile dynamics of these phenomena and the rapid changes of the tourism industry. Yet, some empirical developments have been recently taking place. Models of responsible practice to prevent and counteract trafficking and sex tourism have emerged in the last decade from a variety of tourism stakeholders, including nongovernmental organisations, international governmental organisations, industry and national tourism authorities. They come to complement national laws, including extra-territorial legislation created by many governments to prevent trafficking and sex tourism.

The general aims of tourism industry innovations were, first, to create awareness within the industry regarding its potential preventative role, and, secondly, to equip tourism businesses with the tools to exercise it. Other measures looked into creating alternative opportunities for development for the children at risk, facilitating public awareness, and creating incentives to report sex tourism and trafficking. Several such examples are briefly described in this section, clustered according to the type of stakeholders driving them.

Models of Innovation by Nongovernmental Organisations

The youth Career Initiative Programme of the International Business Leaders' Foundation

The youth career initiative (YCI) is a programme run by the

London-based international business leaders' foundation (IBLF) through their International Tourism Partnership, seeking to increase youth employability in the hotel sector, and by doing so helping to end the cycle of poverty and social exclusion (IBLF, 2007). The programme engages international hotels (Marriott, Sheraton, Pan Pacific, Sol Melia, Starwood, Orient Express, Intercontinental, etc.) to provide five to six months education on the hotel premises for high-school graduates from disadvantaged backgrounds. It includes both theory and practical instruction by hotel staff, in finance, IT, interpersonal skills and personal health and wellbeing. Upon completing the programme, the participants are helped to make further career and education choices. Over 1,300 youth have graduated the programme since its inception in 1995 and with the initial support of UNICEF and the Pan Pacific Hotel in Bangkok. Currently YCI runs in eight countries: Brazil, Ethiopia, Thailand, Philippines, Indonesia, Australia, Romania and Poland (IBLF, 2007). Although the content of the YCI programme is not directly targeting CST or trafficking, it provides a useful example of innovative engagement by the hospitality industry with youth at risk in developing countries. Through the vocational and career skills it instils, YCI is likely to provide an opportunity for youth to start onto a path of healthy development.

'Travel with Care' and 'Child wise Tourism' Programmes of Child Wise™ Australia

The nongovernmental organisation Child Wise is focusing on work in destinations where Australians travel. Child Wise is the Australian representative of the ECPAT International, a network of organisations and individuals working to eliminate the commercial sexual exploitation of children. ECPAT started in 1996 in Thailand, is currently represented in another 62 countries, and has been one of the first organisations to begin campaigning against child prostitution in Asian tourism (ECPAT International, 2007). The approach of Child Wise to protect children builds on the observation that CST involving Australians tends to occur outside the work of the mainstream tourism industry (Hecht, 2001). Consequently, mainstream tourism industry codes of conduct would probably have a limited effect in deterring

Australian child sex tourists. Developed since 1999, 'Child Wise Tourism' is a training and network development programme running throughout the ASEAN region, including training modules and education materials for travel and tourism students, educators and the tourism industry. The programme builds skills for the tourism staff so they become capable of identifying and responding to situations where children may be at risk of sexual exploitation. The programme conducts community-based training sessions in the seven ASEAN countries: Thailand, Indonesia, Cambodia, Philippines, Lao PDR, Vietnam and Myanmar (Child Wise, 2007). Another Child Wise programme, 'Travel with Care', is an intensive travel and tourism industry education module, aimed at increasing awareness of the Australia Child Sex Tourism law. Since December 2003, an awareness raising campaign has been launched with the slogan 'Don't let child abuse travel!' involving distribution of posters, postcards, as well as TV and radio messages.

World Vision 'Child Sex Tourism Prevention Project' and Campaign Targeting US Travellers

World Vision, a Christian humanitarian organisation operating in nearly 100 countries, developed since 2004 through its US branch is a campaign aimed at deterring foreign sex tourists and raising awareness on the extra-territorial legislation against CST. The World Vision campaign slogan 'Abuse a child in this country, go to jail in yours' was used in Cambodia, Thailand, Costa Rica, Mexico and Brazil, targeting mainly American tourists. The campaign also included deterrent messages posted in the US airports, airline in-flight videos, billboards and street signs overseas (World Vision, 2007). ECPAT-USA Inc., a group working since 1996 against CST in the US, estimates that American citizens account for 25 percent of child sex tourists worldwide.

Multi-Stakeholder Models of Innovation

The Code of Conduct for the Protection of Children from Sexual Exploitation in Travel and Tourism (the Code) is an industry-driven multi-stakeholder initiative that seeks to increase protection of children from sex tourism. The companies

— tour operators and their umbrella organisations, hotels, travel agents, airlines, etc. — that endorse the Code, commit themselves to implement six measures. These are elaborating corporate policies against CST; training company staff on how to prevent CST; providing information to the travellers in relation to CST; inserting clauses in contracts with suppliers jointly repudiating CST; working together with 'key persons' in destinations to prevent CST; and finally, reporting annually on the implementation of these measures.

The Code was initiated in 1998 by ECPAT Sweden (member of the ECPAT network) in cooperation with Scandinavian tour operators and the UN World Tourism Organization (UNWTO). Funding was provided by the European Commission for the Code's implementation in six European countries, between 2000 and 2004: Austria, Germany, Sweden, UK, the Netherlands and Italy. Following the launch of the Code in North America in April 2004, UNICEF became a supporting partner and a cofunding body of the Code organisation. Signed by over 600 tour operators, hotels, travel agents and their associations, tourism workers' unions from 23 countries in Europe, Asia, North America, Central and Latin America (Tepelus, 2004), the Code is internationally recognised by UNICEF and the UNWTO as one of the most advanced private sector tools for the prevention and combating of CST. The Code process, however, has a number of shortcomings. Criticisms concern the lack of enforcement mechanisms once a company signs up, and insufficient monitoring of the implementation in destinations. As the structure of the Code is that of a multi-stakeholder process based on support from national partners (ECPAT groups, governments, UNICEF offices, etc.), the rigorousness of implementation varies greatly from country to country. Furthermore, since the Code marketing and promotion proceeded in parallel with attempts to strengthen its own internal organisation, the Code as an industry-driven, self-sustained organisation, independent of the ECPAT network, is still a work in progress.

Innovation through Government-Led Campaigns: Brazil

The Government of Brazil was among the first governments taking a clear and official stand against the phenomenon of CST, launching since 1997 a 'no child sex tourism' campaign. Brazil was the first country to design a logo for the tourism campaign against exploitation of children, logo adopted later by the UNWTO for the global campaign. National awareness started in Brazil since 2001 with the support of EMBRATUR and of the federation of hotels and conventions. More recently, under the presidency of Luiz Inacio Lula da Silva starting in 2002, a Ministry of Tourism was created and a 'Sustainable Tourism and Childhood Thematic Chamber' was institutionalised within the structure of the National Tourism Chamber. The principal objectives of the 'Sustainable Tourism and Childhood' programme are to assist the creation of public policies on the protection of children in relation to tourism, and to promote good practices of the private sector, including the introduction of codes of conduct. The Brazil Ministry of Tourism also spearheaded a regional South American 'Sustainable Tourism and Childhood' programme, by convening annually between 2004 and 2007 a World Tourism Forum for Peace and Sustainable Development. In the context of the Forum, national tourism authorities and tourism ministries from all South American countries came together and issued the 1st Declaration against CST on 26th October, 2005 in Rio de Janeiro. The declaration was followed by plans for a joint South American campaign against CST designed to be running in 12 countries starting in 2007. In its efforts to protect children and teenagers from sexual exploitation in tourism, the Brazilian Federal Government worked together with nongovernmental partners including Save the Children Sweden, World Childhood Foundation Brazil and others.

Engagement of Inter-Governmental Organisations: UNWTO, UNICEF, OSCE, ILO, etc.

Several inter-governmental organisations facilitated tourism innovation against trafficking and CST, mostly by acting as convening bodies for international meetings and by supporting dialogue and information exchange platforms.

UN World Tourism Organization (UNWTO/OMT)

UNWTO has been concerned on the issue of protection of children from sex tourism, providing inputs in the proceedings of the 1st and 2nd Congresses against Commercial Exploitation of Children held in Stockholm in 1996, and in Yokohama in 2001. Following the Stockholm Congress 'Declaration and Agenda for Action', UNWTO established in 1997 a Task Force to Protect Children from Sexual Exploitation in Tourism, a global multi-stakeholder action platform aiming to prevent, uncover, isolate and eradicate the sexual exploitation of children in tourism (UNWTO, 2007a). The Task Force meets bi-annually at the largest international tourism fairs, ITB held in March in Berlin and WTM held in November in London. The framework for the UNWTO position on CST is provided by the Article 2, point 3 of the Global Code of Ethics for Tourism (GCTE), which reads: The exploitation of human beings in any form, particularly sexual, especially when applied to children, conflicts with the fundamental aims of tourism and is the negation of tourism; as such, in accordance with international law, it should be energetically combated with the cooperation of all the States concerned and penalized without concession by the national legislation of both the countries visited and the countries of the perpetrators of these acts, even when they are carried out abroad.

The GCTE is a set of ten principles aiming to guide stakeholders in tourism development, and was recognised by the UN General Assembly in 2001 through the resolution A/RES/56/212. While the GCTE is not a legally binding document, the UNWTO drafted policies and guidelines governing a voluntary implementation mechanism, whereby a World Committee on Tourism Ethics (WCTE) may intervene in the settlement of disputes. Another important contribution of UNWTO is the incorporation of sustainability indicators within the tourism sustainability framework, to better quantify and monitor the increasing CST phenomenon (UNWTO, 2004).

The United Nations Children's Fund (UNICEF)

UNICEF is the UN agency advocating for the protection of children's rights in relation to the provisions and principles of the CRC. The CST and child trafficking issues fall under the 'child protection' focus area of UNICEF's activity. Upon hosting the launch of the tourism industry Code of Conduct in North America in April 2004, UNICEF became a supporting agency of the Code in a tripartite partnership of ECPAT, UNICEF, UNWTO (UNICEF, 2004). In addition to awareness campaigns against CST in various countries including Dominican Republic (2001), Spain (2003), Sri Lanka (2006), Kenya (2006), Gambia (2004), UNICEF has also been actively advocating for the revision of penal codes in countries in Central America and the Caribbean area. The UNICEF Latin America and Caribbean Regional Office organised in 2005 and 2007 training and education courses for officials from national tourism administrations and ministries of tourism from the area.

The Organization for Security and Cooperation in Europe (OSCE)

The Organization for Security and Cooperation in Europe (OSCE) forms the largest regional security organisation in the world, with 56 participating states from Europe, Central Asia and North America, acting for early warning, conflict prevention, crisis management and post-conflict rehabilitation. In 2003, the Office of the Co-ordinator of OSCE Economic and Environmental Activities (OSCE-OCEEA) received a mandate to mobilise and strengthen the private sector's efforts to combat trafficking in human beings by raising awareness and by identifying and disseminating best practices, such as self-regulation, policy guidelines and codes of conduct (OSCE, 2007a).

The OSCE-OCEEA considers that hospitality and tourism, as one of the world's fastest growing sectors, can play an instrumental role in raising the awareness of tourists and business travellers of trafficking, and can help create an environment that does not accept trafficking in human beings and, in particular, the sexual exploitation of minors. OSCE used voluntary instruments such as the Code as 'valuable preventive and awareness raising tools' (OSCE, 2007b) and has supported the extension of the Code to tourism companies operating in south-eastern Europe. OSCE provided as well institutional support for gaining the commitment of the industry and of governments in the prevention and combat of trafficking in human beings and child sex tourism. These measures, as well as training and educational efforts have been undertaken with the support of other local partners since 2004 in Bulgaria, Romania, and as of 2005 also in Albania and Montenegro.

Other UN Agencies: International Labour Organization, UN Office on Drugs and Crimes, International Organization on Migration

Other UN agencies that carried out research to uncover the context of CST include the International Labour Organization(ILO), the UN Office of Drugs and Crimes (UNODC) and the International Organization on Migration (IOM). ILO explored CST in the context of eliminating one of the worst forms of child labour specified under the ILO Convention No. 182 (Black, 1995; Lean, 1998), through its International Program on the Elimination of Child Labour (IPEC). UNODC and IOM have also elaborated guidelines and training materials on the prevention and combat of trafficking in human beings. Although their work is not directly relevant to tourism, it is very informative in the context of smuggling migrants, trafficking and illegal labour, all topics recently connected to tourism (Stipanuk, 2006).

Discussion

The number of child victims of trafficking and CST calls for the mobilisation of tourism stakeholders — academia, private sector and policy-making bodies — to explore these issues more fully. Continuing the innovation on preventive practices is not an easy task, given the complexity of the phenomena and the still predominant perception that tourism is only marginally concerned with these occurrences. Furthermore, the debate is burdened by the confusion, persistent even in academic circles, with other related themes, including smuggling, illegal immigration, illegal labour, adult prostitution, etc. A 'first-generation' of innovations on the prevention of child sex tourism and trafficking, however, emerged in the early 2000s. They were, and some still are, in the process of being pilot tested in various mass tourism destinations. While making an elaborate analysis of the advantages, disadvantages, similarities, differences or interrelationships of each of the models was not the main focus of the paper, the initiatives presented share several key elements relevant from an innovation perspective. What existing models against trafficking and CST seem to have in common irrespective of their location, and who created them, are elements of awareness raising, education and the need for professional training of staff.

A second feature of the examples presented concerns their origin, most of which result from lobbying efforts by civil rights activists and by nongovernmental organisations. The main driver of innovation creation was a reaction, mostly by media and NGOs, but also by inter-governmental bodies, to flagrant and visible violations of children's rights in tourism destinations. The media reports have led to significant damage to the reputation of several destinations whose names remained, for the general public, associated with CST and trafficking. Owing to these negative media reports, the industry was initially forced into a defensive position that mandated immediate reaction. Yet, this external pressure makes it difficult to facilitate innovation beyond the current status quo. Instead, given the sensitive nature of the topic for mainstream tourists, the publicity has arguably not encouraged the private sector to take proactive steps. Current CST and trafficking initiatives, represent innovations of a behavioural nature, and mostly of a voluntary character (guidelines, training kits, codes of conduct, etc.). All these models are still in their initial stages of development. They evolved on an *ad hoc* basis and as continuous trial and error processes. In many circumstances innovation emerged as a result of challenges encountered, rather than being induced by favouring factors. Such challenges included reluctance of governments to acknowledge the existence of the problems, lack or insufficient numbers of skilled trainers, low capacity of local law enforcement, corruption and weak legal systems in tourism destinations particularly in developing countries.

With all their gaps, limitations and even inconsistencies however, innovations so far developed contain valuable knowledge to be applied towards a 'second generation' of prevention programmes. These should ideally evolve beyond voluntary, behavioural measures, and shift in the direction of policies and incentives for responsible behaviour. Based on reviewing the content and extent of currently available innovation models, it is argued here that existing innovation against CST and trafficking needs to increasingly morph towards policy making. From a destination perspective, policies deterring any type of social risk, especially those that potentially tarnish the reputation of destinations, are very desirable. They support destinations to be more competitive in the national and international marketplaces, and intervene to extend the destination's lifecycle. This is also supported by Keller (2003), who notes that, 'the future of traditional destinations will depend on a more innovation-oriented tourism policy'. The need for policy makers not to replace, but to complement CSR measures is also acknowledged by politicians. The head of the Tourism Policy Division of the German Federal Ministry of Economics and Labour, Helmut Kruger, stated, 'in Germany, tourism policy does not intervene in areas where solutions could be found by the industry itself. The industry has the know-how and the necessary momentum needed for innovation,' however, 'the federal government must react to the big challenges and trends of our time'. Hjalager's observations on the role of policy instruments on environmental innovation may also shed some light on the role of policies for tourism social innovations.

Tourism Innovation on Preventing Trafficking and CST

A number of contextual factors may intervene in the morphing from *ad hoc,* pressure-driven innovation, towards innovation-oriented tourism policies. For this to happen, further academic research on tourism CSR needs to incorporate CST and trafficking in the ethical framework for tourism. Academic study of the CST phenomenon focused mostly on definitional aspects, sexuality interferences and representations in rapport to tourism. The academia feedback to the existing actions against CST and trafficking has been extremely limited, although O'Connell (2004) initiates this discussion. There is still insufficient awareness in the tourism academic environment to the global dimensions of CST and trafficking. Emerging CSR research should include these topics in relation to social issues in tourism destinations and along with environmental concerns.

Linkages from the research published in law, social sciences and criminology need to be drawn and incorporated in the research on social impacts and globalization in tourism. As CST and trafficking have been mostly studied in social sciences, legal and law enforcement circles, the body of work currently available may be insufficiently scrutinised by the tourism researchers. Incipient research (Stipanuk, 2006) points to possible implications of illegal labour in US tourism, and calls for the further development of solutions to social impacts of tourism.

Governments and authorities need to create incentives and acknowledge the leaders of socially responsible tourism. Andrews (2004) reported that in 1996, over 25 companies in the US were known to offer <sex tour> package deals to either south-west Asia or other developing countries. While the public promotion of sex tourism has largely stopped in recent years, mostly thanks to the advances in law enforcement, a follow-up step needs to be taken in acknowledging and creating incentives for tourism companies to actively engage in the prevention of CST and trafficking.

Coordination between the relevant UN bodies, tourism policy makers and the civil society has to be improved. As the phenomena of CST and trafficking are closely related to illegal migration, smuggling, international crime and security, there is a strong need for improved interaction and more effective coordination between UN agencies that have the resources to address these issues at a global scale. Some of the concerned agencies include UNWTO, UNICEF, OSCE, ILO, IOM, Interpol, etc. A particularly important role remains for the UNWTO Task Force for the Protection of Children, and the UNWTO WCTE, which are called to support and facilitate exchange of information and to identify emerging international trends. As agendas of different organisations focus on different aspects, the discourse on CST and trafficking risks to become highly politicised, or vulnerable to pressures from the private sector. In order to bring the debate forward, focusing on elements of commonality would prevent territoriality and competition among the agencies concerned.

Hospitality Travel and Tourism Education

In today's rapidly changing business environment, Hospitality Management has come up as a fast growth career for young men and women who possess a pleasant personality, the capacity for hard work and a flair for creativity. Emerging trends for the growth of tourism and expansion of the accommodation sector has necessitated a substantial increase in the additional requirement of trained manpower.

If you have a natural gift for meeting people with a sense and spirit creative hospitality, a healthy dignity of labour, capacity and stamina to ramain cool in ticklish situations.

Hoteliering offers you a very fast-track career. It is the right place for the people who like people.

A career in hospitality management offers glamour, excitement, challenge a fast-track growth and elevated life style. It is in fact a unique and specialised discipline as Engineering, Finance, Medicine, MBA and/or civil services.

5

The Organization of Hospitality

World Tourism Organization

The World Tourism Organization (UNWTO), based in Madrid, Spain, is a United Nations agency dealing with questions relating to tourism. It compiles the World Tourism rankings. The World Tourism Organization is a significant global body, concerned with the collection and collation of statistical information on international tourism. This organization represents public sector tourism bodies, from most countries in the world and the publication of its data makes possible comparisons of the flow and growth of tourism on a global scale. The official languages of UNWTO are Arabic, English, French, Russian and Spanish.

Organizational Aims

The World Tourism Organization plays a role in promoting the development of responsible, sustainable and universally accessible tourism, paying particular attention to the interests of developing countries. The Organization encourages the implementation of the Global Code of Ethics for Tourism, with a view to ensuring that member countries, tourist destinations and businesses maximize the positive economic, social and cultural effects of tourism and fully reap its benefits, while minimizing its negative social and environmental impacts. UNWTO is committed to the United Nations Millennium Development Goals, geared toward reducing poverty and fostering sustainable development.

History

The origin of the World Tourism Organization stems back to 1925 when the International Congress of Official Tourist Traffic Associations ICOTT) was formed at The Hague. Some articles from early volumes of the Annals of Tourism Research, claim that the UNWTO originated from the International Union of Official Tourist Publicity Organizations (IUOTPO), although the UNWTO states that the ICOTT became the International Union of Official Tourist Propaganda Organizations first in 1934.

Following the end of the Second World War and with international travel numbers increasing, the IUOTPO restructured itself into the International Union of Official Travel Organizations (IUOTO). A technical, non-governmental organization, the IUOTO was made up of a combination of national tourist organizations, industry and consumer groups.

The goals and objectives of the IUOTO were to not only promote tourism in general but also to extract the best out of tourism as an international trade component and as an economic development strategy for developing nations.

Towards the end of the 1960's, the IUOTO realized the need for further transformation to enhance its role on an international level. The 20th IUOTO general assembly in Tokyo, 1967, declared the need for the creation of an intergovernmental body with the necessary abilities to function on an international level in cooperation with other international agencies, in particular the United Nations.

Throughout the existence of the IUOTO, close ties had been established between the organization and the United Nations (UN) and initial suggestions had the IUOTO becoming part of the UN. However, following the circulation of a draft convention, consensus held that any resultant intergovernmental organization should be closely linked to the UN but preserve its "complete administrative and financial autonomy".

It was on the recommendations of the UN that the formation of the new intergovernmental tourism organization was based. Resolution 2529 of the XXIVth UN general assembly stated: "[The general assembly] believes that a formula that would allow agreement to be reached more readily among governments for the establishment of an international tourism organization of an intergovernmental, particularly to assist the developing countries would be:

(a) The conversion of the International Union of Official Travel Organizations into an intergovernmental organization through a revision of its statutes:

(b) The establishment of operational links between the United Nations and the transformed Union by means of a formal agreement."

In 1970, the IUOTO general assembly voted in favour of forming the World Tourism Organization (WTO), based on statutes of the IUOTO, and after ratification by the prescribed 51 states, the WTO came into operation on November 1, 1974.

Most recently, at the fifteenth general assembly in 2003, the WTO general council and the UN agreed to establish the WTO as a specialized agency of the UN. The significance of this collaboration, WTO Secretary-General Mr. Frangialli claimed, would lie in "the increased visibility it gives the WTO, and the recognition that will be accorded to [it]. Tourism will be considered on an equal footing with other major activities of human society". As of 2007, its membership included 150 countries, seven territories and some 350 affiliate members, representing the private sector, educational institutions, tourism associations and local tourism authorities. The frequent confusion between the two WTOs – World Tourism Organization and the Geneva-based World Trade Organization – officially ended on 1 December 2005, when the General Assembly approved to add the letters UN (for United Nations) to the start of abbreviation of the leading international tourism body in English and in Russian. UNWTO abbreviation remains OMT in French and Spanish. UNWTO General Assembly concluded its work at its 16th session in Dakar, Senegal, on 2 December 2005.

Secretaries-General of UNWTO

General Assembly

The General Assembly is the supreme organ of the

Organization. Its ordinary sessions, held every two years, are attended by delegates of the Full and Associate members, as well as representatives from the Business Council. It is the most important meeting of senior tourism officials and high-level representatives of the private sector from all over the world.

Regional Commissions

Established in 1975 as subsidiary organs of the General Assembly, the six Regional Commissions normally meet once a year. They enable member States to maintain contact with one another and with the Secretariat between sessions of the General assembly, to which they submit their proposals and convey their concerns. Each commission elects one Chairman and its Vice-Chairmen from among its Members for a term of two years commencing from one session to the next session of the Assembly.

Executive Council

The Executive Council's task is to take all necessary measures, in consultation with the Secretary-General, for the implementation of its own decisions and recommendations of the Assembly and report thereon to the Assembly. The Council meets at least twice a yearly the Council consists of Full Members elected by the Assembly in the proportion of one Member for every five Full Members, in accordance with the Rules of Procedure laid down by the Assembly with a view to achieving fair and equitable geographical distributional The term of office of Members elected to the Council is four years and elections for one-half of the Council membership are held every two years. Spain is a Permanent member of the Executive Council.

Committees

World Committee on Tourism Ethics Programme Committee on Budget and Finance committee on Market and Competitiveness Committee on Statistics and the Tourism Satellite account Sustainable Development of Tourism Committee on Poverty Reduction Committee for the Review of Applications for Affiliate Membership

Secretariat

The Secretariat is led by Secretary-General ad interim Taleb

Rifai of Jordan, who supervises about 110 full-time staff at UNWTO's Madrid Headquarters. He is assisted by the Deputy Secretary-General. These officials are responsible for implementing UNWTO's programme of work and serving the needs of Members. The Affiliate Members are supported by a full-time Executive Director at the Madrid Headquarters. The Secretariat also includes a regional support office for Asia-Pacific in Osaka, Japan, financed by the Japanese Government.

Transport and Tourism

Managing Crises: UK Civil Aviation, BAA Airports and the August 2006 Terrorist Threat

The travel and tourism industry is expanding rapidly, but it has proved itself susceptible to crises which have both internal and external causes. Outside threats originate in the economic, environmental, socio-cultural and political domains and there is increasing concern about terrorism. This paper examines the dynamics and outcomes of a terrorist-related travel and tourism crisis with particular reference to the UK civil aviation industry in the summer of 2006. Reports of a planned terrorist strike against air travellers led to the imposition of unprecedented security measures which brought London's Heathrow Airport, one of the busiest in the world, to a standstill. Disruption was greatest on the day the news became public and continued for a period of ten days with lingering impacts which were felt nationally and globally.

After a brief introduction to the relevant literature, the circumstances are reviewed within the context of a model of the evolution of crises and their management. Phases cover the situation prior to the crisis, the alleged plot and the responses of the principal actors of government, airports and airlines. The focus is on airports run by BAA, formerly the British Airports Authority which was privatised after the 1986 Airports Act and acquired by the Spanish Ferrovial Group in June 2006. Consequences of the events recounted are considered and the paper ends with an overall assessment and some general conclusions derived from the case. Similar incidents seem likely to recur in the future and it is hoped that examination of the particular experiences will improve knowledge of the characteristics of this distinctive type of crisis and afford insights into effective preparation and management. A case study methodology was selected as the most appropriate and the analysis is based on secondary data drawn from a range of electronic and print media sources. The limitations of the absence of an insider perspective and reliance on news reporting are acknowledged, but direct access to decision making by public and private agencies and their documentation was not available to the researcher.

Travel and Tourism Crisis and Crisis Management

Crisis management as a whole has its own literature, but the principles are applicable to the travel and tourism industry and there is a growing volume of specific research. Travel and tourism crises are found to share features common to all crises, but also to possess certain distinctive qualities due to the nature of the product and industry. They often evolve with speed and can have far reaching commercial reverberations (Evans and Elphick, 2005). There is a possibility of personal injury and high fatalities and transport safety failures and accidents are a theme of several studies. Transport crises can also be the result of economic pressures separate from or linked to terrorism, the latter exemplified by the aftermath of what happened in the USA on 11 September 2001 (Nolan *et al.*, 2004; WTO, 2002). The relationship between terrorism and tourism is a topic of mounting interest (Pizam and Smith, 2000; Sonmez, 1998), indicative of the spate of terrorist outrages in the past decade.

There are great variations in scale and crises can be confined to an individual business or embrace a destination (Aktas and Gunlu, 2005). The latter may be engendered by political instability, one manifestation of which is terrorism, but natural disasters are a common catalyst. Management becomes more complex as the geographical area extends and more stakeholders have to be taken into account. Dilemmas were apparent in some of Thailand's coastal resorts after the devastating Indian Ocean tsunami of 2004. Handling of the subsequent tourism crisis was directed by officials and larger tourism businesses and the formal industry was deemed to be nearing recovery while the informal sector of hawkers and small enterprises still faced disruption (Rice, 2005). Inclusiveness and allocation of responsibilities for managing crises are thus important considerations and mechanisms for stakeholder dialogue and participation should be built into any models, although strong leadership is also essential.

Both generic and industry theories of crises and their management suggest that crises unfold in a sequence of steps which can be broadly labelled precrisis, crisis and post-crisis (Fink, 1986; Nankervis, 2000). Management tasks encompass signal detection, preparation, prevention, containment, recovery and learning.

The ultimate aim is the return to normality and restoration of the status quo, although it is appreciated that this may be unrealistic due to fundamental changes engendered by the crisis. Faulkner's (2001) work is frequently cited and his model for managing disasters at destinations.

The model commences with a period when there is no evidence of a looming crisis and, while some can be predicted by means such as environmental scanning, others may be inconceivable in their particularities. Warnings of the imminence of a crisis then ensue, materialising in a situation demanding action.

Recovery commences, divided into shorter and longer term, and resolution concludes the process. Responses comprise activity suitable to each phase with a movement from preparation and adoption of a position of readiness to first reactions and then measures directed at recovery, leading to a final review. These activities both inform and are informed by strategies of risk assessment and crisis management planning through a network of communication loops which also connect to future crises, allowing use to be made of understanding gained in order to prevent recurrence or limit damage when this is impossible. The model seeks to capture the cycle of crisis and is a useful analytical tool. It is employed as a framework for this paper in which the following sections are devoted to the seven phases, questions of the model's shortcomings being returned to in the conclusion.

Phase One: Pre-event and Phase Two: Warning

The parameters of the pre-event phase are not easily delineated in the August 2006 case due to the relatively longstanding hazard in the modern era of terrorists targeting airports and aircraft, illustrated by the history of plane hijackings and occasions like the Pan Am Lockerbie bomb in 1988 (Ray, 1999). A turning point might be 11th of September 2001 that demonstrated the potential for devastation by employing civilian aircraft to further terrorist ends. It signified the enhanced capabilities of terrorists and the sophistication of their methods as well as an intensification of fanaticism, underlining the need for constant vigilance and tighter security (Gunaratna, 2007). The bombings in London in July 2005 were another pivotal incident, confirming the vulnerability of the UK and its capital to terrorist attack (The Economist, 2005).

The onset of the warning phase, however, may predate 2001 and be determined by the political forces which were creating more extreme manifestations of terrorism and a new generation of terrorists, members of which are willing to sacrifice themselves as suicide bombers (Thackrah, 2004). International affairs, especially the circumstances in Iraq, have also engendered hostilities among nations whereby certain countries, their citizens and business interests have become attractive targets. General warnings were thus perhaps implicit in wider developments. Whatever the timetable, the climate in 2006 was one in which government, the air transport industry and passengers had been made keenly aware of the capacity of terrorism to wreak havoc among air travellers. The manner in which this occurred in the UK in August of that year is outlined in the next sections where accounts are founded on information published by two news media during the period under examination and BAA.

Phase Three: Event

Given the prevailing circumstances, the alleged plot was perceived to be highly credible by the UK authorities and deserving of urgent attention. The conspiracy reportedly involved the detonation of liquid explosives, carried onto planes in sports drinks bottles, in as many as ten passenger aircraft flying from the UK to the USA. It had been uncovered after an international surveillance exercise lasting over a year and was linked to the al-Qaeda organisation. British police and intelligence services were told of the threatened strike, expected to take place within 48 h, at 9pm on 9 August and a total of 21 suspects had been arrested by 11.50pm. The British Home Secretary claimed that the country was facing the gravest risk to security since the Second War and senior officials were quoted as saying, had the plan succeeded, it would have meant 'mass murder' on an 'unprecedented' and 'unimaginable' scale.

Whether such language was fitting and the dangers were inflated (Parkes, 2007) are outside the remit of this study. Nevertheless, it must be acknowledged that there had been criticisms of the record of the British security services over their investigations into terrorist suspects. Resultant scepticism in some quarters about the competence of the government and its agencies and underlying agendas constituted an element of the crisis, as did foreign policy decisions, and domestic and international political considerations cannot be entirely overlooked in any evaluation of its root causes and progression.

The discovery of the plan can be seen as the event which precipitated the crisis, although this demarcation is again debatable. Some observers might argue that it was the stances taken by the government and airport authorities that acted as a catalyst and aggravated the scale of the crisis, an interpretation adhered to by a number of airlines. Any such dispute highlights the complexity of the crisis which reverberated across the industry with different implications for government, airports and airlines. The government had responsibility for national security and the safety of citizens as well as obligations to the international community while airports and airlines had to deal with the practicalities of urgently executing radical security measures. Perspectives and priorities varied and there was room for tension and conflict as each party had to contend with its own crisis. However, these were interconnected and all were embroiled in the same drama and united by certain concerns pertaining to averting any further plots and appeasing public anxieties. Decisions made by one had ramifications for others and shaped advances towards individual and collective resolution.

Phase Four: Immediate Emergency

A meeting at 10pm on 9 August of the civil service Civil Contingencies Committee which was led by the Home Secretary, the Prime Minister being overseas, decreed that action must be taken to avert an attack. The UK was put on the maximum state of alert at 2am on 10 August and the Department of Transport announced details of enhanced security at airports. All the baggage of air travellers beginning their journey in the UK or transiting at UK airports was to be conveyed in the hold and they could take only specified essentials into the cabin in a single (ideally transparent) plastic carrier bag. The list covered travel documents, pocket-size wallets and purses, keys, spectacles (without cases), contact lens holders (without solution), tissues and feminine hygiene products (unboxed), prescription medical items (except in liquid form unless verified as authentic) and baby foods and sanitary items for those travelling with an infant. The contents of any bottles of baby milk had to be tasted by their owners. Every passenger would be hand searched and nothing was to be carried in pockets.

Any other liquids and gels, including most types of cosmetics and toiletries and foodstuffs, were not permitted. Prams and walking aids would be screened and only airport wheelchairs could enter the departure area. Those flying to the USA and their belongings would be screened again at the boarding gate. Passengers were advised to postpone travel if possible, to arrive early at the airport and to anticipate lengthy delays. The regime was in force for four days and prolonged completion of airport check-in and security clearance and boarding.

A key agency in the implementation of the scheme was BAA which is in charge of Heathrow, Gatwick, Stansted, Southampton, Aberdeen, Edinburgh and Glasgow airports. Emphasis is given to its role hereafter, but it should not be forgotten that the many other UK airport owners and operators (Humphreys *et al.*, 2007) were also compelled to act. Passengers at Heathrow heard that they could carry only essential hand luggage on board at 5am on 10 August when the first aircraft were scheduled to leave.

Stansted airport asked passengers to travel only if it was essential at 7.30am, extra security personnel were installed at Scottish airports at 8.10am and all incoming services to Heathrow, not already in the air, were suspended at 8.50am.

The American government stated at 1.30pm that the terrorists were focusing on United, American and Continental airlines with the intention of bombing flights to New York, Washington and California.

Most of the approximately 400,000 passengers around the UK directly caught up in the turmoil of 10 August were BAA customers and those journeying to, from and through Heathrow were the worst hit. The airport was so congested that marquees were erected outside the terminals to house the crowds and some, among them travellers with young children and elderly relatives, faced at least a 58 h wait. Individuals interviewed talked of their discontent about the treatment received and paucity of information and being unable to join allocated flights because of overcrowded check-in desks and security screening points.

With regard to airlines, British Airways (BA) cancelled all domestic and short haul international flights from Heathrow and some from Gatwick on 10 August. Passengers flying from Stansted with Ryanair and easy Jet were told to leave the airport and rebook their flights. Most foreign airlines also abandoned their services to London even before the formal suspension of flights. BA offered to refund or rebook customers who chose not to travel from affected airports and volunteers from throughout the company were recruited to assist in staffing the crisis. Cancellations continued on 11 August, but BA anticipated operating 70 percent of its flights on that date while easy Jet and Ryanair cancelled 112 and 30, respectively.

Phase Five: Intermediate

Airport Security

Just after midnight on 14 August, the security threat was downgraded from critical to severe by the government which judged a terrorist attack now to be highly likely rather than imminent. Passenger searches were reduced from 100 to 50 percent and the hand baggage ban was lifted to allow one item, measuring no more than 45 cm long, 35 cm wide and 16 cm deep. Laptops and electronic devices which had previously been forbidden could now be carried if they were contained in the single piece of luggage, but had to be unpacked for security scanning.

Liquids and gels were still banned, apart from baby foods and certain prescribed medication. Liquid, cream or gel essential prescription medicines weighing over 50 ml were not permitted in the cabin while those under 50 ml had to be verified by tasting; if the individual was unable to taste the medicine, they were referred back to the airline and a representative would accompany them to an airport pharmacist for approval. All goods purchased in departure lounges, however, could be taken onboard. These arrangements did not apply to travellers to the USA who could not carry toiletries or cosmetics bought in the departure area or any liquid items and were subjected to secondary searches at the boarding gate.

Changes were implemented immediately at some provincial airports, but BAA said that they would not come into force at Heathrow and Gatwick until Tuesday 15 August at 4.30am in order for time for a full briefing of security staff. Passengers using these airports and Stansted, also serving London, were therefore requested to abide by the original restrictions. The authorities stressed that the rules would persist for as long as it was deemed necessary, despite protests from the airlines. Updated details of regulations were made available on the BAA website and explanatory leaflets were distributed at airports where signage was erected.

The government and BAA expressed their commitment to passenger safety as the further relaxation of restrictions was discussed between the authorities and airlines. More changes were eventually announced on 21 September, effective from 22 September, whereby the internationally agreed standard hand baggage size (56 cm by 45 cm by 25 cm) was restored and musical instruments were again permissable, as were solid cosmetics. Laptops and other electronic equipment were approved, but had to be separately screened and the embargo on nonessential liquids remained. Stricter security was, however, retained for American flights.

There was an opportunity for reflection as well as recrimination in the aftermath of the immediate emergency and speaking at the end of August, the Director General of IATA was quoted as saying that BAA had 'failed miserably in business continuity' by 'stopping the travellers' and that the police and military should have been deployed. While the foiling of the alleged plot was reassuring, deficiencies in airport management had been exposed in what was a 'wake-up call for the industry'. He urged improvements in contingency planning, the acceptance by governments of their obligations and the harmonisation of cross-border security (IATA, 2006a).

Airlines

By mid-August, airlines were cancelling fewer services and the backlog of delayed flights and passengers had eased. August 16 saw 35 BA cancellations from Heathrow and 11 from Gatwick, with 19 the following day, and the company was hopeful that it would be back to normal by 18 August. It did run a full timetable from Heathrow and Gatwick for the first time on 19 August, Ryanair and easy Jet having done so from Stansted on 15 August. There was, however, an additional problem of displaced luggage to deal with and over 20,000 bags were calculated to have gone astray. Most of these belonged to BA customers and arrangements had to be made for their delivery to owners.

The UK's airlines had endorsed the airport authorities and government policy at first, but some started to openly query the way in which the crisis was being handled. BA's Chief Executive said that BAA was 'unable to provide a robust security search process and baggage operation', compelling the airline to cancel flights or leave without all passengers on board (Shah and Mesure, 2006). The chaos and ongoing uncertainty was a victory for the terrorists, in the opinion of the Chief Executive of Ryanair, who called for the army and police to help man airport security. Others practitioners denounced draconian security measures which were unsustainable. There were criticisms of BAA's apparent lack of preparedness and planning and the issue of compensation was raised. Ryanair accused BAA of 'paralysing' its London base of Stansted because of inadequate staffing and condemned baggage policies as 'nonsensical', insisting on the reinstatement of normal security systems. It also launched a campaign to 'get Britain flying again' with a million seats on sale on 100 routes at a price of £25, inclusive of taxes and charges, and a further million at 99 pence subsequently. Ryanair then declared that it would be suing the government for 3m after its seven day ultimatum about a return to the status quo was ignored (Ryanair, 2006).

Air Travellers

From the outset, there was a great deal of confusion about security regulations and complaints from the public who were not always well informed and sometimes received contradictory advice. Airline crews also voiced their dissatisfaction at measures, from which they were not excluded, such as the liquids ban which embraced contact lens solution and toothpaste. Any anger and frustration seemed to give way to resignation after a few days, however, as travellers were pictured in the media waiting patiently in the still lengthy queues.

There were no mass cancellations and the International Air Transport Association (IATA) discounted the idea of a worldwide slump of the magnitude seen in 2001 (IATA, 2006b). Annual comparisons can be misleading, but details of BAA terminal passengers for the month of August over a four-year period hint at negative outcomes of a slowdown in rates of growth and reversals at Heathrow and Edinburgh in 2006. Circumstances appear to have depressed air travel as a whole with BAA's domestic market dipping by 7.6 percent, European charter traffic by 6.8 percent and North Atlantic flyers by 3.3 percent (BAA, 2006b). A similar pattern was observed at non-BAA airports such as Manchester where there was a rise of 1.7 percent in scheduled passengers in contrast to one of 13.8 percent the previous year while Birmingham saw a slump of 7.9 percent (CAA, 2007a).

It can be argued that there were also signs of resilience and that more dramatic cuts might have been expected, many commentators believing that the industry and travelling public were less sensitive to and more stoical about terrorism than in the past (The Economist, 2006a; Harrison, 2006). The fact that the alleged plot had been foiled was also of importance, in marked contrast to previous tragedies. Nevertheless, several occurrences still indicated nervousness among air travellers and airlines. Security alerts incited by disruptive passengers, intentional and unintentional possession of banned items and bomb hoaxes led to flights being delayed and diverted. Heightened sensitivity was apparent elsewhere in Europe, Asia and the USA with a succession of false alarms reported.

Phase Six: Longer Term

Stringent cabin baggage rules were partially relaxed in the UK in a series of steps while efforts were made to secure greater inter-governmental cooperation and consistency in approach. The European Commission (EC) started talks about upgraded counter-terrorism programmes and the exchange of data on airline passengers, pledging investment in research into the detection of liquid explosives. Intelligence gathering and sharing was believed to be a vital tool in stopping terrorists and EU and US officials did come to some agreement regarding trans-Atlantic traveller information, although European privacy laws limited the release of personal data and this complicated discussions. EC nations had concurred about a uniform stance by September 2006 and European wide rules took effect from the beginning of November. These meant that passengers must carry duty-free goods in sealed bags and any fluids in containers no larger than 100 ml in a plastic bag. The ICAO (International Civil Aviation Organisation) also announced its intention to introduce a common policy in all member country airports by March 2007 (ICAO, 2006).

The confrontation between BAA and the airlines became a factor in the five-year review of BAA's landing fees being conducted by the Civil Aviation Authority, price control proposals finally announced in late 2007 (CAA, 2007b). Airlines, which had been critical of BAA's performance prior to August 2006, were prepared to cite the handling of affairs in August as symptomatic of mismanagement. BAA was also under scrutiny by the Office of Fair Trading because of its dominant position which it was accused of abusing by critics who denounced the company as uncaring and unresponsive to the needs of its customers. There was a possibility that BAA would be called on to divest itself of one or more airports and a decision was eventually made at the end of 2006 to refer it to the Competition Commission for more detailed investigation (Office of Fair Trading, 2006). The commercial ramifications of the disclosure of the alleged plot were evidenced by the drop in value of airline shares and disturbed financial markets (Financial Times, 2006). City analysts forecast that easy Jet would forfeit 3m (Shah and Mesure, 2006), Ryanair put its losses at 3m (Ryanair, 2006) and BA stated a figure of 10m for August (BA, 2006). Budget carriers were especially vulnerable as the new measures contradicted their endeavours to accelerate the speed of boarding in order to maximise fleet utility. Ryanair had additionally been encouraging passengers to fly only with hand luggage to reduce turnaround time and its baggage handling fees. The decree that the size of permissible cabin bags be substantially reduced clearly undermined this strategy, albeit on a temporary basis. Airport authorities too faced economic damage and spending attributable to security contributed to BAA losses of 13m in August alone (BAA, 2006c).

Phase Seven: Resolution?

Despite the advance of one year, certain elements of the crisis remained outstanding and this suggests a lingering effect whereby consequences of crises can obscure or delay full and final resolution. Compensation matters and legal disputes may be judged an element of a crisis, for example, and settlements are frequently protracted. Perpetrators of criminal deeds underlying a crisis must be brought to justice before the case is fully closed and the trials of those eventually charged with terrorist offences connected to the bomb plot are due to begin in early 2008.

Debate about the quality of security and responsibilities for setting standards and bearing the costs stimulated by the events of August 2006 has led to ongoing reforms. Certain security procedures adopted seem set be in place indefinitely, reinforced by new steps. Passenger profiling founded on ethnicity and religion as well as age and unusual travel histories was mooted, although opponents complained of its tendency to promote racial stereotyping and discrimination. Other potential tools rely on sophisticated technologies of electronic and biometric analyses, but constraints of resources and reliability will have to be overcome (The Economist, 2006b). Progress will be an international affair given that terrorism and civil aviation both function at a global level and establishing consensus may not be easy, but air travellers can expect to undergo continued rigorous security checks with the attendant inconveniences. The degree to which governments will heed the exhortations of IATA and industry representatives to subsidise security, thereby helping to ameliorate the financial burden imposed on airlines, has not been determined and there is a possibility of higher fares due to mounting security expenses.

In addition, there have been reductions in the duty-free revenues of airport authorities because of the evolving rules governing purchase of liquid goods. Tax paid revenues may also be hit as passenger involvement in lengthy security procedures means less time and money spent on all types of landside and airside shopping. Steady rises in amounts charged to airline customers by airports in a bid to recoup some of this loss would be a blow to a civil aviation industry struggling with escalating fuel bills and competitive pressures. Developments could erode profitability, not least for companies in the budget market, with doubts about the survival of some enterprises.

Regular repetition of chaotic scenes at airports might well provoke interest in alternative modes of transport when these are a viable option, illustrated by the surge in bookings for Eurostar trains between London and Paris and Brussels at the peak of the August 2006 emergency. Nearby destinations could be favoured by holiday makers with a growing partiality for domestic tourism, the latter trend perhaps underway. BTMICE (business travel, meetings, incentives and conferences) participants may also switch to virtual communications (Arnfalk and Kogg, 2003) and facilities such as video-conferencing to escape the stresses and uncertainties of air travel.

Looking ahead, a future of intense security and the persistence of terrorist alarms and outrages can be envisaged.

Flying may come to be widely viewed as excessively arduous for all but the most unavoidable of journeys. Travellers could be unwilling to arrive at the airport at least three, and maybe four, hours before departure for a relatively short flight when they may be prevented from carrying important personal possessions and have to risk the transportation of valuable items in the hold. Business travellers might again be denied use of laptops and equipment which enables them to work while on the move. Passengers and airlines could be approaching a threshold of acceptability and tolerance regarding official air security regimes which they may be reluctant to cross. The crisis exposed the often competing demands of security, passenger comfort and convenience and commercial realities. Identifying and securing an acceptable balance is an ongoing exercise which is perhaps prolonging total resolution.

Travel Agency and Tour Operation

A travel agency is a retail business, that sells travel related products and services to customers, on behalf of suppliers, such as airlines, car rentals, cruise lines, hotels, railways, sightseeing tours and package holidays that combine several products. In addition to dealing with ordinary tourists, most travel agencies have a separate department devoted to making travel arrangements for business travellers and some travel agencies specialize in commercial and business travel only. There are also travel agencies that serve as general sales agents for foreign travel companies, allowing them to have offices in countries other than where their headquarters are located.

Origins

The British company Cox & Kings is sometimes said to be the oldest travel agency in the world, but this rests upon the services that the original bank, established in 1758, supplied to its wealthy clients. The modern travel agency first appeared in the second half of the 19th century. Thomas Cook, in addition to developing the package tour, established a chain of agencies in the last quarter of the 19th century, in association with the Midland Railway. They not only sold their own tours to the public, but in addition, represented other tour companies. Other

British pioneer travel agencies were Dean and Dawson, the Polytechnic Touring Association and the Co-operative Wholesale Society. The oldest travel agency in North America is Brownell Travel; on July 4, 1887, Walter T. Brownell led ten travellers on a European tour, setting sail from New York on the SS Devonia.

Travel agencies became more commonplace with the development of commercial aviation, starting in the 1920s. Originally, travel agencies largely catered to middle and upper class customers, but the postwar boom in mass-market package holidays resulted in travel agencies on the main streets of most British towns, catering to a working class clientèle, looking for a convenient way to book overseas beach holidays.

Operations

As the name implies, a travel agency's main function is to act as an agent, that is to say, selling travel products and services on behalf of a supplier. Consequently, unlike other retail businesses, they do not keep a stock in hand. A package holiday or a ticket is not purchased from a supplier unless a customer requests that purchase. The holiday or ticket is supplied to them at a discount. The profit is therefore the difference between the advertised price which the customer pays and the discounted price at which it is supplied to the agent. This is known as the commission. A British travel agent would consider a 10-12% commission as a good arrangement. In Australia, all individuals or companies that sell tickets are required to be licensed as a travel agent.

In some countries, airlines have stopped giving commission to travel agencies. Therefore, travel agencies are now forced to charge a percentage premium or a standard flat fee, per sale. However, some companies still give them a set percentage for selling their product. Major tour companies can afford to do this, because if they were to sell a thousand trips at a cheaper rate, they still come out better than if they sell a hundred trips at a higher rate. This process benefits both parties. Other commercial operations are undertaken, especially by the larger chains. These can include the sale of in-house insurance, travel guide books and timetables, car rentals, and the services of an on-site Bureau de change, dealing in the most popular holiday currencies.

The majority of travel agents have felt the need to protect themselves and their clients against the possibilities of commercial failure, either their own or a supplier's. They will advertise the fact that they are surety bonded, meaning in the case of a failure, the customers are guaranteed either an equivalent holiday to that which they have lost or if they prefer, a refund. Many British and American agencies and tour operators are bonded with the International Air Transport Association (IATA), for those who issue air tickets, Air Travel Organisers' Licensing (ATOL) for those who order tickets in, the Association of British Travel Agents (ABTA) or the American Society of Travel Agents (ASTA), for those who sell package holidays on behalf of a tour company.

A travel agent is supposed to offer impartial travel advice to the customer. However, this function almost disappeared with the mass-market package holiday and some agency chains seemed to develop a 'holiday supermarket' concept, in which customers choose their holiday from brochures on racks and then book it from a counter. Again, a variety of social and economic changes have now contrived to bring this aspect to the fore once more, particularly with the advent of multiple, no-frills, low-cost airlines.

Commissions

Most travel agencies operate on a commission-basis, meaning that the compensation from the airlines, car rentals, cruise lines, hotels, railways, sightseeing tours and tour operators, etc., is expected in form of a commission from their bookings. Most often, the commission consists of a set percentage of the sale.

In the United States, most airlines pay no commission at all to travel agencies. In this case, an agency usually adds a service fee to the net price.

Types of Agencies

There are three different types of agencies in the UK: Multiples, Miniples and Independent Agencies. The former comprises a number of national chains, often owned by international conglomerates, like Thomson Holidays, now a subsidiary of TUI AG, the German multinational. It is now quite common for the large mass-market tour companies to purchase a controlling interest in a chain of travel agencies, in order to control the distribution of their product. The smaller chains are often based in particular regions or districts.

In the United States, there are four different types of agencies: Mega, Regional, Consortium and Independent Agencies. American Express and the American Automobile Association (AAA) are examples of mega travel agencies.

Independent Agencies usually cater to a special or niche market, such as the needs of residents in an upmarket commuter town or suburb or a particular group interested in a similar activity, such as sporting events, like football, golf or tennis.

There are two approaches of travel agencies. One is the traditional, multi-destination, out-bound travel agency, based in the originating location of the traveller and the other is the destination focused, in-bound travel agency, that is based in the destination and delivers an expertise on that location. At present, the former is usually a larger operator like Thomas Cook, while the latter is often a smaller, independent operator.

Consolidators

Airline consolidators and other types of travel consolidators and wholesalers are high volume sales companies that specialize in selling to niche markets. They may or may not offer various types of services, at a single point of access. These can be hotel reservations, flights or car-rentals, for example. Sometimes the services are combined into vacation packages, that include transfers to the location and lodging. These companies do not usually sell directly to the public, but act as wholesalers to retail travel agencies. Commonly, the sole purpose of consolidators is to sell to ethnic niches in the travel industry. Usually, no consolidator offers everything, they may only have contracted rates to specific destinations. Today, there are no domestic consolidators, with some exceptions for business class contracts.

Criticism and Controversy

"Racking"

Travel agencies have been accused of employing a number of restrictive practices, the chief of which is known as 'racking'. This is the practice of displaying only the brochures of those travel companies whose holidays they wish to sell, the ones that pay them the most commission. Of course, the average customer tends to think that these are the only holidays on offer and is unaware of the possible alternatives.

Conversely, by limiting the number of companies that a travel agency represents, this can bring a better and more profitable, working relationship between the agency and its suppliers. Travel agencies can then obtain special benefits for their customers, from a supplier, by concentrating their bookings with that supplier. Some examples of these special benefits would be room upgrades or the waiver of change and cancellation fees.

("Racking" is a British expression, not used in the United States.)

The Internet Threat

With general public access to the Internet, many airlines and other travel companies began to sell directly to passengers. As a consequence, airlines no longer needed to pay the commissions to travel agents on each ticket sold. Since 1997, travel agencies have gradually been disintermediated, by the reduction in costs caused by removing layers from the package holiday distribution network.

However, travel agents remain dominant in some areas such as cruise vacations where they represent 77% of bookings and 73% of packaged travel. In response, travel agencies have developed an internet presence of their own by creating travel websites, with detailed information and online booking capabilities.

Several major online travel agencies include: Expedia, Voyages-sncf.com, Travelocity, Orbitz, Cheap Tickets, Priceline, Cheap Oair and Hotwire.com. Travel agencies also use the services of the major computer reservations systems companies, also known as Global Distribution Systems (GDS), including: SABRE, Amadeus CRS, Galileo CRS and Worldspan, which is a subsidiary of Travelport, allowing them to book and sell airline tickets, hotels, car rentals and other travel related services. Some online travel websites allow visitors to compare hotel and flight rates with multiple companies for free. They often allow visitors to sort the travel packages by amenities, price, and proximity to a city or landmark.

Travel agents have applied dynamic packaging tools to provide fully bonded (full financial protection) travel at prices equal to or lower than a member of the public can book online. As such, the agencies' financial assets are protected in addition to professional travel agency advice.

All travel sites that sell hotels online work together with GDS, suppliers and hotels directly to search for room inventory. Once the travel site sells a hotel, the site will try to get a confirmation for this hotel. Once confirmed or not, the customer is contacted with the result. This means that booking a hotel on a travel website will not necessarily result in an instant answer. Only some hotels on a travel website can be confirmed instantly (which is normally marked as such on each site). As different travel websites work with different suppliers together, each site has different hotels that it can confirm instantly. Some examples of such online travel websites that sell hotel rooms are Expedia, Orbitz and World Hotel-Link.

The comparison sites, such as Kayak.com, Trip Advisor and Side Step search the resellers site all at once to save time searching. None of these sites actually sell hotel rooms.

Often tour operators have hotel contracts, allotments and free sell agreements which allow for the immediate confirmation of hotel rooms for vacation bookings.

Mainline service providers are those that actually produce the direct service, like various hotels chains or airlines that have a website for online bookings. Portals will serve a consolidator of various airlines and hotels on the internet. They work on a commission from these hotels and airlines. Often, they provide cheaper rates than the mainline service providers as these sites get bulk deals from the service providers. A meta search engine on the other hand, simply culls data from the internet on real time rates for various search queries and diverts traffic to the mainline service providers for an online booking. These websites usually do not have their own booking engine.

Careers

With the many people switching to self-service internet websites, the number of available jobs as travel agents is decreasing. Most jobs that become available are from older travel agents retiring. Counteracting the decrease in jobs due to internet services is the increase in the number of people travelling. Since 1995, many travel agents have exited the industry, and relatively few young people have entered the field due to less competitive salaries. However, others have abandoned the 'brick and mortar' agency for a home-based business to reduce overheads and those who remain have managed to survive by promoting other travel products such as cruise lines and train excursions or by promoting their ability to aggressively research and assemble complex travel packages on a moment's notice, essentially acting as a very advanced concierge.

Cargo

A small number of companies work with cargo airlines and cargo ships.

Who is a travel agent?

A travel agent is any individual or company that:

- Sells, resells, or offers to sell travel tickets
- Makes or offers to make travel arrangements
- Advertises any of those things.

Many businesses are regarded as travel agents, including retail and corporate agents, tour wholesalers, consolidators, inbound tour operators, general sales agents, some bus or coach operators and some airlines.

Travel Technology

Travel technology is a term used to describe applications of Information Technology (IT), or Information and Communications Technology (ICT), in travel, tourism and hospitality industry.

Travel technology may also be referred to as tourism technology or even hospit Definition of Travel Technology

Since travel implies locomotion, travel technology was originally associated with the computer reservations system (CRS) of the airlines industry, but now is used more inclusively, incorporating the broader tourism sector as well as its subset the hospitality industry. While travel technology includes the computer reservations system, it also represents a much broader range of applications, in fact increasingly so. Travel technology includes virtual tourism in the form of virtual tour technologies. Travel technology may also be referred to as *e-travel / etravel* or *e-tourism / etourism* (eTourism), in reference to "electronic travel" or "electronic tourism".

In other contexts, the term "travel technology" can refer to technology intended for use by travellers, such as light-weight laptop computers with universal power supplies or satellite Internet connections. That is not the sense in which it is used here.

Applications of Travel Technology

Travel technology includes many processes such as dynamic packaging which provide useful new options for consumers. Today the tour guide can be a GPS tour guide, and the guidebook could be an audioguide, podguide or I-Tours, such as City audio guides. The biometric passport may also be included as travel technology in the broad sense.

Tour Operator

A tour operator typically combines tour and travel components to create a holiday. The most common example of a tour operator's product would be a flight on a charter airline plus a transfer from the airport to a hotel and the services of a local representative, all for one price. Niche tour operators may specialise in destinations e.g. Italy, activities and experiences e.g. skiing, or a combination thereof. The original raison d'etre of tour operating was the difficulty of making arrangements in far-flung places, with problems of language, currency and communication. The advent of the internet has led to a rapid increase in self-packaging of holidays. However, tour operators still have their competence in arranging tours for those who do not have time to do DIY holidays, and specialize in large group events and meetings such as conferences or seminars. Also, tour operators still exercise contracting power with suppliers (airlines, hotels, other land arrangements, cruises, etc.) and influence over other entities (tourism boards and other government authorities) in order to create packages and special departures for destinations otherwise difficult and expensive to visit.

The two major tour operator associations in the US are the National Tour Association (NTA) and the United States Tour Operator's Association (USTOA), in Europe it is the European Tour Operators Association-ETOA and in the UK it is ABTA and AITO. The primary association for receptive North American inbound tour operators is the Receptive Services Association of America (RSAA).

Tour Operators and Travel Agents

Sometimes there is confusion over the difference in functions of tour operators and travel agents. Tour operators are the organisers and providers of package holidays. They make contracts with hoteliers, airlines and ground transport companies then print brochures advertising the holidays that they have assembled. Travel agents give advice and sell and administer the bookings for a number of tour operators. It is estimated that there are some 7,000 travel agency shops ranging size from the multiples, with several hundred outlets each, to the individual shop. Some travel agents also undertake tour operating-be it on a small scale, e.g. a local agent packaging a group holiday for a local club, or on a larger scale-most famously by the legendary Thomas Cook, who was the first tour operator, and Sir Henry Lunn (Lunn Poly) who is widely credited with "inventing" skiing as a leisure activity. Agents can also sell the 'components' (flights, ferry bookings, car hire etc.) for those who travel independently.

Although most package holidays are sold through travel agents a significant and growing percentage are sold direct to the consumer through advertising -Teletex, TV Travel Shops and the internet.

Package Holiday

A package holiday or package tour consists of transport and accommodation advertised and sold together by a vendor known as a tour operator. Other services may be provided like a rental car, activities or outings during the holiday. Transport can be via charter airline to a foreign country. Package holidays are a form of product bundling. Package holidays are organised by a tour operator and sold to a consumer by a travel agent. Some travel agents are employees of tour operators, others are independent.

Package Tours

An early form of package holiday was organised by Thomas Cook in 1841, offering customers a return trip between Leicester and Loughborough. The first package tour of Europe was organised by Cook in 1855, and by 1872 he was undertaking world-wide tours, albeit with small groups.

Vladimir Raitz, the co-founder of the Horizon Holiday Group, pioneered the first mass package holidays abroad with charter flights between Gatwick airport and Corsica in 1950, and organised the first package holiday to Palma in 1952, Lourdes in 1953, and the Costa Brava and Sardinia in 1954. In addition, the amendments made in Montreal to the Convention on International Civil Aviation on June 14, 1954 was very liberal to Spain, allowing impetus for mass tourism using charter planes.

By the late 1950s and 1960s, these cheap package holidays – which combined flight, transfers and accommodation – provided the first chance for most people in the United Kingdom to have affordable travel abroad. One of the first charter airlines was Euravia, which commenced flights from Manchester Airport in 1961 and Luton Airport in 1962. Despite opening up mass tourism to Crete and the Algarve in 1970, the package tour industry declined during the 1970s. On 15 August 1974, the industry was shaken when the second-largest tour operator, Court Line which operated under the brand names of Horizon and Clarksons, collapsed. Nearly 50,000 tourists were stranded overseas and a further 100,000 faced the loss of booking deposits.

In 2005 a growing number of consumers were avoiding package holidays and were instead travelling with budget airlines and booking their own accommodation. In the UK, the downturn in the package holiday market led to the consolidation of the tour operator market, which is now dominated by a few large tour operators. The major operators are Thomson Holidays and First Choice part of TUI AG and Thomas Cook AG. Under these umbrella brands there exists a whole range of different holiday operators catering to different markets, such as Club 18-30 or Simply Travel. Budget airlines have also created their own package holiday divisions such as Jet2 Holidays.

The trend for package holiday bookings saw a comeback in 2009, as customers sought greater financial security in the wake of a number of holiday and flight companies going bust, and as the hidden costs of 'no-frills' flights increased. Coupled with the search for late holidays as holidaymakers left booking to the last moment, this led to a rise in consumers booking package holidays.

Dynamic Packaging is a method that is becoming increasingly used in package holiday bookings that enables consumers to build their own package of flights, accommodation, and a hire car instead of a pre-defined package. Dynamic packages differ from traditional package tours in that the pricing is always based on current availability, escorted group tours are rarely included, and trip-specific add-ons such as airport parking and show tickets are often available.

Dynamic packages are similar in that often the air, hotel, and car rates are available only as part of a package or only from a specific seller. The term "dynamic packaging" is often used incorrectly to describe the less sophisticated process of interchanging various travel components within a package, however, this practice is more accurately described as "dynamic bundling". True Dynamic Packaging demands the automated recombination of travel components based on the inclusion of rules that not only dictate the content of the package, but conditional pricing rules based on various conditions such as the trip characteristics, suppliers contributing components, the channel of distribution, and terms of sale. Dynamic packages are primarily sold online, but online travel agencies will also sell by phone owing to the strong margins and high sale price of the product.

Free Independent Traveller

Free Independent Traveller (or Tourist) refers to both a way of travelling and, from an industry viewpoint, a sector within the tourism market. FITs practise a form of dynamic packaging but the emphasis is from the end-user point of view and includes the wider economic effects that FITs "spread" in their destination country as opposed to more traditional, consolidated forms of travel.

6

Operation in Hotel Management

Introduction

Tourism and hospitality is the fastest growing industry in the world with over 72.4 million jobs within the industry. Through the growth of e-commerce and globalization, a wide variety of career opportunities have emerged in the meeting and convention, attractions, event planning, travel, gaming, transportations, airline, recreation and food and beverage fields.

Many modern words readily associated with hospitality are evolved from the same hypothetical Proto-Indo-European root ghosti (1) meaning: stranger, guest, host: properly 'someone with whom one has reciprocal duties of hospitality' (American Heritage Dictionary, 2001). The word guest came from the Middle English gest, evolved from Old Norse gestor, and from Old High German gast, both come from Germanic gastiz. Ghosti also evolved to the Latin root hostis, meaning enemy, army, and where host (multitude) and hostile find their origin; and the Latin root hostia, meaning sacrifice, host (Eucharistic). The combination of ghosti and another Proto-Indo-European root poti powerful, gave the compound root ghospot, ghospod-, which evolved to the Latin hospes and eventually into hospice, hospitable, hospital, hospitality, host (giver of hospitality), hostage and hostel. The Greek languages also evolved from the same Proto-Indo-European base; ghosti gave the Greek xenos which has the interchangeable meaning guest, host or stranger.

Hospitality, then, 'represents a kind of guarantee of reciprocity—one protects the stranger in order to be protected from him'.

Grecian Hospitality Mythology

In Ancient Greece, it was not known if the stranger knocking at the door was going to be hostile or hospitable, whether they were a god disguised, or watching from above and passing judgment. This was not considered important for 'it is hard for mortals to see divinity'. Hospitality was a way of honouring the gods, which was so essential, so fundamental to civilized life, that its patron was the god of gods.

In true hospitality, it doesn't matter who the guest is, nor their apparent status in life. Generous hospitality freely given to a stranger was the same as that given to a god.

Reese (1993) in his analysis of the writings attributed to Homer identifies 18 'hospitality' scenes. It is clear from these scenes in the Homeric writings that hospitality brought expectations. As the traveller would not usually be wandering without cause from their home into the dangers of the world.

Hospitality management is the academic study of the hospitality industry. A degree in Hospitality management is often conferred from either a university college dedicated to the studies of hospitality management or a business school with a department in hospitality management studies. Hospitality management is the academic study of the hospitality industry. A degree in Hospitality management is often conferred from either a university college dedicated to the studies of hospitality management or a business school with a department in hospitality management studies.

Hospitality and Tourism Management

In America, Hospitality and Tourism Management (HTM) can be a business major in either a Bachelors of Science, Bachelors of Commerce or a Bachelors of Arts.

Graduate students graduate with a Masters of Business Administration, a Masters or Science, or a Doctorate of Philosophy in Hospitality and Tourism Management. It is a focus that is studied by individuals that are intending to work in the Hospitality Industry, examples of which are; Hotels, Resorts, Casinos, Restaurants, and Events.

Within the HTM concentration there is generally:

- Food Management and Operations (Examples: Food Science, Food Selection and Preparation, Food and Beverage Operations)
- Lodging Operations (Examples: Hotel Operations, Resort Management, Lodging Management, Financial Management and Cost Control for Hospitality Organizations)
- Global Tourism (Examples: Travel and Tourism Management, Tourism Analysis, Hospitality and Research Methods)
- Sustainable Tourism (Examples: Natural Destination Management, Responsible Tourism, Green Tourism and Eco-Tourism, Alternative and more Environmentally friendly ways of working within the whole Tourism industry)
- Tourist Attractions Management (Examples: Heritage Attractions, Arts and Cultural Attractions, Industrial Attractions, City Based Attractions, Retail Attractions, Natural Attractions)
- Entertainment Management (Examples: Theme Park Management, Theatre Management, Cinema Management, Museology, Live Music and Music Festival Management).
- Event Management (Examples: Hospitality Sales, Catering Management, Hospitality Marketing Management).

Several large corporations such as Marriott, IHG, Hyatt, Starwood, Wyndham and Hilton Hotels have summer internships in training programs for students majoring in Hospitality and Tourism Management, to help students get valuable work experience.

Hospitality and Tourism Management

In America, Hospitality and Tourism Management (HTM) can be a business major in either a Bachelors of Science, Bachelors of Commerce or a Bachelors of Arts. Graduate students graduate with a Masters of Business Administration, a Masters or Science, or a Doctorate of Philosophy in Hospitality and Tourism Management. It is a focus that is studied by individuals that are intending to work in the Hospitality Industry, examples of which are; Hotels, Resorts, Casinos, Restaurants, and Events.

Within the HTM concentration there is generally:

- Food Management and Operations (Examples: Food Science, Food Selection and Preparation, Food and Beverage Operations)
- Lodging Operations (Examples: Hotel Operations, Resort Management, Lodging Management, Financial Management and Cost Control for Hospitality Organizations)
- Global Tourism (Examples: Travel and Tourism Management, Tourism Analysis, Hospitality and Research Methods)
- Sustainable Tourism (Examples: Natural Destination Management, Responsible Tourism, Green Tourism and Eco-Tourism, Alternative and more Environmentally friendly ways of working within the whole Tourism industry)
- Tourist Attractions Management (Examples: Heritage Attractions, Arts and Cultural Attractions, Industrial Attractions, City Based Attractions, Retail Attractions, Natural Attractions)
- Entertainment Management (Examples: Theme Park Management, Theatre Management, Cinema Management, Museology, Live Music and Music Festival Management).
- Event Management (Examples: Hospitality Sales, Catering Management, Hospitality Marketing Management).

Several large corporations such as Marriott, IHG, Hyatt, Starwood, Wyndham and Hilton Hotels have summer internships in training programs for students majoring in Hospitality and Tourism Management, to help students get valuable work experience.

Hospitality Industry

The hospitality industry consists of broad category of fields within the service industry that includes lodging, restaurants, event planning, theme parks, transportation, cruise line, and additional fields within the tourism industry. The hospitality industry is a several billion dollar industry that mostly depends on the availability of leisure time and disposable income. A hospitality unit such as a restaurant, hotel, or even an amusement park consists of multiple groups such as facility maintenance, direct operations (servers, housekeepers, porters, kitchen workers, bartenders, etc.), management, marketing, and human resources.

Usage rate is an important variable for the hospitality industry. Just as a factory owner would wish to have his or her productive asset in use as much as possible (as opposed to having to pay fixed costs while the factory isn't producing), so do restaurants, hotels, and theme parks seek to maximize the number of customers they "process".

In viewing various industries, "barriers to entry" by newcomers and competitive advantages between current players are very important. Among other things, hospitality industry players find advantage in old classics (location), initial and ongoing investment support (reflected in the material upkeep of facilities and the luxuries located therein), and particular themes adopted by the marketing arm of the organization in question (such as a restaurant called the 51st fighter group that has a WW2 theme in music and other environmental aspects). Very important is also the characteristics of the personnel working in direct contact with the customers. The authenticity, professionalism, and actual concern for the happiness and well-being of the customers that is communicated by successful organizations is a clear competitive advantage.

Accommodations

- Destination spas
- Floatels
- Hostels
- Hotels
- Inns
- Motels.

Restaurants & Bars

- Cafes
- Nightclubs
- Public houses
- Pubs
- Restaurants.

Travel and Tourism

- Airline Cabin Staff
- Travel agents.

Hotel

A hotel is an establishment that provides paid lodging on a short-term basis. The provision of basic accommodation, in times past, consisting only of a room with a bed, a cupboard, a small table and a washstand has largely been replaced by rooms with modern facilities, including en-suite bathrooms and air conditioning or climate control. Additional common features found in hotel rooms are a telephone, an alarm clock, a television, and Internet connectivity; snack foods and drinks may be supplied in a mini-bar, and facilities for making hot drinks. Larger hotels may provide a number of additional guest facilities such as a restaurant, a swimming pool or childcare, and have conference and social function services. Hotels rooms are usually numbered to allow guests identify their room.

Some hotels offer meals as part of a room and board arrangement. In the United Kingdom, a hotel is required by law to serve food and drinks to all guests within certain stated hours; to avoid this requirement it is not uncommon to come across *private hotels* which are not subject to this requirement. In Japan, capsule hotels provide a minimized amount of room space and shared facilities.

In the United Kingdom, Australia, Canada and Ireland (and rarely in some parts of the United States), the word may also refer to a pub or bar and might not offer accommodation. In India and Bangladesh, the word may also refer to a restaurant.

Etymology

The word *hotel* is derived from the French *hotel* (coming from *hotel* meaning *host*), which referred to a French version of a townhouse or any other building seeing frequent visitors, rather than a place offering accommodation. In contemporary French usage, *hôtel* now has the same meaning as the English term, and *hôtel particulier* is used for the old meaning. The French spelling, with the circumflex, was also used in English, but is now rare. The circumflex replaces the 's' found in the earlier *hostel* spelling, which over time took on a new, but closely related meaning. Grammatically, hotels usually take the definite article-hence "The Astoria Hotel" or simply "The Astoria".

Classification

The cost and quality of hotels are usually indicative of the range and type of services available. Due to the enormous increase in tourism worldwide during the last decades of the 20th century, standards, especially those of smaller establishments, have improved considerably. For the sake of greater comparability, rating systems have been introduced, with the one to five stars classification being most common and with higher star ratings indicating more luxury. Hotels are independently assessed in traditional systems and these rely heavily on the facilities provided. Some consider this disadvantageous to smaller hotels whose quality of accommodation could fall into one class but the lack of an item such as an elevator would prevent it from reaching a higher categorization. In some countries, there is an official body with standard criteria for classifying hotels, but in many others there is none. There have been attempts at unifying the classification system so that it becomes an internationally recognized and reliable standard but large differences exist in the quality of the accommodation and the food within one category of hotel, sometimes even in the same country. The American Automobile Association (AAA) and their affiliated bodies use diamonds instead of stars to express hotel and restaurant ratings levels.

Hotels are also classified by service type ranging for all-inclusive full-service resorts that cater to vacationers to small limited service hotels that cater to transient business travellers. The main categories of hotels are as follows;

- Full Service Upscale :
  - o *Examples include Conrad Hotels, Ritz Carlton, Four Seasons Hotels, and JW Marriott.*
- Full Service :
  - o *Examples include Hilton, Marriott, Doubletree, and Hyatt.*
- Select Service :
  - o *Examples include Courtyard by Marriott and Hilton Garden Inn.*
- Limited Service :
  - o *Examples include Hampton Inn, Fairfield Inn, Days Inn, and La Quinta Inn.*
- Extended Stay :
  - o *Examples include Homewood Suites by Hilton, Residence Inn by Marriott, and Extended Stay Hotels.*
- Timeshare :
  - o *Examples include Marriott Vacation Club, Westgate Resorts, and Disney Vacation Club.*
- Destination Club.

Historic Hotels

Some hotels have gained their renown through tradition, by hosting significant events or persons, such as Schloss Cecilienhof in Potsdam, Germany, which derives its fame from the Potsdam Conference of the World War II allies Winston Churchill, Harry Truman and Joseph Stalin in 1945.

The Taj Mahal Palace & Tower in Mumbai is one of India's most famous and historic hotels because of its association with the Indian independence movement. Some establishments have given name to a particular meal or beverage, as is the case with the Waldorf Astoria in New York City, United States where the Waldorf Salad was first created or the Hotel Sacher in Vienna, Austria, home of the Sachertorte. Others have achieved fame by association with dishes or cocktails created on their premises, such as the Hotel de Paris where the crepe Suzette was invented or the Raffles Hotel in Singapore, where the Singapore Sling cocktail was devised.

A number of hotels have entered the public consciousness through popular culture, such as the Ritz Hotel in London, United Kingdom, through its association with Irving Berlin's song, 'Puttin' on the Ritz'. The Algonquin Hotel in New York City is famed as the meeting place of the literary group, the Algonquin Round Table, and Hotel Chelsea, also in New York City, has been the subject of a number of songs and the scene of the stabbing of Nancy Spungen (allegedly by her boyfriend Sid Vicious). The Waldorf Astoria and Statler hotels in New York City are also immortalized in the names of Muppets Statler and Waldorf.

The luxurious Grand Hotel Europe in Saint Petersburg, Russia achieved fame with its inclusion in the James Bond film GoldenEye.

Unusual Hotels

Many hotels can be considered destinations in themselves, by dint of unusual features of the lodging or its immediate environment:

Treehouse Hotels

Some hotels are built with living trees as structural elements, for example the Costa Rica Tree House in the Gandoca-Manzanillo Wildlife Refuge, Costa Rica; the Treetops Hotel in Aberdare National Park, Kenya; the Ariau Towers near Manaus, Brazil, on the Rio Negro in the Amazon; and Bayram's Tree Houses in Olympos, Turkey.

Bunker Hotels

The Null Stern Hotel in Teufen, Appenzellerland, Switzerland and the Concrete Mushrooms in Albania are former nuclear bunkers transformed into hotels.

Cave Hotels

Desert Cave Hotel in Coober Pedy, South Australia and the Cuevas Pedro Antonio de Alarcon (named after the author) in Guadix, Spain, as well as several hotels in Cappadocia, Turkey, are notable for being built into natural cave formations, some with rooms underground.

Capsule Hotels

Capsule hotels are a type of economical hotel that are found in Japan, where people sleep in stacks of rectangular containers.

Ice and Snow Hotels

The Ice Hotel in Jukkasjarvi, Sweden, and the Hotel de Glace in Duschenay, Canada, melt every spring and are rebuilt each winter; the Mammut Snow Hotel in Finland is located within the walls of the Kemi snow castle; and the Lainio Snow Hotel is part of a snow village near Yllas, Finland.

Garden Hotels

Garden hotels, famous for their gardens before they became hotels, include Gravetye Manor, the home of garden designer William Robinson, and Cliveden, designed by Charles Barry with a rose garden by Geoffrey Jellicoe.

Underwater Hotels

Some hotels have accommodation underwater, such as Utter Inn in Lake Malaren, Sweden. Hydropolis, project cancelled 2004 in Dubai, would have had suites on the bottom of the Persian Gulf, and Jules Undersea Lodge in Key Largo, Florida requires scuba diving to access its rooms.

Other Unusual Hotels

- The Library Hotel in New York City, is unique in that each of its ten floors is assigned one category from the Dewey Decimal System.

- The Burj al-Arab hotel in Dubai, United Arab Emirates, built on an artificial island, is structured in the shape of a boat's sail.
- The Jailhotel Löwengraben in Lucerne, Switzerland is a converted prison now used as a hotel.
- The Luxor, a hotel and casino on the Las Vegas Strip in Paradise, Nevada, United States due to its pyramidal structure.
- The Liberty Hotel in Boston, used to be the Charles Street Jail.
- Built in Scotland and completed in 1936, The former ocean liner RMS *Queen Mary* in Long Beach, California, United States uses its first-class staterooms as a hotel, after retiring in 1967 from Transatlantic service.

Resort Hotels

Some hotels are built specifically to create a captive trade, example at casinos and holiday resorts. Though of course hotels have always been built in popular desinations, the defining characteristic of a resort hotel is that it exists purely to serve another attraction, the two having the same owners. In Las Vegas there is a tradition of one-upmanship with luxurious and extravagant hotels in a concentrated area known as the Las Vegas Strip.

This trend now has extended to other resorts worldwide, but the concentration in Las Vegas is still the world's highest: nineteen of the world's twenty-five largest hotels by room count are on the Strip, with a total of over 67,000 rooms. In Europe Centre Parcs might be considered a chain of resort hotels, since the sites are largely man-made (though set in natural surroundings such as country parks) with captive trade, whereas holiday camps such as Butlins and Pontin's are probably not considered as resort hotels, since they are set at traditional holiday destinations which existed before the camps.

Railway Hotels

Frequently, expanding railway companies built grand hotels at their termini, such as the Midland Hotel, Manchester next to the former Manchester Central Station and in London the ones above St Pancras railway station and Charing Cross railway station also in London is the Chiltern Court Hotel above Baker Street tube station and Canada's grand railway hotels. They are or were mostly, but not exclusively, used by those travelling by rail.

Motels

A motel (Motor Hotel) is a hotel which is for a short stay, usually for a night, for motorists on long journeys. It has direct access from the room to the vehicle (for example a central parking lot around which the buildings are set), and is built conveniently close to major roads and intersections.

World Record Setting Hotels

Largest

In 2006, Guinness World Records listed the First World Hotel in Genting Highlands, Malaysia as the world's largest hotel with a total of 6,118 rooms.

Oldest

According to the Guinness Book of World Records, the oldest hotel still in operation is the Hoshi Ryokan, in the Awazu Onsen area of Komatsu, Japan which opened in 718.

Tallest

Burj Al Arab in United Arab Emirates is the tallest building used exclusively as a hotel. However, the Rose Tower, also in Dubai, which has already topped Burj Al Arab's height at 333 m (1,093 ft.), will take away this title upon its opening.

Hotel Rooms as an Investment

Some hotels sell individual rooms to investors. The buyer is allowed to stay in the room without charge or at a reduced rate for a given number of days each year.

The investor is paid a share of the takings for the room. Rooms can be sold on a leasehold basis, sometimes on a 999 year lease. Room owners are free to sell at any time.

Living in Hotels

A number of public figures have notably chosen to take up semipermanent or permanent residence in hotels.

Actor Richard Harris lived at the Savoy Hotel while in London. Hotel archivist Susan Scott recounts an anecdote that when he was being taken out of the building on a stretcher shortly before his death he raised his hand and told the diners "it was the food".

Fictitious Hotels

Hotels have been used as the settings for television programmes such as the British situation comedies Fawlty Towers and I'm Alan Partridge, the British soap opera Crossroads, and in films such as the Bates Motel in Hitchcock's 1960 film Psycho.

Hospitality Service

The concept of Hospitality Exchange, also known as "accommodation sharing", "hospitality services" (short "hospex"), and "home stay networks", refers to centrally organized social networks of individuals, generally travellers, who offer or seek accommodation without monetary exchange. Generally, these services connect users via the internet.

History

In 1949, Bob Luitweiler founded the first hospitality service called Servas Open Doors as a cross national, nonprofit, volunteer run organization advocating interracial and international peace. In 1965, John Wilcock set up the Traveller's Directory as a listing of his friends willing to host each other when travelling. In 1988, Joy Lily rescued the organization from imminent shutdown, forming Hospitality Exchange. In 2000, Veit Kuhne founded Hospitality Club, the first Internet-based service. In 2004, Casey Fenton started CouchSurfing, now the largest hospitality exchange organization.

How they Work

Generally, after registering, members have the option of providing very detailed information and pictures of themselves and of the sleeping accommodation being offered, if any. The more information provided by a member improves the chances that someone will find the member trustworthy enough to be their host or guest. Names and addresses may be verified by volunteers. Members looking for accommodation can search for hosts using several parameters such as age, location, sex, and activity level. Home stays are entirely consensual between the host and guest, and the duration, nature, and terms of the guest's stay are generally worked out in advance to the convenience of both parties. No monetary exchange takes place except under certain circumstances (e.g. the guest may compensate the host for food). After using the service, members can leave a noticeable reference about their host or guest.

Instead of or in addition to accommodation, members also offer to provide guide services or travel-related advice. The websites of the networks also provide editable travel guides and forums where members may seek travel partners or advice. Many such organizations are also focused on "social networking" and members organize activities such as camping trips, bar crawls, meetings, and sporting events.

Some networks cater to specific niche markets such as students, activists, religious pilgrims, and even occupational groups like police officers.

Benefits

Monetary Savings

As these networks provide accommodation at no charge, monetary savings can be significant.

Local Contact

Hospitality exchange gives travellers the chance to experience what life is like for people living in other places. In addition, making interpersonal connections and fostering understanding of different cultures may in the long run also be important to international relations. During hospitality exchanges, hosts may show off their local knowledge and exciting places "off the tourist map". Not only may travellers get a distinct experience, but they will also get a feel for the everyday lives of local residents.

Reciprocity

These systems foster richer and more convenient travel experiences not so much on the premise of altruism, but on the basis of social exchange theory. Implicit in the agreement to host travellers is the ability to ask to be hosted by them in the future. If one enjoys having interesting guests in their home, this works out well for both parties. It works comparatively better if you are visited by travellers from a locale you find particularly attractive.

Thus, hosting someone from New York City in Gainesville, Florida seems to be an unbelievable opportunity. Moreover, if you are a Westerner visiting someone in a developing country, your stay might be the only way that this individual or family could afford a trip to a rich nation. This may mean more than just a relaxing vacation for such disadvantaged parties.

Drawbacks

Lack of Guarantee

There is no contractual agreement between users in these systems. Reservations are made, but if they are for some reason broken, there is no higher authority to which one could plead for a refund or other compensation.

The only repercussion will be the poor rating you give that user and your only consolation will be that your warning will deter others from visiting or hosting them. For those who feel insecure unless their travel arrangements are written in stone before departure, this system will not be comforting.

Potential Interpersonal Conflict or Awkwardness

There is a chance that guest and host will not get along. Perhaps there will be scheduling or ideological conflicts. Maybe you will find that hosts or visitors have misrepresented themselves. Perhaps the experience will not live up to your expectations.

Intense interpersonal communications in advance and a flexibility once you have arrived is your best bet. These experiences require additional planning and courtesy towards the demands of your host. Thus, your living conditions, length of stay, and overall experience will be circumscribed by the living conditions you enter into.

Digital Divide and Demographic Segregation

As use of these services generally requires access to the internet and knowledge of the English language, the sample population found in searches of these databases is really much less diverse than a geographical representation of worldwide users might suggest.

Security

Staying in someone's house, or inviting people into your house leaves open the possibility of being taken advantage of.

Example Networks

There are countless websites that serve the idea of hospitality service, with new ones appearing as this phenomenon becomes more popular. While this page is not intended to be a directory listing, here is a small sample of the well-established and long-standing networks:

- CouchSurfing-A very active network with over 1.3 million members in more than 200 countries
- Hospitality Club-A very active network with over 550,000 members in more than 200 countries
- Servas International-human rights and global peace oriented since 1949. A relatively small network now with over 15,000 members(?) with a very long history.
- BeWelcome.

Hilton Hotels Corporation Announces Global Sustainability Goals

Hilton Hotels Corporation recently announced short and long term goals and objectives towards building sustainability into the core fabric of its businesses worldwide. Christopher J. Nassetta, President & CEO, outlined directional targets for improvement in the company's sustainability performance throughout the next five years within systemwide hotels globally. By 2014, goals for the Hilton Family of Hotels are to:

- Reduce energy consumption from direct operations by 20%
- Reduce CO_2 emissions by 20%
- Reduce output of waste by 20% and
- Reduce water consumption by 10%.

"Upon becoming a truly global company with the acquisition of Hilton International and following the acquisition of our company by Blackstone late last year, we are in an ideal position to lay down a framework for sustainability within our global hotels and corporate offices," said Nassetta.

As a global business serving more than a quarter billion guests a year in more than 3000 hotels across 74 countries, the Hilton family of Hotels, including Hilton, Conrad Hotels & Resorts, Doubletree, Embassy Suites Hotels, Hampton Inn and Suites, Hilton Garden Inn, Hilton Grand Vacations, Homewood Suites by Hilton and The Waldorf=Astoria Collection, are well-positioned to make a difference environmentally, socially, culturally and economically.

"Population growth and global industrialization are accelerating the depletion of our natural resources. Around the world, demand for energy continues to grow and fresh water scarcity is becoming a global reality. How we respond to these challenges will determine the sustainability of our future lifestyles, the sustainability of our communities as we know them, and ultimately the sustainability of our planet.

"To meet the growing demand of increased travel around the world, we must be able to do so in a sustainable fashion while still delivering unsurpassed levels of hospitality, including a better night's sleep, an enhanced dining experience and a more productive meeting," Nassetta continued.

"We must operate our business in ways that provide for our current needs while allowing future generations to meet their own needs.

This is the essence of sustainability and the path we must follow. Not only is it the right thing to do as responsible global citizens, it's the right thing to do for our business."

Long-Term, High-Impact Goals

In addition to the stated measurable short-term targets, the company also has committed to focus on several high-impact areas that offer significant long-term benefits. Sustainable buildings and operations, including the advancement of sustainable design and construction, operations, chemical management and purchasing will be one key area. The company is also committed to the advancement of renewable energy as a source of power for its operations, not only to reduce its carbon footprint but to develop a viable commercial infrastructure for powering hotels and corporate offices.

External Assessment by Leading Consulting Group

In the past year, Hilton Hotels Corporation conducted a thorough assessment of its global operations with the goal of identifying current impacts, and creating a strategy to define, galvanize and build sustainability into the business. To lead this effort, HHC brought in Blu Skye Sustainability Consulting, led by company founder and CEO Jib Ellison. Blu Skye visited a cross-section of Hilton Family hotels, interviewed various business units and analyzed the company's operating procedures. As a result of these efforts, corporate and brand management teams, together with Blu Skye, were able to identify specific areas of focus to build the company's sustainability framework focusing on short and long term value creation. "Hilton is building on its strong history of environmental stewardship by launching these ambitious goals," said Ellison. "Their comprehensive sustainability strategy has put them on a path to leadership in the hospitality industry."

Support Strategy

Under the direction of a newly appointed vice president – global sustainability Christopher Corpuel, HHC will build out a team to develop and implement its sustainability strategy. This team will support all of HHC's core businesses and work closely with hotel ownership and management groups to achieve its stated goals.

In addition, Hilton Hotels Corporation is supporting its portfolio of commitments in a number of ways, by:

- Building out educational and engagement programs for all brands and team members, including online learning, centralized web content, and various training modules.
- Measuring and reporting on our progress. The internal environmental management tool used within company-managed hotels will be extended to all properties, allowing us to track and report on our commitments and design processes and programs that identify areas of opportunity to drive innovation and efficiencies.
- Revising brand operational, and design and construction standards for 2009 to ensure both internal and external best practices are shared, adopted and transparent around the globe.
- Evaluating all current and future purchasing policies and practices across the brands to ensure that the range of products placed in hotels not only enhance the guest experience but drive value for owners while supporting the company's overall sustainability efforts.

Current Practices

Hilton Hotels Corporation has demonstrated its commitment to sustainability with several projects that currently are underway. In the European region, energy and water consumption already have been reduced by 10% during the last two years. In the U.K. and Ireland, the introduction of carbon-free electricity has reduced CO2 emissions in participating Hilton hotels by more than 64,000 tons, or 56% of our carbon footprint. In the United States, Hilton was the first in the industry to complete the installation of a commercial fuel cell power system, atop the Hilton New York, delivering one of the cleanest power generating technologies available today.

Galvanizing the spirit demonstrated by its recent and past successes together with its current commitments, Hilton Hotels Corporation has created a Mission Statement that will carry forward throughout its business practices.

Mission Statement

The Hilton Family of Hotels will manage our business

through a lens of sustainability to benefit this generation and those that follow. Through action and innovation, we will lead our industry in products and programs that:

- Enhance the guest experience
- Engage our employees
- Improve operational efficiency
- Advance building design
- Strengthen our partnerships
- Serve our communities
- Protect our global environment
- Enrich our Family of Brands.

Summary

"If we can use the lens of sustainability and find ways to enhance our leadership position in the industry, I am confident we will not only drive business value in the short and long term, but innovate our products and offerings in ways we never imagined," said Nassetta. "We can create better experiences for our guests, better business opportunities for our partners and investors, better work facilities for our colleagues, and better serve our communities, giving back in ways that actually restore resources instead of removing them, and improving the well-being of all involved. The platform for change we create now is one that will serve us for many years to come and support our goal of being the world's preeminent hospitality company."

About the Hilton Hotels Corporation

Hilton Hotels Corporation is the leading global hospitality company, with more than 3,000 hotels and 500,000 rooms in 74 countries, with more than 135,000 team members worldwide. The company owns, manages or franchises some of the best known and highly regarded hotel brands including Hilton®, Conrad® Hotels & Resorts, Doubletree®, Embassy Suites Hotels®, Hampton Inn®, Hampton Inn & Suites®, Hilton Garden Inn®, Hilton Grand Vacations™, Homewood Suites by Hilton® and The Waldorf=Astoria Collection™. Hilton Hotels Corporation is an Official Sponsor of the U.S. Olympic Team, which will extend through the 2010 Olympic and Paralympic Winter Games in Vancouver, the 2012 Olympic and Paralympic Games in London, the 2010/2012 U.S. Paralympic Team and the 2011 U.S. Pan American Team.

The Hilton Family of Hotels adheres to founder Conrad Hilton's philosophy that, "It has been, and continues to be, our responsibility to fill the earth with the light and warmth of hospitality." The company put a name to its unique brand of service that has made it the best known and most highly regarded hotel company: be hospitable®. The philosophy is shared by all brands in the Hilton Family of Hotels, and is the inspiration for its overarching message of kindness and generosity.

Selecting and Attracting the Right Customers

The following case is completely against the above statement made by Ratan Tata. One day in the month of December Mr.X and his friend Mr.Y went to deposit cash in one of the leading Multi National commercial Bank, They entered the bank premises found one of their executives attending only selective customers which they felt that it is unfair treatment but still they approached him, enquired for pay-in-slip they got it and filled it, later joined the queue with other customers towards the teller counter to deposit the cash which took more than five minutes, employee at the teller counter said "please collect the token for depositing the cash", They left the queue and went to the token machine and opted for non customer with deposit of Rupees less than 50000 and they got the token with (NW72) number and they were waiting for their turn to come and also observing the pattern of calling the customers, customers who came after them were provided priority services, in first 10-12 minutes they came to a conclusion that first preference was given to the customers of the bank itself, They immediately went to the token machine and opted for an another token as customer of the bank with deposit of Rupees less than 50000 and got the token with (CD81) number, their turn came just after fourth customer. They deposited the money and went to see the manager and put forth their complaint to him that the treatment what a non customer is getting is unreasonable and it is unfair on the part of the bank, the bank manager says that "this is a system where in non customers have been provided a separate counter and as an when their turn comes they will get the service and he was arguing with them and goes on explaining the system, procedure etc., But Mr. X & Y were not at all impressed with his justification and his indifferent comments on the problem made them felt awful, They thanked the Bank Manager and left his cabin.

This is nothing but over automation where in there is no personal touch or humane touch in their approach. This conversation have created an permanent negative image of the bank in their minds that they would never ever be a customer of such Bank or its sister concern and will never suggest any of their friends, relatives and even strangers to be a customer of that bank. Does any customer wants to hear "what are the company's systems and procedures, rules & regulations etc., As a direct or indirect customer one would never want to hear all those justifications, they just want quick service. And there is every possibility that automation of customer service will be abandoned in the frontline and induction of specialists in customer services in front office will be a future trend now which can be observed in Aviation industry. As of now few financial institutions are serving their customers in depositing money, withdrawals, financial planning and tax planning etc., at customer's premises.

The following example explains how indirectly a customer can be a valuable asset for an organization.

Eg: An individual who spends merely an average dollar amount per month with a wireless phone provider might be considered even more valuable if the wireless company knew the customer's spouse was responsible for selecting the wireless service plan for 5,000 workers at a large company.

In general there is misconception in the peoples mind that Public sector undertakings are poor at customer service, to some extent this comment may be right, but not completely true. Here are two public sector banks 'C' Bank (CB) and 'O' Bank (OB). Whose services are far better than that of Indian Multi National Bank. In the month of December Mr. X have been to CB to collect a Demand Draft, it took him more than half an hour when he asked about the time delay in issuing Demand Draft the Assistant Manager was courteous enough to say that "Sir, please wait for few minutes it will be done" and he did it in next ten minutes. Though Mr. X felt bad about the delay in issuing the draft but Mr. X was pleased by the response of the Assistant Manger. This episode haven't made him much disappointed and have not provoked him to erase completely CB from his mind; He still wanted to open an account because it is convenient for him to transact and staff's aptitude to handle customer services are better. And Mr. X still felt CB is bankable and there are better chances that he would suggest his friends to bank at CB. Unfortunately on the same day itself a situation came, where in he was forced to take one more Demand Draft, he visited OB and enquired about DD form at the counter, the employee just shown the place where they were, with a pathetic face, he took the form and his first question to the bank employee was "How much time does it take to issue a Demand Draft" there was no response from that bank employee who was sitting at the counter, suddenly there was a unexpected response which he heard from an unusual person, a middle aged woman, who is just a Peon " Sir it will just take five minutes" He was convinced with her approach of attending him, he simply paid the amount at the teller and stood near the counter, rest she took over the Job. During this time, she was doing her job simultaneously interacting with him by posing soft questions like "Are you in a hurry Sir?"

Where do you come from? And other few similar questions. By the time he answered her questions, the Demand Draft was ready. It took only seven minutes as compared to official time to make a DD is twenty minutes, though it was delayed by two minutes as promised, he was extremely satisfied with that Lady's service. He felt like it would have been better if she would have placed in front office as an executive instead of Peon. Mr. X was extremely impressed by that lady's ability to engage customer at POP, One would definitely feel that the big companies and their big projects of Customer Relationship Management are of no use when there are no people to implement it all the levels.

"According to a research by Reichheld and Sasser in the Harvard Business Review, 5% increase in customer retention can increase profitability by 35% in banking business, 50% in insurance and brokerage, and 125% in the consumer credit card market. Therefore, banks are now stressing on retaining customers and increasing market share".

The above situations like these are definitely creating an impression in the mind of customers that the corporate are denying legitimate right, needs and requirements.

Right from the days of customer centric market, this has been a regular activity that there are problems in customer care. In today's business environment there is no such industry, where customer care problems does not exist, even in the field of hospitality industry and service industry where in these industry's core business is custom care and the gap between the customers and their expectations and the service providers are increasing day by day. Today in the Heighten world lot many new innovative products and services are being invented, but at the same time does any company thought that the product/ service they offer are really needed by the customers or it is just because the products are being produced and are dumped into the market.

As people are very much aware that there are whole variety of products and services available in the market. But how many of them do really buy them even though they are of top quality, with marvelous features and at affordable prices.

Managers at middle level and supervisory levels of Indian corporate are not ready to treat customers equally. Unless the attitude of the managers changes towards customers problems pertaining to service will always exist.

How companies are responding to the bad experiences of using the product or service, what are the measures taken to avoid such experiences by the customers. Companies must ensure that customers get a new experience in purchasing and using their products and the impact of such purchase must be for a long time and which can be encased into new opportunities in the long run. And differentiating from competitors, there by extending the change in purchasing experience.

One would definitely agree that, it is not always possible to give such a kind of experience and personal attention to each and every customer, but a company must make sure that customers should not leave the premises without satisfaction, and it is the right of the customer to expect highest degree of respect, let it be in the case of, hospitality, product availability, price, features or any other service (E.g.: Fiat is known for its best designed and engineered cars in the world, but in India it could not capture the market as expected because, after sales service levels were not up to the expectations of the customer, In order to boost sales in India, Tata Motors and Fiat came together and announced a strategic relationship in passenger car segment for sales and marketing of Fiat cars through Tata dealerships. Through these dealerships display a wide selection of Fiat cars along with service and spares will be provided across Tata dealerships in India. Dealers will display the Fiat models along with Tata cars).

And most importantly the consumer complaining behavior process is unique; it has to deal with at most importance. And it distinguishes between negative word-of-mouth that occurs prior to seeking redress (or in lieu of seeking redress) and negative word-of-mouth that occurs after seeking redress.

There is an argument from the company's point of view i.e. how can any company spend time and manpower to attend a default and fraudulent customer and how treat them in the same manner as genuine and productive customer. Certainly they must be treated in a cordial way but one should not forget that they too deserve some importance in one way or the other.

There is every possibility that companies make mistakes but they must be such that they should be forgivable by the customer, meaning even though companies make mistakes and try to rectify at the earliest and inform customers that the mistake which has been committed is been rectified and at most precautions have been taken, not to repeat the mistake.

Eg: What Cadbury has done by giving advertisements in the media, that it has rectified its mistakes and promised the customer that it won't repeat the same mistake again.

If a person is a regular customer of friendly neighborhood

grocery shop or any other shop or bank, one will definitely know the painless punch of corporate businesses. They might misguide, mislead with the bashing effect, display, intense publicity, promotion and enchasing on personal intimacy. One should be aware that in one way or the other the suppliers are the customers and consumers of their own produce. The individuals who supply the produce at certain rate cannot afford to purchase the same product just because it is been packed and placed in fully decorated place. In this kind of situation, are you (customer) the beneficiary, just ask yourself. Who do you think is the real beneficiary; if your answer is, neither the supplier nor the consumer, then one will get to know there is nothing, which is called as "Service".

Most Indians are habituated to have every thing fresh and never had tradition of packing food, let it be cooked or uncooked food, they prefer to have them in a natural way.

Eg: Fresh vegetables and fruits, do they really need packing, is there any need for branding products which are grown naturally or cultivated, does anyone feel it is absolutely necessary?

The ever changing customer expectations are forcing the corporate to provide excellent service which is not possible to each an every company, organizations which provides service beyond customer expectations will survive the future rest will be out of business. Organizations who wanted to survive are exploring, proliferating them selves by establishing new businesses in big way, there by depending on higher volumes. Some of them are collaboratively sharing their customer data there by offering vide variety of products to the same customer and leveraging customer base. These strategies adopted by the companies constantly put the pressure on the customer by offering vide range of product and there is fare chance that one might ignore such product offerings which are marketed by different departments, which are in a race generate revenue of their own. There is always a risk that customer may encounter different service levels of the different department of the same company. For many years, Indian economy has been guarded from invasion of foreign companies in the form of Joint venture or fully owned or capitalistic form of economy. Only some state owned companies which were in key areas like Defense, Telecom, Oil and other essential commodities. A set of few private owned companies who were into consumer items, engineering and manufacturing prospered during that period. Right from the days of closely guarded economy and till the days of economic liberalization in late 1990, the private owned companies in the seller's market were very successful. But the whole scenario chanced after post liberalization.

Ever since the golden days (customer centric market) i.e. Since last thirty years to till date, marketers have been saying "Customer is the King" but, is the customer really a king? This is the main question which comes to everybody's mind and other questions such as how customers are treated? What quality of products do marketers offer? Are the products are user friendly? Etc., if these questions are answered completely with good outlook, a company can build up a brand which will be unique in any or combination of all the following attributes Price, Design, Quality, Usability, Service and shopping experience there by creating own and distinguished Brand. As an human being every individual expects to be treated with courtesy, similarly it is prime duty of marketers to treat customer with at most respect which he/she deserves. Here is a situation where CRM come in to picture, the essence of CRM should be understood as any activity which is completely customer centric and which enhances customer's expectations and satisfaction levels by giving him/her a wow effect with a human touch, at the same time maximize revenues from such services.

> *"CRM would help organizations to serve the customers on an individual basis, to enjoy a long-term relationship and to get rid of barriers and distortions created by non-value adding intermediaries. He also says that CRM would also help organizations to reduce marketing costs, target specific customers by focusing on their needs and to track the effectiveness of a given marketing action" by Dr. Thapan K. Panda, IIM Indore.*

"CRM has power to help bankers quickly and directly improve customer satisfaction. CRM is an added dimension to ensure that what the customer expects is consistent with what the bank is prepared to deliver. One expert in bank CRM initiatives recently said that CRM is an approach that is less focused on providing the right services to the customer than attracting customers who are the right fit for what the bank has to offer. Further, the primary value of CRM is its potential as a customer retention tool. People are starting to measure CRM in terms of increased customer satisfaction rather than ROI" by Rob Keene, Director, Banking Practice.

In the vide spectrum of business, in after adopting and practicing latest technologies like CRM, people soft and other similar technologies. How do people interpret and understand the meaning of Customer Relationship Management, many experts expressed their view in different forms but there are few seminaries which revolve round the "Customer's needs, expectations and satisfaction".

In the field of consumer service management, many unexpected problem do arise and they pose challenges to be solved, a doubt may arise in the minds of individuals that adopting all these CRM technologies are of waste of money and time. May be not, as per the latest studies, customer service problems are marginalized to some extent but could not overcome them completely. We cannot imagine big businesses without such customer service technologies. Company's internal environment (employees) and external environment (Customer traffic, Business expansion etc.,) do influence on implementation of such technologies, Employees must be trained continuously to implement it and also change their mind set to adapt to such changing environment (customer centric).

Unless people from top to bottom level in all departments focus and act on, what they actually wanted achieve in customer relationship management, interactive Customer Relationship Management software solutions will never deliver expected results.

It can be concluded that if any company intends to survive in today's competitive market it is essential that they must to treat customer as a king irrespective of using any technology. And giving at most importance to the direct or an indirect customer. Who knows a non productive customer of yours, may be a highly productive customer of your competitor.

International Trade Theory, Practice and Policy

International trade is exchange of capital, goods, and services across international borders or territories. It refers to exports of goods and services by a firm to a foreign-based buyer (importer) In most countries, it represents a significant share of gross domestic product (GDP). While international trade has been present throughout much of history, its economic, social, and political importance has been on the rise in recent centuries.

Industrialization, advanced transportation, globalization, multinational corporations, and outsourcing are all having a major impact on the international trade system. Increasing international trade is crucial to the continuance of globalization. International trade is a major source of economic revenue for any nation that is considered a world power. Without international trade, nations would be limited to the goods and services produced within their own borders.

International trade is in principle not different from domestic trade as the motivation and the behavior of parties involved in a trade do not change fundamentally regardless of whether trade is across a border or not. The main difference is that international trade is typically more costly than domestic trade. The reason is that a border typically imposes additional costs such as tariffs, time costs due to border delays and costs associated with country differences such as language, the legal system or culture.

Another difference between domestic and international trade is that factors of production such as capital and labour are typically more mobile within a country than across countries. Thus international trade is mostly restricted to trade in goods and services, and only to a lesser extent to trade in capital, labour or other factors of production. Then trade in goods and services can serve as a substitute for trade in factors of production. Instead of importing a factor of production, a country can import goods that make intensive use of the factor of production and are thus embodying the respective factor. An example is the import of labour-intensive goods by the United States from China. Instead of importing Chinese labour the United States is importing goods from China that were produced with Chinese labour.

International trade is also a branch of economics, which, together with international finance, forms the larger branch of international economics.

Models

Several different models have been proposed to predict patterns of trade and to analyse the effects of trade policies such as tariffs.

Ricardian Model

The Ricardian model focuses on comparative advantage and is perhaps the most important concept in international trade theory. In a Ricardian model, countries specialize in producing what they produce best. Unlike other models, the Ricardian framework predicts that countries will fully specialize instead of producing a broad array of goods.

Also, the Ricardian model does not directly consider factor endowments, such as the relative amounts of labour and capital within a country. The main merit of Ricardin model is that it assumes technology differences between countries. Technology gap is easily included in the Ricardian and Ricardo-Sraffa model.

The Ricardian model makes the following assumptions:

1. Labour is the only primary input to production (labour is considered to be the ultimate source of value).
2. Constant Marginal Product of Labour (MPL) (Labour productivity is constant, constant returns to scale, and simple technology.)
3. Limited amount of labour in the economy
4. Labour is perfectly mobile among sectors but not internationally.
5. Perfect competition (price-takers).

The Ricardian model measures in the shortrun, therefore technology differs internationally. This supports the fact that countries follow their comparative advantage and allows for specialization.

Modern Development of the Ricardian Model

The Ricardian trade model was studied by Graham, Jones, McKenzie and others. All the theories excluded intermediate goods, or traded input goods such as materials and capital goods. McKenzie(1954), Jones(1961) and Samuelson (2001) emphasized that considerable gains from trade would be lost once intermediate goods were excluded from trade.

In a famous comment McKenzie pointed that "A moment's consideration will convince one that Lancashire would be unlikely to produce cotton cloth if the cotton had to be grown in England."

Recently, the theory was extended to the case that includes traded intermediates. Thus the "labour only" assumption was removed from the theory. Thus the new Ricardian theory, or the Ricardo-Sraffa model, as it is sometimes named, theoretically includes capital goods such as machines and materials, which are traded across countries. In the time of global trade, this assumption is much more realistic than the Heckscher-Ohlin model, which assumes that capital is fixed inside the country and does not move internationally.

Heckscher-Ohlin Model

In the early 1900s an international trade theory called factor proportions theory emerged by two Swedish economists, Eli Heckscher and Bertil Ohlin. This theory is also called the Heckscher-Ohlin theory. The Heckscher-Ohlin theory stresses that countries should produce and export goods that require resources (factors) that are abundant and import goods that require resources in short supply.

This theory differs from the theories of comparative advantage and absolute advantage since these theory focuses on the productivity of the production process for a particular good. On the contrary, the Heckscher-Ohlin theory states that a country should specialise production and export using the factors that are most abundant, and thus the cheapest. Not to produce, as earlier theories stated, the goods it produces most efficiently.

The Heckscher-Ohlin model was produced as an alternative to the Ricardian model of basic comparative advantage. Despite its greater complexity it did not prove much more accurate in its predictions. However from a theoretical point of view it did provide an elegant solution by incorporating the neoclassical price mechanism into international trade theory.

The theory argues that the pattern of international trade is determined by differences in factor endowments. It predicts that countries will export those goods that make intensive use of locally abundant factors and will import goods that make intensive use of factors that are locally scarce. Empirical problems with the H-O model, known as the Leontief paradox, were exposed in empirical tests by Wassily Leontief who found that the United States tended to export labour intensive goods despite having a capital abundance.

The H-O model makes the following core assumptions:

1. Labour and capital flow freely between sectors
2. The production of shoes is labour intensive and computers is capital intensive
3. The amount of labour and capital in two countries differ (difference in endowments)
4. free trade
5. technology is the same across countries (long-term)
6. Tastes are the same.

The problem with the H-O theory is that it excludes the trade of capital goods (including materials and fuels). In the H-O theory, labour and capital are fixed entities endowed to each country. In a modern economy, capital goods are traded internationally. Gains from trade of intermediate goods are considerable, as it was emphasized by Samuelson (2001).

Reality and Applicability of the Heckscher-Ohlin Model

The Heckscher-Ohlin theory is preferred to the Ricardo theory by many economists, because it makes fewer simplifying assumptions. In 1953, Wassily Leontief published a study, where he tested the validity of the Heckscher-Ohlin theory. The study showed that the U.S was more abundant in capital compared to other countries, therefore the U.S would export capital-intensive goods and import labour-intensive goods. Leontief found out that the U.S's export was less capital intensive than import.

After the appearance of Leontief's paradox, many researchers tried to save the Heckscher-Ohlin theory, either by new methods of measurement, or either by new interpretations. Leamer emphasized that Leontief did not interpret HO theory properly and claimed that with a right interpretation paradox did not occur. Brecher and Choudri found that, if Leamer was right, the American workers consumption per head should be lower than the workers world average consumption.

Many other trials followed but most of them failed. Many of famous textbook writers, including Krugman and Obstfeld and Bowen, Hollander and Viane, are negative about the validity of H-O model. After examining the long history of empirical research, Bowen, Hollander and Viane concluded: "Recent tests of the factor abundance theory [H-O theory and its developed form into many-commodity and many-factor case] that directly examine the H-O-V equations also indicate the rejection of the theory."

Heckscher-Ohlin theory is not well adapted to the analyse South-North trade problems. The assumptions of HO are less realistic with respect to N-S than N-N (or S-S) trade. Income differences between North and South is the one that third world cares most. The factor price equalization [a consequence of HO theory] has not shown much sign of realization. HO model assumes identical production functions between countries. This is highly unrealistic. Technological gap between developed and developing countries is the main concern of the poor countries.

Specific Factors Model

In this model, labour mobility between industries is possible while capital is immobile between industries in the shortrun. Thus, this model can be interpreted as a 'short run' version of the Heckscher-Ohlin model. The specific factors name refers to the given that in the shortrun, specific factors of production such as physical capital are not easily transferable between industries. The theory suggests that if there is an increase in the price of a good, the owners of the factor of production specific to that good will profit in real terms. Additionally, owners of opposing specific factors of production (i.e. labour and capital) are likely to have opposing agendas when lobbying for controls over immigration of labour. Conversely, both owners of capital and labour profit in real terms from an increase in the capital endowment. This model is ideal for particular industries. This model is ideal for understanding income distribution but awkward for discussing the pattern of trade.

New Trade Theory

New Trade theory tries to explain several facts about trade, which the two main models above have difficulty with. These include the fact that most trade is between countries with similar factor endowment and productivity levels, and the large amount of multinational production (i.e.foreign direct investment) which exists. In one example of this framework, the economy exhibits monopolistic competition and increasing returns to scale. There are three basic theories that global marketer has to comprehend: 1. Comparative Advantage Theory 2. Trade or product trade cycle theory 3. Business orientation theory

Gravity Model

The Gravity model of trade presents a more empirical analysis of trading patterns rather than the more theoretical models discussed above. The gravity model, in its basic form, predicts trade based on the distance between countries and the interaction of the countries' economic sizes. The model mimics the Newtonian law of gravity which also considers distance and physical size between two objects. The model has been proven to be empirically strong through econometric analysis. Other factors such as income level, diplomatic relationships between countries, and trade policies are also included in expanded versions of the model.

Regulation of International Trade

Traditionally trade was regulated through bilateral treaties between two nations. For centuries under the belief in mercantilism most nations had high tariffs and many restrictions on international trade. In the 19th century, especially in the United Kingdom, a belief in free trade became paramount. This belief became the dominant thinking among western nations since then. In the years since the Second World War, controversial multilateral treaties like the General Agreement on Tariffs and Trade (GATT) and World Trade Organization have attempted to promote free trade while creating a globally regulated trade structure. These trade agreements have often resulted in discontent and protest with claims of unfair trade that is not beneficial to developing countries.

Free trade is usually most strongly supported by the most economically powerful nations, though they often engage in selective protectionism for those industries which are strategically important such as the protective tariffs applied to agriculture by the United States and Europe. The Netherlands and the United Kingdom were both strong advocates of free trade when they were economically dominant, today the United States, the United Kingdom, Australia and Japan are its greatest proponents. However, many other countries (such as India, China and Russia) are increasingly becoming advocates of free trade as they become more economically powerful themselves. As tariff levels fall there is also an increasing willingness to negotiate non tariff measures, including foreign direct investment, procurement and trade facilitation. The latter looks at the transaction cost associated with meeting trade and customs procedures.

Traditionally agricultural interests are usually in favour of free trade while manufacturing sectors often support protectionism. This has changed somewhat in recent years, however. In fact, agricultural lobbies, particularly in the United States, Europe and Japan, are chiefly responsible for particular rules in the major international trade treaties which allow for more protectionist measures in agriculture than for most other goods and services.

During recessions there is often strong domestic pressure to increase tariffs to protect domestic industries. This occurred around the world during the Great Depression. Many economists have attempted to portray tariffs as the underlining reason behind the collapse in world trade that many believe seriously deepened the depression. The regulation of international trade is done through the World Trade Organization at the global level, and through several other regional arrangements such as MERCOSUR in South America, the North American Free Trade Agreement (NAFTA) between the United States, Canada and Mexico, and the European Union between 27 independent states. The 2005 Buenos Aires talks on the planned establishment of the Free Trade Area of the Americas (FTAA) failed largely because of opposition from the populations of Latin American nations. Similar agreements such as the Multilateral Agreement on Investment (MAI) have also failed in recent years.

Risk in International Trade

Companies doing business across international borders face many of the same risks as would normally be evident in strictly domestic transactions. For example,

- Buyer insolvency (purchaser cannot pay);
- Non-acceptance (buyer rejects goods as different from the agreed upon specifications);
- Credit risk (allowing the buyer to take possession of goods prior to payment);
- Regulatory risk (e.g., a change in rules that prevents the transaction);
- Intervention (governmental action to prevent a transaction being completed);
- Political risk (change in leadership interfering with transactions or prices); and
- War and other uncontrollable events.

In addition, international trade also faces the risk of unfavorable exchange rate movements (and, the potential benefit of favorable movements).

The Measurement of Efficiency and Productivity

Market orientation efficiency is conceptualized as the speed by which a company gathers information about customers and competitors, disseminates the information throughout the organization, arrives at a shared meaning, and implements a response. A reliable scale with demonstrated content and convergent validity is developed and the impact of market orientation efficiency on business performance is assessed based on multiple informant data drawn from two industries. From a managerial perspective, the scale can be used to evaluate a given firm's level of market orientation efficiency as a baseline measure and again as a measure of success once strategies designed to improve market orientation efficiency are set into motion.

Ultimate Goal of Operations Research

The term Operations Research (OR) describes the discipline that is focused on the application of information technology for informed decision-making. In other words, OR represents the study of optimal resource allocation. The goal of OR is to provide rational bases for decision making by seeking to understand and structure complex situations, and to utilize this understanding to predict system behavior and improve system performance. Much of the actual work is conducted by using analytical and numerical techniques to develop and manipulate mathematical models of organizational systems that are composed of people, machines, and procedures. This article introduces some of the methods and application that are affiliated with OR, and elaborates on some of the benefits that may be gained by incorporating OR into the actual business framework.

OR Activities

OR's role in both, the public and the private sectors is increasing rapidly. In general, OR addresses a wide variety of issues in transportation, inventory planning, production planning, communication operations, computer operations, financial assets, risk management, revenue management, and many other fields where improving business productivity is paramount. In the public sector, OR studies may focus on energy policy, defense, health care, water resource planning, design and operation of urban emergency systems, or criminal justice. To reiterate, OR reflects an analytical method of problem solving and decision-making that is useful in the management of organizations. In OR, problems are (1) decomposed into basic components and (2) solved via mathematical analysis. Some of the analytical methods used in OR include mathematical logic, simulation, network analysis, queuing theory, and game theory. The actual

OR process can in general be described via three steps. (1) A set of potential solutions to a problem is identified and developed (the set may be rather large). (2) The alternatives derived in the first step are analyzed, and reduced to a smaller set of solutions (the solutions have to be feasible and workable). (3) The alternatives derived in the second step are subjected to simulated implementation and, if feasible, exposed to an actual analysis in a real-world environment. It has to be pointed out that in the final step, psychology and management sciences often play a rather important role. Generally speaking, OR improves the effectiveness and the efficiency of an institution, hence some of the benefits offered by OR include:

- Decrease Cost or Investment
- Increase Revenue or Return on Investment
- Increase Market Share
- Manage and Reduce Risk
- Improve Quality
- Increase Throughput while Decreasing Delays
- Achieve Improved Utilization form Limited Resources
- Demonstrate Feasibility and Workability.

OR Functions and Methods

OR may assist decision-makers in almost any management function. To illustrate, OR supports the key decision making process, allows to solve urgent problems, can be utilized to design improved multistep operations (processes), setup policies, supports the planning and forecasting steps, and measures actual results. OR can be applied at the non-manager levels as well, as engineers or consumers alike can benefit from the improved and streamlined decision-making process.

When first encountered, the methods commonly utilized in OR may seem obscure. Technical labels such as multi-criteria decision analysis, linear and non-linear programming, discrete-event Dominique A. Heger, Fortuitous Technology, Austin, TX, 2006 simulation, queuing and stochastic process modeling, conjoint analysis, or neural networking further foster this general impression. Despite the wealth of labels available in the filed of OR, most projects apply one of three broad groups of methods, which may be described as:

- *Simulation methods,* where the goal is to develop simulators that provide the decision-maker with the ability to conduct sensitivity studies to (1) search for improvements, and (2) to test and benchmark the improvement ideas that are being made.
- *Optimization methods,* where the goal is to enable the decision maker to search among possible choices in an efficient and effective manner, in environments where thousands or millions of choices may actually be feasible, or where some of the comparing choices are rather complex. The ultimate goal is to identify and locate the very best choice based on certain criteria's.
- *Data-analysis methods,* where the goal is to aid the decision-maker in detecting actual patterns and interconnections in the data set. This method is rather useful in numerous applications including forecasting and data mining based business environments.

Within each of the three basic groups, many probabilistic methods provide the ability to assess risk and uncertainty factors.

OR in Manufacturing

As OR has made (over the years) significant contributions in virtually all industries, in almost all managerial and decision-making functions, and at most organizational levels, the list of OR applications is prodigious. Hence, this article focuses in the next few paragraphs on the manufacturing industry, and introduces some of the application where OR is being used.

The term operations in OR may suggests that the manufacturing application category represents the original home of OR. That is not quite accurate, as the name originated from military operations, not business operations. Nevertheless, it is a true statement that OR's successes in contemporary business pervade manufacturing and service operations, logistics, distribution, transportation, and telecommunication. The myriad applications include scheduling, routing, workflow improvements, elimination of bottlenecks, inventory control, business process reengineering, site selection, or facility and general operational planning. Revenue and supply chain management reflect two growing applications that are distinguished by their use of several OR methods to cover several functions. Revenue management entails first to accurately forecasting the demand, and secondly to adjust the price structure over time to more profitably allocate fixed capacity. Supply chain decisions describe the who, what, when, and where abstractions from purchasing and transporting raw materials and parts, through manufacturing actual

products and goods, and finally distributing and delivering the items to the customers. The prime management goal here may be to reduce overall cost while processing customer orders more efficiently than before. The power of utilizing OR methods allows examining this rather complex and convoluted chain in a comprehensive manner, and to search among a vast number of combinations for the resource optimization and allocation strategy that seem most effective, and hence beneficial to the operation.

Production Systems

Businesses and organizations frequently face challenging operational problems whose successful solution requires certain expertise in applied statistics, optimization, stochastic modeling, or a combination of these areas. To illustrate, a company may need to design a sampling plan in order to meet specific quality control objectives. In a manufacturing environment, operations that compete for the same resources must be scheduled in a way that deadlines are not violated.

The manager of a supermarket must determine how many checkout lines to keep open at various times during the day and evening so that shoppers are not unnecessarily delayed. Or as a final example, the size of the areas reserved for storing work in process at a Dominique A. Heger, Fortuitous Technology, Austin, TX, 2006 number of bottleneck stations has to be determined so that a smooth flow of work results, even at the busiest (peak) production times.

The area of operations research that concentrates on real-world operational problems is called production systems. Production systems problems may arise in settings that include, but are not limited to, manufacturing,. telecommunications, healthcare delivery, facility location and layout, and staffing. The area of production systems presents special challenges for operations researchers. Production problems are operations research problems, hence solving them requires a solid foundation in operations research fundamentals. Additionally, the solution of production systems problems frequently draws on expertise in more than one of the primary areas of operations research, implying that the successful production researcher can not be one-dimensional. Furthermore, production systems problems can not be solved without an in-depth understanding of the real problem, since invoking assumptions that simplify the mathematical structure of the problem may lead to an elegant solution for the wrong problem. Common sense and practical insight are common attributes of successful production planners. At the current time, the filed of OR is extremely dynamic and ever evolving. To name a few of the contemporary (primary) research projects, current work in OR seeks to develop software for material flow analysis and design of flexible manufacturing facilities using pattern recognition and graph theory algorithms. Further, approaches for the design of reconfigurable manufacturing systems and progressive automation of discrete manufacturing systems are under development. Additional OR projects focus on the industrial deployment of computer-based methods for assembly line balancing, business process reengineering, capacity planning, pull scheduling, and setup reduction, primarily through the integration of the philosophies of the Theory of Constraints and Lean Manufacturing.

Identifying Sources of Operational Risk

An operational risk is a risk arising from execution of a company's business functions. As such, it is a very broad concept including e.g. fraud risks, legal risks, physical or environmental risks, etc. The term operational risk is most commonly found in risk management programs of financial institutions that must organize their risk management program according to Basel II. In Basel II, risk management is divided into credit, market, liquidity and operational risk management. In many cases, credit and market risks are handled through a company's financial department, whereas operational risk management is perhaps coordinated centrally but most commonly implemented in different operational units (e.g. the IT department takes care of information risks, the HR department takes care of personnel risks, etc.)

More specifically, Basel II defines operational risk as the risk of loss resulting from inadequate or failed internal processes, people and systems, or from external events. Although the risks apply to any organization in business, this particular way of framing risk management is of particular relevance to the banking regime where regulators are responsible for establishing safeguards to protect against systemic failure of the banking system and the economy.

Background

Since the mid-1990s, the topics of market risk and credit risk have been the subject of much debate and research, with the result that financial institutions have made significant progress in the identification, measurement and management of both these forms of risk. However, it is worth mentioning that the near collapse of the U.S. financial system in September 2008 is a clear indication that our ability to measure market and credit risk is far from perfect.

Globalization and deregulation in financial markets, combined with increased sophistication in financial technology, have introduced more complexities into the activities of banks and therefore their risk profiles. These reasons underscore banks' and supervisors' growing focus upon the identification and measurement of operational risk.

Events such as the September 11 terrorist attacks, rogue trading losses at Societe Generale, Barings, AIB and National Australia Bank serve to highlight the fact that the scope of risk management extends beyond merely market and credit risk.

The list of risks (and, more importantly, the scale of these risks) faced by banks today includes fraud, system failures, terrorism and employee compensation claims. These types of risk are generally classified under the term 'operational risk'.

The identification and measurement of operational risk is a real and live issue for modern-day banks, particularly since the decision by the Basel Committee on Banking Supervision (BCBS) to introduce a capital charge for this risk as part of the new capital adequacy framework (Basel II).

Definition

The Basel Committee defines operational risk as: "The risk of loss resulting from inadequate or failed internal processes, people and systems or from external events." However, the Basel Committee recognizes that operational risk is a term that has a variety of meanings and therefore, for internal purposes, banks are permitted to adopt their own definitions of operational risk, provided the minimum elements in the Committee's definition are included.

Scope Exclusions

The Basel II definition of operational risk excludes, for example, strategic risk-the risk of a loss arising from a poor strategic business decision.

Other risk terms are seen as potential consequences of operational risk events.

For example, reputational risk (damage to an organization through loss of its reputation or standing) can arise as a consequence (or impact) of operational failures-as well as from other events.

Basel II Event Type Categories

The following lists the official Basel II defined event types with some examples for each category:

1. Internal Fraud-misappropriation of assets, tax evasion, intentional mismarking of positions, bribery
2. External Fraud-theft of information, hacking damage, third-party theft and forgery

3. Employment Practices and Workplace Safety-discrimination, workers compensation, employee health and safety
4. Clients, Products, & Business Practice-market manipulation, antitrust, improper trade, product defects, fiduciary breaches, account churning
5. Damage to Physical Assets-natural disasters, terrorism, vandalism
6. Business Disruption & Systems Failures-utility disruptions, software failures, hardware failures
7. Execution, Delivery, & Process Management-data entry errors, accounting errors, failed mandatory reporting, negligent loss of client assets.

Difficulties

It is relatively straightforward for an organization to set and observe specific, measurable levels of market risk and credit risk. By contrast it is relatively difficult to identify or assess levels of operational risk and its many sources. Historically organizations have accepted operational risk as an unavoidable cost of doing business.

Methods of Operational Risk Management

Basel II and various Supervisory bodies of the countries have prescribed various soundness standards for Operational Risk Management for Banks and similar Financial Institutions. To complement these standards, Basel II has given guidance to 3 broad methods of Capital calculation for Operational Risk

- Basic Indicator Approach-based on annual revenue of the Financial Institution
- Standardized Approach-based on annual revenue of each of the broad business lines of the Financial Institution
- Advanced Measurement Approaches-based on the internally developed risk measurement framework of the bank adhering to the standards prescribed (methods include IMA, LDA, Scenario-based, Scorecard etc.)

The Operational Risk Management framework should include identification, measurement, monitoring, reporting, control and mitigation frameworks for Operational Risk.

Operational disasters in financial institutions have grabbed any number of headlines in newspapers around the world in the last few years-as the case studies on our Wheel of Misfortune demonstrate.

For managers, these tales of incompetence, corruption and simple bad luck are both entertaining and disconcerting.

Disconcerting because, as the tally has risen, it's become clear that gross operational error and failure is much less isolated from the problem of day-to-day management than the financial industry had imagined.

Researchers now reckon that catastrophic events are the visible part of a wider spectrum of cover-ups, "near misses", and costly but undramatic events that plague most firms-and signal a failure in risk management practice and technology.

Operational risk has also turned out to be more costly in terms of capital than most institutions realised-recent estimates put it at 25% or more of risk capital. And that's rising, as operational risk emerges from beneath New Economy business models such as Internet banking, electronic trading and the outsourcing of core bank functions.

Meanwhile, as our scroll-over timeline explains, the regulators of international banking are about to ask major banks to set aside specific amounts of capital for operational risk. It's part of their long-term project to tie capital charges more directly to risk-taking.

Bank regulators are not alone in demanding a new approach. Corporate governance experts and stockmarket analysts have begun to address disingenuous questions to all sorts of financial institutions. Shouldn't top executives be able to name any "sudden death" risks that their firm is exposed to? Or at least have some idea of the scale of potential operational losses in their industry?

Top executives are themselves wondering whether decisions based on risk-adjusted return on capital (RAROC) might be flawed if operational risk is not taken into account. Might they simply exchange business lines with transparent market or credit risks for those with hidden risks?

All this explains why controlling operational risks at business-line level-simply "getting it right"-is no longer enough for many professionals. But, so far, financial institutions lack a framework of methodologies and tools to push operational risks through a coherent risk management cycle.

Operational Risk Management Cycle;

1. Identify and assess
2. Analyse risk controls
3. Rank/score/measure/track
4. Cost
5. Contextualise and communicate
6. Monitor
7. Assume risk
8. Assume but reduce frequency
9. Assume but mitigate severity
10. Assume but risk finance
11. Avoid/Remove
12. Transfer .

In this piece of the Risk Jigsaw, we'll tell how the financial industry-led by bankers and their regulators-is constructing that framework.

Some of the new ideas have grown out of established risk management disciplines in financial institutions such as Audit and Market Risk, while others are drawn from activities as diverse as healthcare and the space industry.

As we go along, we'll explain the new concepts that are driving operational risk management, hear from some Expert Witnesses, and offer links to key information points on the web.

Saying what You Mean-The Definitional Problem

Defining operational risk sounds easy-it's the risk of something going unexpectedly wrong! Bankers add the caveat "outside of market and credit risk" because they already have specialist risk managers for these areas.

But general definitions are less useful when a manager or regulator tries to do something about enterprise-wide operational risk-such as improve operational risk controls across the board, or reserve capital against operational risk.

Counting something, or controlling it, means putting a line around it. Soon, regulators and RAROC analysts will need to decide whether to include, say, strategic business risks or reputational risk in their allocation of regulatory and enterprise-wide capital.

And managers will need to know whether their assessment of operational risk in a business line should include, say, the risk of a trader misunderstanding a sophisticated financial model. Some experts are sure model risk should be included, while others are sure it forms a more natural component of market risk-the button below maps out some other tricky boundary clashes. Luckily, busy practitioners can sidestep this industry debate by selecting a suitable definition from those below. For the moment, there's really no "right" general definition save one that's boldly drawn and fits the purpose.

Definitions developed by industry bodies and regulators have some practical advantages, so let's take a closer look at the components of operational risk as defined by the London-based British Bankers Association-a body that has been active in developing standard approaches to operational risk.

For the BBA, "Operational risk is the risk of direct or indirect loss resulting from inadequate or failed internal processes, people, and systems or from external events."

Patching up Processes

Historically, most financial institutions have built expert "ways of doing things" to achieve their objectives-whether that's administering a checking account in the retail business, or confirming the details of a million-dollar swap transaction in the money markets.

Processes of a more or less formal kind surround many of the risky activities of a bank. Some are routines performed by humans while others are part of the core infrastructure of the institution. The button below lists some key processes surrounding a capital markets trader.

Connecting a discrete set of actions into a procedure, and than a formal process, offers huge benefits to financial institutions-as it does to manufacturing industries-in terms of scaling, risk control and standardisation.

Processes also help to defuse risk by institutionalising skills that would otherwise reside in a single individual. But processes can make a firm vulnerable in other ways.

Few employees understand a complex bank process as a whole, so the implications of sloppiness or breakdowns in the process chain are often unclear. And devious individuals find a process easier to exploit than a savvy manager because there's no immediate "sense check" of their actions.

Meanwhile, because turning a procedure into a process is usually associated with an increase in business line volumes and notional amounts at the expense of profit margins, processes tend to concentrate and leverage any existing operational risks. If something goes wrong, it goes wrong big time.

This cycle continues as processes speed up and are automated using the institution's computer systems-automation tends to improve consistency but it does not guarantee that the underlying process is structurally safe.

In financial institutions, most processes are designed with audited failsafes and checking procedures. These might be built into the process itself or take the form of independent monitoring by risk control groups such as Compliance.

But because processes interact with other risky variables-the external environment, business strategy, people-it's difficult to sound the all clear. For example, are the failsafes and "checks and balances" of the process appropriate now that the firm has opened offices in a new jurisdiction?

Given the new products a firm has introduced, could the firm suffer a massive loss if a step in the procedure is compromised? Does the process efficiently manage transactions that are exceptions to the norm, or are staff barely coping? Is risk information flowing from the process to decision-makers speedily enough to match market developments?

These questions help to show why the problem of risk managing processes has become more urgent over the over the last ten years as the rate of change in the financial industry has accelerated.

Institutions have automated processes, re-engineered them after mergers and acquisitions, and adapted them to improvements in industry-wide infrastructure and communications capabilities. Increasingly, banks have been rewarded with high margins for entering immature markets where, by definition, safe processes are not yet established.

They have also extended their activities overseas-beyond the easy reach of their established process infrastructure and monitoring capabilities.

And they have introduced new processes to monitor underlying processes-New Product Approval Process and formal Technology Audits being only two examples.

The Problem with People

It's said that the greatest asset of a services business goes up and down in the office lift every day. But like any other asset, people are a source of risk as well as reward.

Until recently, the risk associated with the staff of financial institutions was largely thought of in terms of simple fraud. The figures here remain eye-opening-FBI statistics for 1998 show that some 32% of convictions for crimes against US financial institutions involved bank employees. The internet age has also opened up a new frontier for fraudsters.

But people also cause damage to institutions through incompetence, error, bad decision-making and rule breaking.

And institutions can become dangerously dependent on key individuals, or on teams that are suffering a high staff turnover rate. As we explain below, some firms are starting to identify this kind of key dependency and to monitor business lines for the key people risk indicators. Even in the case of fraud, greed in its simplest form is not always the most important factor.

Traders who exceed their trading limits-rogue traders-often seem to incur the most damaging losses as they try to gamble themselves back into a break-even position.

The original rule-breaking might be motivated by an attempt to improve a bonus, but it's the fear of discovery and its consequences that encourages traders to go for double-or-quits.

That's why, as our next Expert Witness explains, there's increasing interest in the psychology of risk and decision taking.

Modern electronic trading and information systems can help by physically preventing certain actions as well as by automatically reporting infringements to risk managers and escalating key information through the management hierarchy. These increasingly intelligent process control tools help to turn reliance on people into reliance on properly designed systems.

But even where a business line or market has the electronic infrastructure to make this kind of monitoring practical-many derivatives markets, for example, continue to rely on phone and fax trading-people risk is reduced, not removed. Systems that are used by people are always vulnerable to compromise by them. And a real-time risk report delivered by a state-of-the-art system is of little use if managers do not react to it appropriately.

It's also difficult to enforce control through automatic systems when businesses are immature or when volumes have grown suddenly. Other kinds of financial business-such as advisory services or those dependent on third-party agency sales-are structurally reliant on people for expertise or distribution in a way that is difficult to engineer away.

That's why financial institutions have started to look at individual and group behaviour as a way of understanding risk. Researchers believe the reason why individuals break rules-more crucially, why their colleagues let them get away with it-is sometimes rooted in the corporate culture of an institution.

Does the institution reward success without looking closely at how it is achieved? Do senior managers favour dominant personalities and connive with the bullying of subordinates?

Making sure that reporting systems are independent of business lines, risk sensitive, automatic, consistent and secure is an important aspect of the control of operational risk. But in many cases on our Wheel of Misfortune, losses spiralled out of control because a compromised executive was high enough in the hierarchy to disguise the losses.

Often, the problem is a fatal reliance upon an individual by senior managers and committees, compounded by the reluctance of staff further down the reporting line to break rank and voice concern.

Increasingly, corporate governance rules around the globe are encouraging firms to establish formal mechanisms for individuals to step outside the normal reporting line-to blow the whistle on wrong doing that has either a social cost or a cost to shareholders.

And as our last Expert Witness mentioned, the way that groups of professionals take critical decisions is also coming under scrutiny. Many disastrous losses-often misleadingly recorded as credit and market risk losses-happen because a group of managers or an oversight committee take a decision in a way that, with hindsight, seems to ignore extreme risks in favour of attaining preagreed goals. One palliative is to make sure the person or committee with the power to take action on the risk information understands what they are being told, and its implications. This is, in part, a problem of risk communication. The development of methodologies such as value-at-risk in recent years is, in part, an attempt to get to grips with this problem.

But confused or wrong-headed decisions are also rooted in poor corporate governance and tie in with the problem of enterprise-wide risk management.

All Systems Down

The reliance of most financial institutions on computer systems and technology infrastructure is absolute, as the avalanche of reports produced in advance of the millennium date-change made clear.

From individual business lines to the core support functions of an institution, systems are the principal means for storing and managing vast amounts of transactional, financial and corporate data.

They are used to analyse that information, to automate all or part of many critical bank processes, and to communicate with customers.

It's a mistake to think of these systems as an interconnected whole. Instead, most institutions rely on a series of partially interconnected systems of various shape, size and age.

Often, management information systems or data warehouses are used to extract information from underlying systems and present it to managers to help them in making strategic and risky decisions.

Some of the most intractable system risks reside in the relationship between the system and an institution's business plans. Technicians cannot plan for flexibility in capacity, levels of redundancy or absolute levels of security without clear directions from business managers.

As business plans or volumes change, it's important that these decisions are revisited and that the firm as a whole monitors its system dependencies. If a system is left unaltered, a risk decision has been taken-albeit unconsciously.

Systems audits can help to make these tacit decisions more transparent, but they do not necessarily help managers in weighing up the risks and rewards of new system investments. Some researchers believe that the new science of real options-the application of financial options concepts to the valuation of decisions about physical assets-will help managers in the future.

But at a more practical level, as our Expert Witness explains, the most pressing problem for senior managers is to identify, monitor and manage critical risks in the huge range of systems supporting their institution-including those supporting emerging e-commerce and multi-channel banking initiatives.

Enemy at the Gate-external Risks

External risks take many forms, but they have one defining feature-it's difficult for firms to influence whether the risk event takes place. So the risk management of an external event focuses on mitigating its effect.

The most dramatic external risks are natural and man-made physical catastrophes such as the bombing of Canary

Wharf, London's financial district, by terrorists in 1992. The direct physical impact of these risks is insurable. But payouts cannot compensate for an interrupted relationship with a customer, or for the effect on future business plans or staff.

The problem of ensuring that a business can continue despite a physical catastrophe-business continuity-has evolved into a small industry.

Major banks now spend millions of dollars each year to ensure that, if disaster strikes, they can relocate within hours to a functional version of their main or trading offices-complete with IT systems that are constantly primed with backup data from the bank.

But this cannot remove the vulnerability of institutions to public or financial market infrastructure. A recent and dramatic example of this was the systems failure at the London Stock Exchange in the summer of 2000 which prevented the exchange from opening.

Fundamental social and technological trends can also threaten institutions-from a rise in general fraud to sustained attacks on corporate web sites by external hackers and fraudsters.

In the summer of 2000, the UK's financial services regulator Howard Davies echoed the concerns of regulators around the world when he claimed that banks systems were being "probed for weaknesses hundreds of times a day"-and that there was sometimes insufficient segregation between the internal systems of banks. But regulators are themselves a source of external risk. An unforeseen shift in the regulatory or political environment can ruin the profitability of an institution, or leave it vulnerable to catastrophic litigation.

The Big Picture

Many of the operational risks described above are already managed by specific risk functions within institutions-line managers, operations managers, market risk, credit risk, technology risk, internal audit, security, legal, compliance, insurance and so on.

But most of these functions have responsibility for specific risks, services or business lines. They cannot give a firm a wide-angle view of its operational risks. The reasons why institutions and experts think this wider view is important tend to vary according to individual priorities. But the most pressing are the efficient monitoring of critical risks across an organisation, the interaction of risks, risk measurement and the efficient use of capital, and corporate support for risk-reducing investments at business-line level.

Some leading financial institutions have established specific operational risk managers at a senior level to give them this wider view-the purist approach, in that the operational risk function can then itself be checked over by the institution's internal audit group.

Other firms have extended the remit of internal audit to include operational risk management, arguing that their audit group has to hand the skills, infrastructure and manpower to take action on operational risk.

Some firms report that giving internal audit a wider remit makes the function more efficient. Rather than simply ensuring that the proper reporting and control procedures are in place in each unit, audit can take a more active view of risk/reward and reduce duplicated checks and controls. Whatever the framework, taking the wider view means bringing together information about risk in a consistent fashion so that corporate management and the specific owners of the risk can take action.

The button opposite offers easy access to some of the new information management tools that are being marketed to help managers do this more efficiently.

One interesting aspect of these tools is that by making approaches to operational risk control and measurement more consistent within and across firms, they also make it easier for firms to benchmark their risk standards and publish this information to external audiences of regulators, investors-and key customers.

Seeing the Wood for the Trees-Critical Dependencies and what-if Scenarios

One approach to identifying operational risk is to look for critical dependencies in people, processes, systems and external structures. Once identified, the dependencies can be managed or engineered away by adding failsafes and system redundancies.

This approach is commonsensical, and has the great advantage that the risk of an event happening does not have to be measured in any quantitative way. It simply has to be identified as critical to the safety of the firm or process.

Many of the formal ideas that have come into the financial industry for system and process analysis have their roots in engineering-appropriately enough, given the increasing dependence of financial institutions on technology.

For example, some consulting firms now specialise in identifying the critical dependencies in power, communication and security systems-such as the failure of a critical power line, cable or firewall. Click the dependency diagram opposite to read how our next Expert Witness tracks back to a specific critical risk.

Dependencies often arise out of the interplay between business plans, process design and system architecture-which means that senior managers and business line managers must be involved in risk identification as well as risk management solutions.

And because a disaster would affect the whole firm, senior managers need to understand enough about the risks and their relationships to take the right decision.

It's not just a question of identifying physical dependencies. Many firms have begun to bring together groups of experts to discuss all the various risks in their part of a financial business line or process.

These structured discussions are different from most traditional forms of risk audit in financial institutions because they concentrate not on checking control procedures, or on the filling in of periodic reports, but on risk identification, the promotion of risk awareness in business line personnel, and detailed risk scenario building.

Risk scenarios are important because they help managers to work through what might happen if a particular mishap occurred. These "what if" scenarios are often simply descriptive and hypothetical. But some institutions are experimenting with more formal, quantitative techniques that model firms as systems.

The approaches include applying the latest scientific ideas on network topologies and complexity theory.

At the moment, though, it's difficult to apply this kind of sophisticated analysis to whole firms-so it's mainly being used to track down dependencies in specific business lines and processes.

The Data Game-more Questions than Answers

When a risk threatens a whole firm, and can be removed simply and cheaply, decision-making is easy. But some decisions demand hard numbers.

It costs money to install redundant systems-how much should be spent? If the chosen means of managing the risk is to reserve capital, how much capital is required? If a company decides to insure itself, how does it assess whether a high premium is worth paying?

It's difficult for firms to answer these questions-and move through the risk management decision cycle we identified earlier-without first answering three questions that depend upon data.

- How frequent are the events that generate each specific risk?
- How costly will any loss event be if it occurs?
- How likely is it that risk control efforts will reduce either of these numbers?

These questions are similar to those asked by market and credit risk specialists. But operational risk is a more difficult nut to crack because of the paucity of data, the many different frequencies and severities of loss, the multiple categories of risk that have to be considered, and the difficulty of linking a loss event to a single cause.

As our next Expert Witness explains, some key concepts here are expected, unexpected and catastrophic types of event. These concepts can help managers compare the character of risk profile associated with different business lines, and they also help explain part of the data problem. Take the case of a failure to process a transaction of some kind. In institutions that process large volumes of transactions, these failures are relatively frequent. Firms are likely to be able to gather significant data on the more common low-impact costs associated with these breaks-fines, penalties, reimbursement to customers or counterparties, cost of mending the transaction, and so on.

Other kinds of medium-impact risk, such as significant bank fraud, are more difficult for banks to analyse because they do not have enough data on loss and frequency within the institution to support a valid statistical analysis. This is not always because data do not exist-sometimes it's a question of availability and quality.

For example, in the US bank fraud and money laundering data is already gathered systematically by the regulatory authorities. But it was only in October 2000, after pressure from industry associations, that the US Treasury's Financial Crimes Enforcement Network indicated it might publish the data periodically in association with the American Banking Association.

It is not yet clear whether the data will be released with enough contextual detail to make it useful for quantifying the risk of different kinds of fraud in different kinds of institutions.

For many kinds of medium-frequency, medium-impact risk, however, there are simply no readily available databases of loss. So one of the most exciting developments in operational risk is the emergence of banking industry initiatives to solve this problem.

In the summer of 2000, the British Bankers Association announced that over 20 financial firms were joining together to collect data on operational risk events. By autumn 2000, some of the firms were actually supplying their internally collected data to the BBA, using the association's standard categorisation of loss and risk types.

The BBA pools the data and removes any identifying tags before republishing the complete dataset to contributing banks. A similar venture, MORE, has been set up by Connecticut-based risk consultancy NetRisk, with the support of industry associations and various Canadian and US banks.

The most important feature of both these efforts is the attempt to produce a rich but standard set of data that will help banks quantify risk and link it to root causes, while at the same time preserving bank confidentiality.

These initiatives should help the banking industry to put numbers against the operational risks that are frequent and also those that are unexpected. But they will not solve the problem of the most extreme and infrequent events.

Extremely high impact, but low frequency, risks pose a different kind of problem. This kind of loss is difficult to conceal from shareholders, and is often reported in the press, so some data is publicly available. Bringing this data together in a consistent form is a significant task, but a number of consultancies-listed in our Operational Risks Tools button above-offer such public loss databases as packages.

But the real problem is that, even at an industry level, there are not enough extreme events of a particular type to allow the statistical modelling of their frequency or severity. Most firms respond to these extreme risks through attempting to prevent them or by insuring against them, rather than by reserving specific amounts of capital against them.

But they can't be ignored in the numbers game, or institutions will be building a blind spot for the most deadly risks of all. The regulators are also keen that these risks are accounted for in the total levels of capital available to the financial industry.

One of the cutting-edges of operational risk research is therefore the application of a body of theory known as Extreme Value Theory to the scarce data that is available on catastrophic risks. Although highly technical, EVT offers some hope that it will become possible to put meaningful figures against the risk of massive operational failure.

But EVT cannot help solve a more fundamental data problem. Data takes time to collect and it often has to be aggregated across institutions to make the sample large enough for statistical analysis. Some experts point out that aggregate historical data cannot help banks identify the risks specific to their institution, or the risks that are lie in wait over the horizon of the data sample.

Risk Indicators and Scorecards

Collecting historical loss data at an industry or institutional level is one way to put a number against operational risk-but it's not the only way.

Institutions can also try to identify sets of quantitative "risk indicators" that seem likely to be related to the level of operational risk in a business line. As our next Expert Witness explains, quantitative risk indicators could bring a valuable element of objectivity to traditional operational risk assessment techniques.

For example, in a business line that depends upon the safe handling of transactions, some key quantitative risk indicators might include the ratio of reported transaction "breaks" or failures compared to transaction volumes, the ratio of transaction volume to trained staff, and the ratio of system downtime to uptime.

After all, a back-office operation with high volumes, skeleton staff and poor systems would seem more likely to make operational errors than a similar low-volume operation with longer-serving employees and a robust systems infrastructure.

Quantitative risk indicators can be transformed into weighted components of a more general risk scorecard for a business line or whole firm with the help of expert judgement. But this introduces a subjective element into the measurement.

So some leading banks are starting to apply statistical techniques, such as discriminant analysis and principal components analysis, to explore the relationship between a risk indicator and loss levels, and to weight the indicator's relative importance within a larger set of indicators.

In an ideal world, all operational risk indicators would be quantitative, and their weighting within the overall risk score of a business line would be decided statistically, and backtested.

Operational risk modelling would end up looking something like advanced credit modelling-a series of weighted risk ratios backtested against the available data.

In the real world, some bankers say it's difficult to avoid assessing operational risk using qualitative factors. That's why the new science of quantitative operational risk management sometimes begins to sound like the rather older art of risk auditing-armed with new information management tools and risk/reward concepts.

Indeed, some practitioners argue that risk managers who try to track operational risk at group level should simply incorporate audit scores for each business line into their enterprise-wide risk assessments.

The tension between quantitative and qualitative assessments of risk is likely to be a continuing theme in operational risk management. The problem is at its greatest in business lines and support functions such as fund management or legal risk that that rely heavily on individual expertise and integrity.

But even techniques for awarding qualitative scores can be improved. For example, qualitative scoring can be linked more closely related to risk levels, rather than control levels. That is, the weighting given to each element of the control environment can be modified to reflect the severity of any loss given a failure of control, and the scoring can be made independent, and benchmarked for consistency.

Moving from Measurement to Capital Allocation

Quantitative measures and improved scorecards can be used to compare the risk levels in different business lines, track risk trends, improve controls and prioritise risk management efforts. But some firms are also starting to use them to allocate portions of economic risk capital to particular business lines.

There are various ways to approach this problem. One is to work out the total capital the bank ought to set aside to cover operational risk by looking at the amounts of capital other banks set aside (the benchmarking methodology) or by a statistical analysis of industry-level operational losses in the relevant business lines. Internal scorecards can then be used to adjust the portion of the capital charge allocated to each particular business line.

This mixed methodology is not the only approach to calculating or allocating capital for operational risk. In the past, firms that allocated capital to operational risk tended to use non-interest expense as a rule of thumb or, alternatively, examined the revenue/expense volatility associated with a business.

Into the future, many firms hope they will be able to a purely statistical/actuarial approach that links the analysis of data collected at business-line level to firm-and industry-wide loss and risk data.

But for the moment, scorecards have some practical advantages from the point of view of forward-looking line managers and enterprise-wide risk managers.

For a start, the cause of a high score is transparent because it can easily be traced back to the scores on the card. By contrast, if a business line is deemed "risky" because of historical or industry-wide data, it is often unclear what the manager can do to reduce the risk score.

So scorecards help motivate managers to reduce the amount of economic capital allocated to their business line by ironing out problem areas. Likewise, group managers can quickly establish stronger incentives for line managers to improve controls.

From Risk Insurance to Alternative Risk Transfer

Some operational risks are impossible to engineer away or to risk manage adequately. Others are so difficult to identify and scale that an institution can never be sure that its internal risk management has been effective.

Where the potential losses seem likely to be of medium severity, a financial institution can reserve capital or use self-insurance techniques to mitigate their impact. But in the case of a catastrophic risk, institutions either have to accept the risk as part of doing business, or transfer the risk to external providers of risk capital.

Over the last few years, new kinds of insurance and alternative risk transfer mechanisms have held out hope that this kind of risk transfer will become more practical and cheaper.

Insurance has developed in two ways. Firstly insurance policies have developed to cover types of operational risk that are ill-served in traditional bank cover. Our next Expert Witness believes an improved set of insurance products will offer a stiff challenge to some novel ideas that have recently been mooted within the banking industry-such as mutual insurance techniques.

Secondly, insurers have begun to offer coverall policies for extreme levels of risk, arguing that the massive amounts of capital available to insurers gives them a special role in managing catastrophic risk.

But critics of the insurance strategies for operational risk claim that the insurance market is an opaque and inefficient way of pricing risk. They say the delay and uncertainty associated with insurance payouts might destroy a wounded institution.

In the case of alternative risk transfer mechanisms, on the other hand, capital would already in the hands of the wounded bank. ART tools-so far only a concept in the financial institutions sector-would take the form of structured instruments sold to the capital markets by the bank itself.

For example, some time in the near future a financial institution might sell a special bond to investors that offered an above-market interest rate, with the stipulation that the bank would cease paying any interest on the billion-dollar principal in the event of an operational disaster.

The premium the bank had to pay to the market to accept this embedded option would be, in effect, the market price of its operational risk-and the world would have seen the first operational risk derivative for a financial institution.

Some investment bankers say this kind of traded market in operational risk would price major bank risks more efficiently than the traditional insurance market. But the banking industry's own internal insurance specialists are more cautious.

They say they are still trying to work out how well their existing insurance polices complement the risks the bank is running. They don't think they'll be in a position to understand the cost reduction and risk management benefits of newfangled instruments for some time to come.

But it would be a pleasant irony if the derivatives technology that lay behind some of the most famous operational losses in the 1990s eventually helped to tame the most unpredictable piece of the risk jigsaw.

7

Challenges and Strategies of Hospitality Industry

Competitiveness refers to-*the ability and willingness to compete* and two most important underlying criteria of competitiveness are-'Profitability' and 'Productivity', that is, increased competitiveness is reflected in sustained growth in productivity and profitability. Since 'productivity' and 'profitability' are vital for all organizations, industries, sectors and nations, it indicates that the concept of competitiveness is equally applicable to each of these entities, so it is a must that they appreciate the conceptual framework of competitiveness and the various forms that it takes, (commercial competitiveness, market competitiveness etc.) along with the fact that it is a complex ongoing process affected by a range of factors/inputs. Although, 'competitiveness' in parlance of business (and industries) is not a new phenomenon and is usually discussed in terms of – the decisions it makes, the resources it has, and the environmental factors which surrounds the business, but lately, the trend of categorizing and evaluating nations on basis of their competitiveness has become a norm among economists, policy makers, business executives and investors.

Liberalization, Privatization and Globalization (LPG) have worked together for reducing protection and creating a rapidly changing competitive environment resulting in fierce international competition 'in' and 'for' the world-market. With this, there has been a growing realization that avoiding the rigors of competition is not possible and developing strategies for enhancing sustainable competitiveness has emerged as a 'must do' exercise for all. However, the context of 'competitiveness' might vary for business, industries and nations, depending on their-objectives, form, nature and functions – that is-from completely social to hardcore commercial.

Competitiveness of Nations and the Service Sector-Most of the (developing) economies are in rapid transit towards becoming 'service economies" and therefore 'competitiveness of service sector' is emerging as a crucial factor influencing the overall competitiveness of a country, and India is no exception to this, where the share of services is increasingly getting higher in the total GDP, and also the growth rate of India's 'service exports' is higher then the world average, hence for India, out of the three pillars of competitiveness, one is certainly it's service sector (agriculture and manufacturing are the remaining two.)

Variables of Competitiveness at country, industry and firm level-The paper deals with the issue of competitiveness at all the three levels (country, industry and firm) taking-'India' as the variable for 'country' and 'Indian Tourism and Hospitality Industry' as the variable for 'industry', and at the firm level, the paper identifies cases from many different organizations, rather then taking a particular organization as a variable, because a broader canvas is required to capture the diversity of businesses operating in this domain, and any one organization cannot symbolize the complete tourism and hospitality industry because this industry is formed by a combination of very different businesses.

(Only infrastructure business, or only hotel business or only aviation business can not represent this industry alone, but all these businesses jointly do so).

Competitiveness Challenges of Indian Tourism and Hospitality Industry – as mentioned above, different diverse businesses jointly form this industry *(transportation, hotels, infrastructure, aviation etc.)*, and a balanced development of all these different businesses and high coordination amongst all the participants is a prerequisite for enhancing competitiveness of this industry and creating this 'fine blend' of such 'polar elements' is a tough challenge in itself.

This industry can be called as the "industry of big paradoxes", first, on one hand it has almost unbeatable competitive advantages, huge potential and high growth rates *(in terms of-generating foreign exchange, growth rates, & employment generation),* and on the other hand, inspite of above mentioned positives, Indian Tourism and Hospitality Industry is still way behind even from its small neighbours in South-East Asia, not to mention the large counterparts like China.

Second paradox is that, on one hand, in order to be competitive, this industry needs the cooperation of both public and private sector players as both play a vital role in it, and on the other hand, cut throat competition also exists between the two in this industry itself.

Finally, the 'offering' of this industry is also paradoxical. For India, where 'history' is an important attraction for tourists, this industry has to offer 'history', but it can not loose sight of modernization either, in other words, Indian Tourism and Hospitality Industry has to be a 'historian' and a 'futurist' simultaneously.

Thus, in order to find a sustainable solution to the competitiveness issue of this industry, the paper suggest that it is important to identify the reasons behind its lack of competitiveness and then to search for 'breakthrough solutions' to face the unique challenges it offers, by undertaking a study of the innovative and best practices developed and adopted by players of this industry in the global arena which are applicable in Indian conditions and finally, redefining the role of government and private players to create a more competitive landscape might also be an effective part of the overall solution.

Case Study: Hongkong

The tourism industry has been a major source of revenue for Hong Kong. Along with the boom of tourism is the increase investment in hotel industry. Indeed, these two sectors have been indispensable that the subsequent decline in tourism following the economic crisis has impacted hotel operations significantly. The tourism and hotel industry in Hong Kong has been suffered major decline although it has manifested recovery during the previous years. The factors contributing to the decline include high rates due to the high cost of living, the outbreak of SARS, deteriorating image of Hong Kong as shopper's paradise and the development of tourist attractions in other countries in the region. The following section will review the development of the tourism industry from its subsequent decline and its way to recovery.

Part A

Macro Analysis

The business environment is generally successful and attractive. The gross domestic product has grown consistently and became the envy of developed and developing systems. The unemployment rate has always been in a low rate while the demand for the employment remains to be buoyant. With this, there appeared to be an increase in the standard of living explaining the social stability in the country. The government policy on the other hand has adopted a policy of positive non interventionism. In general, the business environment of the country is favourable for investors.

Hotel Industry

Hong Kong's hotel industry is a popular channel of investment along with the booming of the tourism industry. Tourism is a major revenue earner in Hong Kong. It has become the second largest source of foreign exchange. Hong Kong serves as the travel gateway for the vast majority of business and recreational travels to China and as the primary travel hub for South East Asia. The hotel industry was geared to the tourist trade especially at the upper end (Gerzenberg, 1994).

In the years prior to the hand back to China, hotel room rates rose to high levels. Room rates may have been slashed and two for one flight promotions run but the image of Hong Kong as expensive destination has been fixed in the minds of potential tourist travellers.

Tourism and hotel industry has slumped badly during the Asian financial crisis. Despite the major rebound in the number of tourists coming during 1999-2000, the actual revenue received has declined. Explanations for the decline in revenue from tourists differed but include the high costs of living compare to other locations in the region. In addition to this, HK is no longer seen as a shopper's paradise. It has been characterized by the lack of initiatives to provide tourist attractions and above all the high level of pollution affects the territory.

In 1999, hotel prices in Asia rose again as the region recovered from the economic crisis of 1997-1998. Room rates in South Korea, Japan and Taiwan rose by 32%, 38% and 30% in euros. However, China and Hong Kong experienced continued fall in room rates by 31.5% though it stabilized slightly in 1999 and towards the end of that year. Yet the reality remains that hotels are property and properties are major investments and assets in Hong Kong. By 2000, room rates and occupancy are again at high levels (Joseph, 2005). One of the bright spot for Hong Kong hoteliers is the climbing of tourism.

By the end of last year, there were about 612 hotels and tourist guest houses in Hong Kong with 52, 512 rooms. The average occupancy rates in all hotel categories were 87% for the whole of 2006. This marked a one-percentage-growth as compared to 2005 regardless of the 7.4% increase in room supplies between December 2005 and December 2006. During 2006, about 62.75 of all visitors stayed one night and longer, a trend which reflects the importance of Hong Kong as a regional transport hub.

Today, the Hong Kong tourism and hotel industry is gambling its future as a tourist destination for Disneyland. The industry is expecting a boost from the increased number of tourists especially those coming from mainland China.

In 2003, Beijing has eased the travel rules for mainland tourist to Hong Kong which allowed people for Chinese cities to travel individually rather than in organized groups. It has also doubled the currency allowed for mainland tourists to take with them when traveling abroad. These new polices are part of the series of measures to help stimulate Hong Kong's' flagging tourism, lift property and share prices (Bezlova, 2004). As a result, China has become the major source of tourist arrivals in Hong Kong.

Competitor Analysis

The erosion of Hong Kong's price competitiveness resulting from regional currency turmoil and depreciation has made other destinations such as Thailand, Malaysia and Singapore to become more competitive. Thus, the industry must try harder to attract the foreign market by providing competitive packages, attractive tourism products and high quality services and satisfactory experiences. The need for such initiatives has been illustrated by the decreasing rate of hotel occupancy despite increase of visitor arrivals. There are increasing worries that the current tourism boom may fade in the years to come as wealthy mainland travellers set their destinations to Paris and London. Hong Kong is also competing with the nearby Macau. For the next decade, it plans to create 60,000 new hotel rooms (Joseph, 2005). Macau is also planning to penetrate the untapped market of China by investing in the monopolized gaming industry. It is next to Hong Kong which is likely to benefit from the ease of travel rules from China. As Chinese people enjoy more and longer holidays, the urban rich are traveling in great numbers to Macau for gaming activities. The influx of mainland Chinese has already uplifted the economic growth of Macau which is highly dependent on tourism (Bezlova, 2004).

The local competition in the hotel industry is intense. The choices are vast and there are so many competitors. Few cities offer large numbers of first rate hotels and few places competes with the services that made the Hong Kong hotel industry legendary. Most of the hotels and guest houses are situated on Hong Kong Island and in Kowloon but there are also selections in the New Territories (including the outlying islands). The keen competition and the laws of supply and demand have ensured that these hotels maintain the highest standards.

Pestle Analysis

This analysis audits the impact on the market of large and usually long terms factors: political, economic, social, technological, legal and environmental changes going around the industry. These factors have dramatic impact on the working dynamics of the marketplace.

Political factors such as government intervention distort the marketplace. Economic factors include the cycles of growth and decline that impact business. For instance, the increase or decrease in consumer spending impact the host of businesses from consumer goods. Social factors such as the increasing number of double income families impact the standard of living which may increase the purchasing power of consumers.

Technological factors are changes in technology which created the need for people to upgrade their skills to remain employable and for businesses to engage in new technologies so that they are not left behind by their competitors. Legal factors involve general legislations that affect all organizations such as employment laws and other industry specific regulations. Lastly are the environmental factors such as pollution control and the spread of diseases such as SARS that has affected businesses in the Asian region.

Political Factors

- Government Policy of non Interventionism on Businesses
- Autonomy from People's Republic of China.

Economic Factors

- High Gross Domestic Product
- High Purchasing Power
- Low unemployment rate
- High Operating Costs.

Social Factors

- Social Stability
- Increase in the Standard of Living
- Lack of Skilled workers.

Technological Factors

- Use of Information and Communication Technology in the Hotel industry
- Technology transfer arrangements with foreign investors The use of Information Technology in various aspects of the industry.

Legal Factors

- Ease of Travel Rules from Mainland China
- Accommodations are subject for 3 percent government tax.

Environmental Factors

- High Levels of Pollution
- Fear of SARS outbreak.

Five Forces Analysis

This analysis discusses five competitive forces governing the tourism and hotel industry.

Force	*Strength*	*Trend*	*Comments*
Entry	High	Changing	Developers are seeing new hotel prospects at the South side of Hong Kong. This would mean new entrants in the industry. Also, 37 percent increase in hotel development is expected until 2008.
Suppliers	Low	Changing	Suppliers can negotiate prices and agreements based on the quantity of goods supplied.
Buyers	High	Increasing	The high purchasing power and increase in disposable income would mean that tourists are likely to spend more in exchange for satisfaction and best experience. This would require the hotels to improve their service standards if they are to remain competitive. Conversely, this may cause tourist to go other destinations such as Paris and London.
Substitutes		Low	Not ChangingHotels are not the only means for lodging. Hotels may also compete with lodging services such as tourists' guest houses and resorts.
Rivalry	High	Increasing	The competition for tourist with neighbouring countries is likely to increase. The development of tourist attractions such as casinos in Macau is likely to affect arrivals in Hong Kong. Also, the competitiveness of Thailand, Malaysia and Singapore in terms quality and price competitiveness is likely to impact the industry

Mobility Barriers

Ownership

Hostels and Guesthouses have minimal capital investment and are traditionally small hotels owned by an individual or family. The dependence of small hotels on individual and the type of security available for loan are among the factors that mitigates against the availability of external finance from lending institutions. While independently owned hotels may till be dominant in the industry, the growth of the industry has been greatly associated with the emergence of hotel groups. The increase in the size of hotel has resulted from these firms building or acquiring hotels in various locations under a central management. These hotels may be grouped in a restricted geographical area or distributed within the country or between countries. International hotels have essentially national companies with a head office in a particular country and engage to a greater extent of hotel operations in the country and other countries.

Marketing and Distribution Systems

Hostels and Guesthouses rely on personal recommendation and repeated visits rather than systematic promotion. On the other hand hotel groups have the marketing capability to promote its services. The international hotels are more advantageous in this aspect due to broad scope of the marketing activities in different countries. These last two groups have larger market and can formulate operations to meet market needs through employing promotion on a wider scale. Another barrier is in terms of the suppliers. Hotel groups has economies of buying because it can buy bulk and negotiate with advantageous prices and terms with suppliers of a wide range of goods. This is something which small hotels could not afford.

Part B

Future Scenarios for the Industry

Hotels in Hong Kong can be described as being capable of providing high levels of services and facilities. More than 20 million tourists are expected to visit the city every year mainly from mainland China. Developers are building up to nine new hotels in the remote industrial sectors on the south side of Hong Kong. Overall, the numbers of hotel rooms are expected to increase by 37 percent by mid 2008 to 56,816 rooms. Occupancy rates among the highest worldwide has already declined to 86 percent in 2005 from 88 percent in the previous year.

The introduction of the seven day free visa in 1993 and the five day work week in China had positive impacts in its outbound travel to Hong Kong. This implied that positive policies such as simplified visa application and extended visa-free status play an important role in attracting international tourists to Hong Kong. HK tourism authorities emphasized the importance of positive policies for the China outbound travel market and the top agenda is to make visas easier for Chinese tour groups. Further, the relaxation on the issue of travel document formalities boosts travel numbers.

The tourism industry of Hong Kong has lobbied the Chinese government to increase daily quotas and this allowed additional 358 tourists into Hong Kong each day. With the increasing standard of living and further relaxation of the outbound travel, mainland Chinese travellers will continue to be the most important tourist market for Hong Kong in the future. Tourism related industry such as Hotels must strive to ensure that they provide the best experience and satisfaction possible. With the political and economic condition in China, outbound vacation travel will continue to expand and Hong Kong will be the first to benefit from this growing trend. In order to maximize and get fast return, Hong Kong must shift its emphasis to the China Market and design appropriate marketing strategies.

Conclusion

The tourism and hotel industry has been characterized by significant development, subsequent decline and recovery. This industry has been considered to be one of the major sources of revenues for the country. However, it has declined greatly following the economic crisis and the outbreak of epidemic in the country. This can also be attributed to the high cost of living and the lack of tourist attractions that will entice tourist to visit the country. The condition was even worsen by the intense competition with other international destinations such as Malaysia, Thailand and Singapore. All of which are offering relatively low prices with the quality services.

To date, the industry is recovering by developing attractions such as the Disneyland. While this will boost the industry, competition will also strengthen as other countries are developing their tourist attractions such as casinos in Macau. Indeed, the hotel industry must improve its competitive position by enhancing the experience of guests through quality services, innovation and affordable prices.

Recommendations

- Enhance Hong Kong's image as Asia's world city by leveraging endorsements in a wide audience reach. This would entail making use of traditional channels to communicate the essence of unique Hong Kong experiences to the targeted market segments.
- Introduce and develop major tourism attractions that will boost tourist's stay in Hong Kong. The construction of Disneyland has helped in promoting the country as a tourist destination. Also, Macau's concept of casino and gaming activities is a good example of tourist attraction.
- The importance of offering high quality experiences meaningful to the hotel guests is unquestionable. They should maximize the arrivals of visitors, length of stay, repeat visits and satisfaction through initiatives that will enhance visitor's experiences. Chinese mainland tourists are expected to be the most important market of the industry and hotels must ensure that they offer the best experience through quality service and modern facilities.
- Hoteliers must find a way of offering competitive prices that will suit the budget of travellers. The high costs of living has always been the problem of Hong Kong and this has led to the lost of potential tourist to other competitive locations in Asia.
- Offer promotional packages. A great example of this was the cooperation of HKTB and 53 Hong Kong Hotels

in 2004 to offer discounted room rates to bona fide employees of airlines, tour operators, travel agents and tourist offices outside Hong Kong. The promotion showed the range of experiences Hong Kong offers so that these key influencers could in turn motivate and inform their customers about the city.

- Develop e-business. This will help hoteliers to better serve e-consumers by improving the quality of their online offers, expanding the quality of services and developing more competitive e-distribution channels.

The Importance of the Small Hotel

Boutique Hotel

Boutique hotel is a term popularised in North America and the United Kingdom to describe intimate, usually luxurious or quirky hotel environments. Boutique hotels differentiate themselves from larger chain/branded hotels and motels by providing personalized accommodation and services/facilities. Sometimes known as "design hotels" or "lifestyle hotels", boutique hotels began appearing in the 1980s in major cities like London, New York, and San Francisco. Typically boutique hotels are furnished in a themed, stylish and/or aspirational manner. They usually are considerably smaller than mainstream hotels, often ranging from 3 to 50 guest rooms. Boutique hotels are always individual and are therefore extremely unlikely to be found amongst the homogeneity of large chain hotel groups. Guest rooms and suites may be fitted with telephony and Wi-Fi Internet, air-conditioning, honesty bars and often cable/pay TV, but equally may have none of these, focusing on quiet and comfort rather than gadgetry. Guest services are often attended to by 24-hour hotel staff. Many boutique hotels have on-site dining facilities, and the majority offer bars and lounges that may also be open to the general public.

Despite this definition, the popularity of the boutique term and concept has led to some confusion about the term. Boutique hotels have typically been unique properties operated by individuals or companies with a small collection. However, their successes have prompted multi-national hotel companies to try to establish their own brands in order to capture a market share.

The most notable example is Starwood Hotels and Resorts Worldwide's W Hotels, ranging from large boutique hotels, such as the W Union Square NY, to the W 'boutique resorts' in the Maldives, to true luxury boutique hotel collections, such as the Bulgari collection, Kimpton Hotels & Restaurants, SLS Hotels, Thompson Hotels, Joie De Vie hotels, The Keating Hotel, and O Hotel, among many others.

There is some overlap between the concept of a small boutique hotel and a bed and breakfast.

In the United States, New York remains the centre of the boutique hotel phenomenon, as the original Schrager-era boutique hotels remain relevant and are joined by scores of independent and small-chain competitors, mainly clustered about Midtown and downtown Manhattan. The French Quarter and Garden District, New Orleans have several dozen boutique hotels, most of which are located in old homes or inns. These usually provide an ambience based on 19th-century antiques, artwork with New Orleans themes, vintage or reproduction furniture and decor and/or interesting historical associations. Miami and Miami Beach also have several boutique hotels, found mostly along the beachfront streets Ocean Drive and Collins Drive. Most of these are in buildings from the heyday of the Art Deco period. Their attractions include the Art Deco ambiance, beach access, nouvelle and Latin cuisines, and tropical-themed interior decor.

The concept of boutique or design hotels has spread throughout the world. Including European countries like Spain, and East Asian countries such as Thailand, where many boutique or design hotels are sprouting, especially in resort locations, such as Phuket and Hua Hin. Other Far Eastern cities in which boutique and design hotels are becoming increasingly popular include Bangkok, Singapore, and Hong Kong. Boutique hotels are even appearing in such places as Indonesia, mainland China, Iceland, Peru, and Turkey, demonstrating that the concept has penetrated beyond the typical design capitals of the world and is entering new markets.

Hotels and Other Accommodations

Significant Points

- Service occupations account for almost two-thirds of the industry's employment—by far the largest occupational group.
- Hotels employ many young workers and first-time job holders in part-time and seasonal jobs.
- Job opportunities should be good as low entry requirements for many jobs lead to high turnover and replacement needs.

Nature of the Industry

People travel for a variety of reasons, including for vacations, business, and visits to friends and relatives. For many of these travellers, hotels and other accommodations will be where they stay while out of town. For others, hotels may be more than just a place to stay; they are destinations in themselves. Resort hotels and casino hotels, for example, offer a variety of activities to keep travellers and families occupied for much of their stay.

Goods and services. Hotels and other accommodations are as different as the many family and business travellers they accommodate. The industry includes all types of lodging, from luxurious five-star hotels to youth hostels and RV (recreational vehicle) parks. While many provide simply a place to spend the night, others cater to longer stays by providing food service, recreational activities, and meeting rooms. In 2008, 64,300 establishments provided accommodations to suit many different needs and budgets.

Hotels and motels comprise the majority of establishments in this industry and are generally classified as offering either full-service or limited service. Full-service properties offer a variety of services for their guests, but they almost always include at least one or more restaurant and beverage service options other than self-service—from coffee bars and lunch counters to cocktail lounges and formal restaurants. They also usually provide room service. Larger full-service properties usually have a variety of retail shops on the premises, such as gift boutiques, newsstands, and drug and cosmetics counters, some of which may be geared to an exclusive clientele. Additionally, a number of full-service hotels offer guests access to laundry and valet services, swimming pools, beauty salons, and fitness centres or health spas. A small—but growing—number of luxury hotel chains also manage condominium units in combination with their transient rooms, providing both hotel guests and condominium owners with access to the same services and amenities.

The largest hotels often have banquet rooms, exhibit halls, and spacious ballrooms to accommodate conventions, business meetings, wedding receptions, and other social gatherings. Conventions and business meetings are major sources of revenue for these properties. Some commercial hotels are known as conference hotels—fully self-contained entities specifically designed for large-scale meetings. They provide physical fitness and recreational facilities for meeting attendees, in addition to state-of-the-art audiovisual and technical equipment, a business centre, and banquet services.

Limited-service hotels are free-standing properties that do not have on-site restaurants or most other amenities that must be provided by a staff other than the front desk or housekeeping. They usually offer continental breakfasts, vending machines or small packaged items, Internet access, and sometimes unattended game rooms or swimming pools in addition to daily housekeeping services. The numbers of limited-service properties have been growing. These properties are not as costly to build and maintain. They appeal to budget-conscious family vacationers and travellers who are willing to sacrifice amenities for lower room prices.

Hotels can also be categorized based on a distinguishing feature or service provided by the hotel. *Conference hotels* provide meeting and banquet rooms, and usually food service, to large groups of people. *Resort hotels* offer luxurious surroundings with a variety of recreational facilities, such as swimming pools, golf courses, tennis courts, game rooms, and health spas, as well as planned social activities and entertainment. Resorts typically are located in vacation destinations or near natural settings, such as mountains, seashores, theme parks, or other attractions. As a result, the business of many resorts fluctuates with the season. Some resort hotels and motels provide additional convention and conference facilities to encourage customers to combine business with pleasure. During the off season, many of these establishments solicit conventions, sales meetings, and incentive tours to fill their otherwise empty rooms; some resorts even close for the off-season.

Extended-stay hotels typically provide rooms or suites with fully equipped kitchens, entertainment systems, office space with computer and telephone lines, fitness centres, and other amenities. Typically, guests use these hotels for a minimum of 5 consecutive nights, often while on an extended work assignment or lengthy vacation or family visit. *All-suite hotels* offer a living room or sitting room in addition to a bedroom.

Casino hotels combine both lodging and legalized gaming on the same premises. Along with the typical services provided by most full-service hotels, casino hotels also contain casinos where patrons can wager at table games, play slot machines, and make other bets. Some casino hotels also contain conference and convention facilities.

In addition to hotels, *bed-and-breakfast inns, RV parks, campgrounds,* and *rooming and boarding houses* provide lodging for overnight guests and are included in this industry. *Bed-and-breakfast inns* provide short-term lodging in private homes or small buildings converted for this purpose and are characterized by highly personalized service and inclusion of breakfast in the room rate. Their appeal is quaintness; they typically provide unusual service and unique decor.

RV parks and campgrounds cater to people who enjoy recreational camping at moderate prices. Some parks and campgrounds provide service stations, general stores, shower and toilet facilities, and coin-operated laundries. While some are designed for overnight travellers only, others are for vacationers who stay longer. Some camps provide accommodations, such as cabins and fixed campsites, and other amenities, such as food services, recreational facilities and equipment, and organized recreational activities. Examples of these overnight camps include children's camps, family vacation camps, hunting and fishing camps, and outdoor adventure retreats that offer trail riding, white-water rafting, hiking, fishing, game hunting, and similar activities.

Other short-term lodging facilities in this industry include *guesthouses*, or small cottages located on the same property as a main residence, and *youth hostels*—dormitory-style hotels with few frills, occupied mainly by students traveling on limited budgets. Also included are *rooming and boarding houses*, such as fraternity houses, sorority houses, off-campus dormitories, and workers' camps. These establishments provide temporary or longer term accommodations that may serve as a principal residence for the period of occupancy. These establishments also may provide services such as housekeeping, meals, and laundry services.

Industry organization. In recent years, the hotel industry has been dominated by a few large national hotel chains. To the traveller, familiar chain establishments represent dependability and quality at predictable rates. Many chains recognize the importance of brand loyalty to guests and have expanded the range of lodging options offered under one corporate name to include a full range of hotels from limited-service, economy-type hotels to luxury inns. While these national corporations own some of the hotels, many properties are independently owned but affiliated with a chain through a franchise agreement or management contract. Increasingly, hotel chains are moving away from owning properties to managing them. As part of a chain, individual hotels can participate in the company's national reservations service or incentive program, thereby appearing to belong to a larger enterprise. For those who prefer more personalized service and a unique experience, *boutique hotels* are becoming more popular. These smaller hotels are generally found in urban locations and provide patrons good service and more distinctive decor and food selection.

Although there are nationwide RV parks and campgrounds, most small lodging establishments are individually owned and operated by a single owner, who may employ a small staff to help operate the business.

Recent developments. The lodging industry is moving towards more limited-service properties mostly in suburban, residential, or commercial neighborhoods, often locating hotels near popular restaurants. Many full-service properties are limiting or quitting the food service business altogether, choosing to contract out their food service operations to third party restaurateurs, including long-term arrangements with chain restaurant operators. Urban business and entertainment districts are providing a greater mix of lodging options to appeal to a wider range of travellers.

Increased competition among establishments in this industry has spurred many independently owned and operated hotels and other lodging places to join national or international reservation systems. This allows travellers to make multiple reservations for lodging, airlines, and car rentals with one telephone call or Internet search. Nearly all hotel chains and many independent lodging facilities operate online reservation systems through the Internet or maintain Web sites that allow individuals to book rooms. Online marketing of properties is so popular with guests that many hotels promote themselves with elaborate Web sites and allow people to investigate availability and rates.

Working Conditions

Hours. Because hotels are open around the clock, employees frequently work varying shifts or variable schedules. Employees who work the late shift generally receive additional compensation. Many employees enjoy the opportunity to work part-time, nights or evenings, or other schedules that fit their availability for work and the hotel's needs.

Hotel managers and many department supervisors may work regularly assigned schedules, but they also routinely work longer hours than scheduled, especially during peak travel times or when multiple events are scheduled. Also, they may be called in to work on short notice in the event of an emergency or to cover a position. Those who are self-employed, often owner-operators of small inns, camp sites, or RV parks, tend to work long hours and often live at the establishment or nearby.

Office and administrative support workers generally work scheduled hours in an office setting, meeting with guests, clients, and hotel staff. Their work can become hectic—processing orders and invoices, dealing with demanding guests, or servicing requests that require a quick turnaround. Job hazards typically are limited to muscle and eye strain common to working with computers and office equipment.

Computer specialists, information technology technicians, and audiovisual technicians who are employed mostly by larger convention hotels typically maintain standard hours servicing the property's Web sites and computer and communications networks. However, they often work long hours setting up and testing equipment for events that require their services. Work environment. Work in hotels and other accommodations can be demanding and hectic. Hotel staffs provide a variety of services to guests and must do so efficiently, courteously, and accurately. They must maintain a pleasant demeanor even during times of stress or when dealing with an impatient or irate guest. Alternately, work at slower times, such as the off-season or overnight periods, can seem slow and tiresome. Still, hotel workers must be ready to provide guests and visitors with gracious customer service at any hour.

Food preparation and food service workers in hotels must withstand the strain of working during busy periods and being on their feet for many hours. Kitchen workers lift heavy pots and kettles and work near hot ovens and grills. Job hazards include slips and falls, cuts, and burns, but injuries are seldom serious. Food service workers often carry heavy trays of food, dishes, and glassware. Many of these workers work part time, including evenings, weekends, and holidays.

Employment

Hotels and other accommodations provided 1.9 million wage and salary jobs in 2008. Employment is concentrated in cities and resort areas. Compared with establishments in other industries, hotels and other accommodations tend to be small. About 74 percent employed fewer than 20 workers and 54 percent employed fewer than 10. As a result, lodging establishments offer opportunities for those who are interested in owning or running their own business. Although establishments tend to be small, the majority of jobs are in larger hotels—those with more than 100 employees.

Hotels and other lodging places often provide first jobs to many new entrants to the labour force. In 2008, about 19 percent of the workers were younger than age 25, compared with about 13 percent across all industries.

Occupations in the Industry

The vast majority of workers in this industry—83 percent in 2008—were employed in service and office and administrative support occupations. Workers in these occupations usually learn their skills on the job. Postsecondary education is not required for most entry-level positions; however, college training may be helpful for advancement in some of the occupations. For those in administrative support—mainly hotel desk clerks—and service occupations, positive personality traits and a customer-service orientation may be more important than formal schooling. The most important traits for success in the hotels and other accommodations industry are good communication skills; the ability to get along with people in stressful situations; a neat, clean appearance; and a pleasant manner.

Service occupations. Service workers are by far the largest occupational group in the industry, accounting for 65 percent of the industry's employment. Most service jobs are in housekeeping occupations, including *maids and housekeeping cleaners* and *janitors and cleaners*, and in food preparation and serving jobs, including *waiters and waitresses, bartenders, fast food and counter workers*, and various other kitchen and dining room workers. The industry also employs many *baggage porters and bellhops, gaming services workers*, and *grounds maintenance workers*.

Workers in cleaning and housekeeping occupations ensure that the lodging facility is clean and in good condition for the comfort and safety of guests. *Maids and housekeeping cleaners* clean lobbies, halls, guestrooms, and bathrooms. They make sure that guests not only have clean rooms, but have all the necessary furnishings and supplies. They change sheets and towels, vacuum carpets, dust furniture, empty wastebaskets, and mop bathroom floors. In larger hotels, the housekeeping staff may include assistant housekeepers, floor supervisors, housekeepers, and executive housekeepers. *Janitors* help with the cleaning of the public areas of the facility, empty trash, and perform minor maintenance work.

Workers in the various *food preparation and serving* occupations deal with customers in the dining room or at a service counter. *Waiters and waitresses* take customers' orders, serve meals, and prepare checks. In smaller establishments, they often set tables, escort guests to their seats, accept payment, and clear tables. In larger restaurants, some of these tasks are assigned to other workers.

Bartenders fill beverage orders for customers seated at the bar or from waiters and waitresses who serve patrons at tables. *Dining room and cafeteria attendants* and *bartender helpers* assist waiters, waitresses, and bartenders by clearing, cleaning, and setting up tables, replenishing supplies at the bar, and keeping the serving areas stocked with linens, tableware, and other supplies. *Fast food and counter workers* take orders and serve food at fast-food counters and in coffee shops; they also may operate the cash register.

A variety of food preparation workers prepare food in the kitchen. Larger hotels employ *chefs and head cooks* who create menus, develop recipes, and oversee food preparation operations and personnel. *Food preparation and serving supervisors* direct workers and supervise specific tasks, such as overseeing banquet cooks or bartenders and servers at a private function, while the chef tends to other activities. *Restaurant cooks* specialize in the preparation of many different kinds of foods and menu items, generally cooking from scratch and typically only when ordered by diners. They may have titles such as salad chef, grill chef, or pastry chef. Individual chefs may oversee the day-to-day operations of different kitchens in a hotel, such as a full-service restaurant that specializes in fine-dining, a casual or counter-service establishment, or banquet operations. Chef positions generally are attained after years of experience and, sometimes, formal training, including apprenticeships. Larger establishments also employ *executive chefs* and *food and beverage directors* who plan menus, purchase food, and supervise kitchen personnel for all of the kitchens in the property. *Food preparation workers* shred lettuce for salads, cut up food for cooking, and perform simple cooking steps under the direction of the chef or head cook. Beginners may advance to more skilled food preparation jobs with experience or specialized culinary training.

Many full-service hotels employ a uniformed staff to assist arriving and departing guests. *Baggage porters and bellhops* carry bags and escort guests to their rooms. *Concierges* arrange special or personal services for guests. They may take messages, arrange for babysitting, make restaurant reservations, provide directions, arrange for or give advice on entertainment and local attractions, and monitor requests for housekeeping and maintenance. *Doorkeepers* help guests into and out of their cars, summon taxis, and carry baggage into the hotel lobby.

Hotels also employ the largest percentage of *gaming services* workers because a large share of gaming takes place in casino hotels. Some gaming services positions are associated with oversight and direction—supervision, surveillance, and investigation—while others involve working with the games or patrons themselves, by tending the slot machines, handling money, writing and running tickets, dealing cards, and performing related duties.

The industry also employs a large number of *recreation and fitness workers*. At resort hotels and at vacation and recreational camps, recreation workers organize and conduct recreation activities for guests and campers. *Camp counselors* lead and instruct children and teenagers in outdoor-oriented forms of recreation, such as swimming, hiking, horseback riding, and camping. In addition, counselors at vacation and resident camps also provide guidance and supervise daily living and general socialization. Other types of campgrounds may employ trail guides for activities such as hiking, hunting, and fishing.

Office and administrative support occupations. These positions accounted for 19 percent of the jobs in hotels and other accommodations in 2008. Hotel desk clerks, bookkeeping and accounting clerks, and switchboard operators ensure that the front office operates smoothly. *Hotel, motel, and resort desk clerks* process reservations and guests' registrations and checkouts, monitor arrivals and departures, handle complaints, and receive and forward mail. The duties of hotel desk clerks depend on the size of the facility. In smaller lodging places, one clerk or a manager may do everything. In larger hotels, a larger staff divides the duties among several types of clerks.

Management, business, and financial operations occupations. Hotels and other lodging places employ many different types of managers to direct and coordinate the activities of the front office, kitchen, dining room, and other departments, such as housekeeping, accounting, personnel, purchasing, publicity, sales, security, and maintenance.

Lodging managers, typically the general manager and assistant managers, make decisions that affect the general operations of the hotel, including setting room rates, establishing credit policy, and having ultimate responsibility for resolving problems. In smaller establishments, lodging managers also may perform many of the front-office administrative tasks. In the smallest establishments, the owners—sometimes a family team—do all the work necessary to operate the business. Other managers are responsible for different phases of hotel operations. For example, *food and beverage managers* oversee restaurants, lounges, and catering or banquet operations. *Rooms managers* look after reservations and occupancy levels to ensure proper room assignments and authorize discounts, special rates, or promotions. Large hotels, especially those with conference centres, use an executive committee structure to better facilitate departmental communications and coordinate activities. Other managers who may serve on a hotel's executive committee include *public relations* or *sales managers, human resource directors, executive housekeepers,* and *heads of hotel security.*

Other occupations. Hotels and other accommodations employ a variety of workers found in many other industries. *General maintenance and repair workers* fix leaky faucets, do some painting and carpentry, make sure that heating and air-conditioning equipment works properly, mow lawns, and exterminate pests. The industry also employs cashiers, accountants, personnel workers, and entertainers. As properties acquire and use more sophisticated computer systems, they employ more *computer specialists* to help maintain these systems as well as the hotel's Web site, and computer connections for guests. Also, many additional workers inside a hotel may work for other companies under contract to the hotel or may provide personal or retail services directly to hotel guests from space rented by the hotel. This group includes guards and security officers, barbers and cosmetologists, fitness trainers and aerobics instructors, valets, gardeners, and parking attendants.

Training and Advancement

Most large hotel properties employ persons in occupations that require a wide range of skills and experience. Most entry-level jobs require little or no previous training; basic tasks usually can be learned in a short time. Lodging managers and many department heads usually require some formal training, or years of hospitality industry experience, or both. All positions in this industry require employees to maintain a customer-service orientation. Almost all workers in the hotel and other accommodations industry undergo some on-the-job training provided under the supervision of an experienced employee or manager to acclimate new employees to any unique characteristics of the property or the local area. Hotel managers and owners recognize the importance of personal service and attention to guests, so they look for persons with positive personality traits and good communication skills when filling many guest services positions, such as desk clerk and host and hostess positions.

Many hotel managers place a greater emphasis on customer service skills while providing specialized training in other skill areas, such as computer technology and software. Vocational courses and apprenticeship programs in food preparation, catering, and hotel and restaurant management, offered through restaurant and lodging associations and trade unions, provide training opportunities. Programs range in length from a few months to several years.

Service workers. Most service workers need only a high school diploma or equivalent to get hired, but some can be hired with even less. Some entry-level jobs are filled by students looking for part-time or seasonal work. Most hotels, particularly the chain hotels, have some formal training sessions for new employees that may include video or online training. Advancement opportunities for service workers in the hotel industry vary widely.

Some workers, such as housekeepers and janitors, generally have few opportunities for advancement. In large properties, some may advance to supervisory positions. Advancement opportunities for chefs and cooks are better than those for most other service occupations. Cooks often advance to chef or to supervisory and management positions, such as executive chef, restaurant manager, or food service manager. Hotel desk clerks sometimes advance to supervisory or managerial front-office positions.

Promotional opportunities often are greatest for those who are willing to take on a new assignment in a different department. Advancement for those who excel at customer service and demonstrate a willingness to learn front-office jobs can serve as a steppingstone to jobs in public relations, advertising, sales, and management.

Management, business, and financial operations occupations. Many hotels fill first-level manager positions by promoting staff from within—particularly those with good communication skills, a solid educational background, tact, loyalty, and a capacity to endure hard work and long hours. People with these qualities still advance to manager jobs, but, more recently, lodging chains have primarily been hiring persons with 4-year college degrees in the liberal arts or other fields and starting them in assistant manager or management trainee positions.

Bachelor's and Master's degree programs in hotel, restaurant, and hospitality management provide the strongest background for a career as a hotel manager, with nearly 150 colleges and universities offering such programs. Graduates of these programs are highly sought by employers in this industry because of their familiarity with technical issues and their ability to learn related skills quickly. Eventually, they may advance to a top management position in a hotel or a corporate management position in a large chain operation.

Upper management positions, such as general manager, food service manager, or sales manager, generally require considerable formal training and job experience. Some department managers, executive housekeepers, and executive chefs, generally require some specialized training and extensive on-the-job experience. To advance to positions with more responsibilities, lodging managers frequently change employers or relocate within a chain to a property in another area.

Office and administrative support occupations. For office and administrative support workers, advancement opportunities in the hotel industry vary widely. These occupations offer excellent entry-level job prospects and can serve as a steppingstone to jobs in hospitality, public relations, advertising, sales, and management.

Outlook

The hotels and other accommodations industry is expected grow by 5 percent over the 2008-18 period. The industry employs large numbers of part-time and younger workers who typically do not stay in these jobs for very long. The need to replace these workers will create job opportunities in an array of occupations and localities. Employment change. Wage and salary employment in hotels and other accommodations is expected to increase by 5 percent between 2008 and 2018, compared with 11 percent growth projected for all industries combined. Travel and tourism typically grows during expansion periods in the economy, which results in a greater need for transient rooms. The hotel market is expected to see increases in the number of rooms, but the greatest number of rooms is expected to open in limited service hotels that do not provide food service. Many of these newer hotels are being built in the suburbs where a growing population is increasingly based and a foundation of business establishments is being developed.

Employment outlook varies somewhat by service class of hotel and occupation. Growth of full-service hotels, casino hotels, and the smaller luxury hotel market that specializes in personal service will cause employment of lodging managers to grow more slowly than the average.

The accelerating trend among chain-affiliated hotels to establish regional management and staffing teams among several properties and across service classes should provide current assistant managers or department managers with opportunities to demonstrate their readiness for advancement, but may also limit the prospects for new manager positions. Opportunities should be more limited for self-employed managers or owners of small lodging places, such as bed-and-breakfast inns, because of the competition from long-established chains as they move into untapped markets that were once friendly to the quainter properties. Job opportunities at outdoor recreation and RV parks should grow as RVs and driving vacations gain popularity in the United States. Also, gaming services and gaming manager occupations should grow as more casino hotels are built.

Employment of hotel, motel, and resort desk clerks is expected to grow faster than some other occupations in the industry in part because the growing numbers of limited-service hotels still require desk clerks. However, employment of dishwashers will decline within the industry—reflecting the increasing number of hotels and other accommodations that either do not offer full-service restaurants or contract them out to other food service establishments.

Job prospects. Although most of the hotels opening over the next decade will be limited-service hotels, most of the job openings will arise in full-service hotels, including convention, casino, and resort hotels, because they employ the most workers. Limited-service properties do not operate restaurants or lounges; therefore, these establishments offer a narrower range of employment opportunities. The streamlined organizational structure, however, offers a faster route to the general manager level for those more interested in running or owning their own hotel. Job opportunities will be concentrated in the largest hotel occupations, such as building cleaning workers and hotel, motel, and resort desk clerks. These workers are found in all types of hotels and accommodations, from the limited-service economy hotels to posh casino hotels. They also are important to the luxury hotel segment that emphasizes personal service. Some occupations in this industry have relatively high numbers of workers who leave their jobs and must be replaced. Many young people, and those looking only for seasonal or part-time work, take food service and administrative jobs that require little or no previous training. To attract and retain workers, the hotel and other accommodations industry is placing greater emphasis on training and retaining employees. Job opportunities in this industry should be good for first-time jobseekers, people with limited experience, and those interested in making a career in the lodging industry.

Earnings

Industry earnings. Earnings in hotels and other accommodations generally are much lower than the average for all industries. In 2008, average earnings for all nonsupervisory workers in this industry were $402 a week, compared with $608 a week for workers throughout private industry. Some workers in this industry earn the Federal minimum wage, which was $7.25 per hour as of July 2009. Some States have laws that establish a higher minimum wage.

Food and beverage service workers, as well as hosts and hostesses, maids and housekeeping cleaners, concierges, and baggage porters and bellhops, derive their earnings from a combination of hourly wages and customer tips. Waiters and waitresses often derive the majority of their earnings from tips, which vary greatly depending on menu prices and the volume of customers served. Many employers also provide free meals and furnish uniforms. Food service personnel may receive extra pay for working at banquets and on other special occasions.

The Chain Hotel Concept

Prior to examining the concept and the idea behind hotel chains and what exactly they are, it's important to have a peek at the interesting aspects of what a hotel is, what its mission supposed to be and how its operations are being carried out. With such an understanding, it's easier to see the value, purpose and the excitement behind hotel chains as opposed to a hotel.

As we all know, a hotel is regarded as an institution and or a service provider's establishment to offer paid lodging facilities to customers on limited time or short term basis. These facilities provided include, accommodation consisting of a room with a bed and other furniture (limited to the product bought), meals on room and board basis, attached bathrooms, air conditioning and climate control facilities, as well as, telephone facilities, cable television, internet connectivity and access plus the desirable mini bar. These are only some of the items included in a hotel room.

Apart from the facilities provided in the rooms of these hotels to the guests, there are many other additions and assortments available for a person staying in these hotels. They come in the form of, multi cuisine restaurants, swimming pools, fitness training centres, spas, conference and banquet halls and many others.

Another aspect that anyone comes across with hotels is the classification. As a result of the tourism industry worldwide expanding at a rapid rate during recent decades, for purposes of comparability and standards, rating systems have been introduced. This rating system takes the form of one to five stars classification where the most stars bearing hotels provide the best product and the lower star hotels provide a mediocre or average product to their guests. 'Some consider this disadvantageous to smaller hotels whose quality of accommodation could fall into one class but the lack of an item such as an elevator would prevent it from reaching a higher categorization. In some countries, there is an official body with standard criteria for classifying hotels, but in many others there is none. There have been attempts at unifying the classification system so that it becomes an internationally recognized and reliable standard but large differences exist in the quality of the accommodation and the food within one category of hotel, sometimes even in the same country.

With a proper understanding of the concept, idea and the purpose behind a hotel, it is helpful now to look at the term hotel chain. The term hotel chain traits back its origins to the 1920s where a great trend began which shifted individual ownership of hotels to corporate ownership as a result of increasing costs of building and operating hotels. As the corporate world took over the hotel business, they didn't believe in a single hotel at a single location but a chain of hotels at different locations with the same name but not necessarily with the same capacity and product range. Chain operations of 'hotels allows for efficient management through the use of mass purchasing, central reservations and billings, and extensive advertising and promotion campaigns. Today about 30 percent of all American hotels and motels are affiliated with chains or franchised groups.

Going International

In general, to be called a hotel, an establishment must have a minimum of six letting bedrooms, at least three of which must have attached (ensuite) private bathroom facilities. Although hotels are classified into 'Star' categories (1-Star to 5-Star), there is no standard method of assigning these ratings, and compliance with customary requirements is voluntary. A US hotel with a certain rating, for example, is may look very different from a European or Asian hotel with the same rating, and would provide a different level of amenities, range of facilities, and quality of service. Whereas hotel chains assure uniform standards throughout, non-chain hotels (even within the same country) may not agree on the same standards.

In Germany, for example, only about 30 percent of the hotels choose to comply with the provisions of the rules established by the German Hotels & Restaurants association. Although both WTO and ISO have been trying to persuade hotels to agree on some minimum requirements as worldwide norms, the entire membership of the Paris-based International Hotel & Restaurant (IH&RA) opposes any such move.

According to IH&RA, to harmonize hotel classification based on a single grading (which is uniform across national boundaries) would be an undesirable and impossible task.

As a rough guide: A 1-Star hotel provides a limited range of amenities and services, but adheres to a high standard of facility-wide cleanliness. A 2-Star hotel provides good accommodation and better equipped bedrooms, each with a telephone and attached private bathroom. A 3-Star hotel has more spacious rooms and adds high-class decorations and furnishings and colour TV. It also offers one or more bars or lounges. A 4-Star hotel is much more comfortable and larger, and provides excellent cuisine, room service, and other amenities.

A 5-Star hotel offers most luxurious premises, widest range of guest services, as well as swimming pool and sport and exercise facilities. The Official Hotel Guide (published in the US, and followed world wide) has its own classification scheme that ranks hotels in nine categories as (1) Moderate Tourist Class, (2) Tourist Class, (3) Superior Tourist Class, (4) Moderate First Class, (5) Limited Service First Class, (6) First Class, (7) Moderate Deluxe, (8) Deluxe, and (9) Superior Deluxe.

Marriott International

Marriott International, Inc. (NYSE: MAR) is a worldwide operator and franchisor of a broad portfolio of hotels and related lodging facilities. Founded by J. Willard Marriott, the company is now led by son J.W. (Bill) Marriott, Jr. Today, Marriott International has about 3,150 lodging properties located in the United States and 67 other countries and territories.

Marriott's operations are grouped into the following five business segments:

- Full-service lodging-65%
- Select-service lodging-11%
- Extended-stay lodging-5%
- Timeshare-15%
- Synthetic fuel-4% (primarily a tax shelter).

History

Marriott was founded by J. Willard Marriott 1927 when he and his wife opened a root beer stand in Washington D.C.. As a missionary in the sweltering, humid summers in Washington, Marriott was convinced that what the city needed was a such a place to get a cool drink. They later expanded their enterprises into a chain of restaurants and hotels.

The Key Bridge Marriott in Arlington, Virginia is Marriott International's longest operating hotel, and celebrated its 50th anniversary in 2009. Their son and current Chairman and Chief Executve Officer, J.W. (Bill) Marriott, Jr. has led the company to spectacular worldwide growth. Today, Marriott International has about 3,150 lodging properties located in the United States and 67 other countries and territories.

Marriott International was formed in 1992 when Marriott Corporation split into two companies, Marriott International and Host Marriott Corporation.

In 2002 Marriott International began a major restructuring by spinning off many Senior Living Services Communities (which is now part of Sunrise Senior Living) and Marriott Distribution Services, so that it could focus on hotel ownership and management. The changes were completed in 2003.

In April 1995, Marriott International acquired a 49% interest in the Ritz-Carlton Hotel Company LLC. Marriott International believed that it could increase sales and profit margins at the Ritz, a troubled chain with a significant number of properties either losing money or barely breaking even. The cost of Marriott's initial investment was estimated to be about $200 million in cash and assumed debt. The next year, Marriott spent $331 million to take over the Ritz-Carlton Atlanta and buy a majority interest in two properties owned by William Johnson, a real estate developer who had purchased the Boston Ritz Carlton in 1983 and expanded his Ritz holdings over the next twenty years.

The Ritz began expansion into the lucrative timeshare market among other new initiatives made financially possible by the deep pockets of Marriott, which also lent its own in-house expertise in certain areas. There were other benefits for Ritz-Carlton flowing from its relationship with Marriott, such as being able to take advantage of the parent company's reservation system and buying power. The partnership was solidified in 1998 when Marriott boosted its interest in Ritz-Carlton to 99 percent. By 1999 revenues from the 35 hotels it operated around the world totaled about $1.4 billion. Marriott International owned Ramada International Hotels & Resorts until its sale on September 15, 2004 to Cendant. It is the first hotel chain to serve food that is completely free of trans fats at all of its North American properties. In 2005, Marriott International and Marriott Vacation Club International comprised two of the 53 entities that contributed the maximum of $250,000 to the second inauguration of President George W. Bush.

On July 19, 2006, Marriott announced that all lodging buildings they operate in the United States and Canada would become non-smoking beginning September 2006. "The new policy includes all guest rooms, restaurants, lounges, meeting rooms, public space and employee work areas."

Terrorist Attacks

Several Marriott hotels around the world have been the target of bombings.

- 2001 Marriott world trade centre 9/11 atacks
- 2003 Marriott Hotel bombing
- 2008 Islamabad Marriott bombing
- 2009 Jakarta bombings.

Great America Parks

Marriott also developed three and ultimately opened two theme parks entitled Marriott's Great America from 1976 until 1984. The parks were located in Gurnee, Illinois, Santa Clara, California and a proposed but never-built location in the Washington, DC area, and were themed celebrating American history. The American-themed areas under Marriott's tenure of ownership included "Carousel Plaza" (the first section beyond the main gates); small-town-themed "Hometown Square"; "The Great Midwest Livestock Exposition At County Fair" with a Turn of the Century rural-fair theme; "Yankee Harbor", inspired by a 19th century New England port; "Yukon Territory," resembling a Canadian/Alaskan logging camp; and the French Quarter-modeled "Orleans Place". At opening, both parks were laid out nearly identically. In 1984, Marriott disposed of its theme park division; both parks were sold and today are associated with national theme park chains.

The Gurnee location was sold to Six Flags Theme Parks where it operates today as Six Flags Great America. The Santa Clara location was sold to the City of Santa Clara, who retained the underlying property and sold the park to Kings

Entertainment Company, renamed Paramount Parks in 1993. From 1993 to 2006, the Santa Clara location was known as Paramount's Great America. In 2006, Paramount Parks was acquired by Cedar Fair Entertainment Company; the Santa Clara park operates today as California's Great America. In the years after their sale, the layouts of the parks have diverged substantially.

Marriott Brands

Full Service Lodging

- Marriott Hotels & Resorts
- JW Marriott Hotels & Resorts
- Renaissance Hotels & Resorts
- Marriott Conference Centres
- Ritz-Carlton Hotels & Resorts
- BVLGARI Hotels & Resorts
- Edition Hotels & Resorts
- Autograph Collection Hotels & Resots.

Select Service Lodging

- Courtyard by Marriott
- Fairfield Inn by Marriott
- SpringHill Suites by Marriott.

Extended Stay Lodging

- Residence Inn by Marriott
- TownePlace Suites by Marriott
- Marriott ExecuStay
- Marriott Executive Apartments.

Timeshare

- Marriott Vacation Club International (MVCI)
- Marriott Grand Residence Club
- The Ritz-Carlton Club
- The Ritz-Carlton Destination Club.

Marriott Rewards

Marriott International also offers Marriott Rewards, a loyalty ("rewards") program that allows members to earn points or airline miles for their stays at participating Marriott brand hotels, in addition to other membership benefits.

20 Largest Hotels in the World

Las Vegas is famous for many items! Besides gambling, wedding, conventions, destination resorts, Las Vegas is famous for the size of the hotels. Below we have listed the 20 largest hotels in the world, 15 of the 20 are located within a two-mile radius within Las Vegas. Also, 21 of the top 28 hotels are located within the same two-mile radius.

Ranked number one, the First World Hotel has topped the list. It is not located in Las Vegas, but in Malaysia. Pictured on the right, this multicolor structure is a real eye catcher.

The MGM Grand is also pictured to the right, it reigned as the number one largest hotel for years, now taking the number two seat.

Size	*Hotel*	*Location*	*Rooms*
1.	First World Hotel	Malaysia	6,118
2.	MGM Grand	Las Vegas	5,690
3.	Luxor	Las Vegas	4,408
4.	Mandalay Bay (Inc. The Hotel)		
	3,223 & 1118	Las Vegas	4,341
5.	The Venetian	Las Vegas	4,027
6.	Excalibur	Las Vegas	4,008
7.	Bellagio	Las Vegas	3,993
8.	Circus Circus	Las Vegas	3,774
9.	Planet Hollywood	Las Vegas	3,697
10.	Shinagawa Prince Hotel Tokyo	Tokyo	3,680
11.	Ambassador City Jomtien	Thailand	3,610
12.	Flamingo Las Vegas	Las Vegas	3,565
13.	Palazzo	Las Vegas	3,443

14.	Hilton Hawaiian Village	Honolulu	3,386
15.	Caesar's Palace	Las Vegas	3,349
16.	Mirage	Las Vegas	3,044
17.	Monte Carlo	Las Vegas	3,002
18.	The Venetian Macao	Macau	3,000
19.	Las Vegas Hilton	Las Vegas	2,956
20.	Paris Las Vegas	Las Vegas	2,916
Honorable Mention			
21.	Treasure Island	Las Vegas	2,895
22.	Gaylord Opryland	Nashville	2,883
23.	Disney's Pop Century	Orlando	2,880
24.	Bally's	Las Vegas	2,814
25.	Wynn Las Vegas	Las Vegas	2,716
26.	Imperial Palace	Las Vegas	2,635
27.	Harrah's Las Vegas	Las Vegas	2,576
28.	Stratosphere	Las Vegas	2,444

Largest Hotel

The largest hotel in the world is the First World Hotel in Genting Highlands, Malaysia. This biggest hotel took the title from the MGM Grand Las Vegas in Las Vegas, Nevada. The First World Hotel hass 6,118 rooms with prices starting as low as $60.00 USD/night.

IHG (InterContinental Hotels Group)

Is the worlds largest and most global hotel chain. IHG's brands include: InterContinental Hotels, Crowne Plaza, Hotel Indigo, Holiday Inn, Holiday Inn Express, Staybridge Suites, and Candlewood Suites.

As of March 2009 they had over 4,200 hotels in their portfolio representing over 621,000 Rooms.

Best Western uses the tag line "The Worlds Largest Hotel Chain"; however with a portfolio of just under 4,000 hotels representing 303,000 rooms. They come in number 7 behind IHG, Wyndham, Marriott, Hilton, Accor, and Choice Hotels.

Revenue Management Techniques in Hospitality Industry – A comparison with Reference to Star and Economy Hotels

The hospitality industry is part of a larger enterprise known as the travel and tourism industry. It is one of the oldest industries in the world. In early days, traders, explorers, missionaries and pilgrims needed a break in their journeys requiring food, shelter and rest.

People opened their homes and kitchens to these weary travellers, and an industry was born. Although accommodation today is varied and their services have changed and expanded over the ages, one thing about the hospitality industry has remained the same, guests are always welcome! From a friendly greeting at the door, room service, breakfast, to a host of facilities' the hospitality industry offers travellers a home away from home.

Hospitality is defined as "the friendly reception and treatment of strangers". For most people, hospitality means entertaining guests with courtesy and warmth. Hospitality is also an industry made up of businesses that provide lodging, food and other services to travellers. The main components of this industry are hotels, motels, inns, resorts and Restaurants.

In a broad sense, the hospitality industry might refer to any group engaged in tourism, entertainment, transportation or lodging including cruise lines, airlines, railways, car rental companies and tour operators.

However the two main segments are the lodging industry also called the hotel industry, and the food and beverage industry, also called the restaurant industry. The lodging industry is made up of businesses providing temporary housing, and such a business is called a lodging establishment and the people who stay in it are called guests or clients.

What is Revenue Management?

Revenue Management is a technique to optimize the revenue earned from a fixed, perishable resource. The challenge is to sell the right resources to the right customer at the right time. Revenue Management implements the basic principles of supply and demand economics in a tactical way to generate incremental revenues. There are three essential conditions for revenue management to be applicable:

- That there is a fixed amount of resources available for sale.
- That the resources sold are perishable. This means that there is a time limit to selling the resources, after which they cease to be of value.
- That different customers are willing to pay a different price for using the same amount of resources.

Revenue Management is of especially high relevance in cases where the constant costs are relatively high compared to the variable costs. The less variable costs there are, the more the additional revenue earned will contribute to the overall profit.

To illustate this, we can take the example of the luxury hotel which charges different prices for different customers. In India it is generally practiced in star hotels to maximise the revenues. The customer who is price sensitive and time conscious generally pays lesser tariffs than a customer who is willing to pay more and books the room one or two days before the stay.

Revenue Management in other words tries to maximise revenues by managing the tradeoff between a low occupancy and higher room rate senario (business customers) versus a high occupancy and lower room rate (vacation customers).

Demand forecasting: Pricing and demand are inter-related and need to be coordinated. In the hospitality industry, demand for a room is cyclic in nature and follows a trend. Revenue management models help pinpoint demand by minimising uncertainity and producing the best possible forecast.

Allocation: the revenue management also puts light on the allocation of inventory (hotel rooms) among different segments. For example, if a hotel has two price categories of rooms, say Rs.4500 and Rs. 6000.

Since the pricing is different for the two rooms, these rooms are each targeted at a different customer set. Based on the historical preference pattern of customers in each segment, it would be possible to estimate the number of customers who would be willing to pabuy these rooms at a given price with a reasonable variance. For example, an average 50 customers may be willing to pay Rs. 6000 for some rooms, but it could also mean that the actual number of customers who turn up for Rs. 6000 could be 60 or even 40 with some probability, or 80 or 30 with a lesser probability.

Overbooking: Overbooking is a practice of intentionally selling more rooms than available in order to offset the effect of cancellations. For example, suppose in the hotel industry, there are 180 rooms available, there is no certainity that all the rooms would be booed at a point of time. In the same way, during the season, there is a possibility of over booking.

Therefore if the booking is done 181 customers instead of 180, the hotel may end up with only 173 or less than 180 customers, since the probability of exactly 181 customers turning up is low, the revenue from that aditional customer generally compensates more than the expected cost.

Classification of Hotels

Hotels are classified into five main types:

- Economy/limited-service hotels
- Mid-market hotels
- All-suite hotels
- First class or executive hotels
- Luxury or deluxe hotels.

For the purpose of our research, Economy and Executive hotels are selected.

Normally hotels have four rate categories: (1) Rack rates, (2) Group and tour rates, (3) Special and promotional rates and (4) package rates.

(1) Rack rates are normal room rates. It is based on the category of the room, type of bedding and occupancy. Unless specified, guests are quoted the rack rates and are charged for the same.

(2) Group and Tour rates are a discounted room rate for an organisation, which has blocked a large number of

rooms. Most hotels have group rates that are lower than the rack rates. This rate is generally extended to a trade association or fraternal organisation that has scheduled a meeting, seminar or conference at the hotel. Discounts are also offered to a tour operator, in return for a commitment to purchase a minimum number of rooms over a given period of time.

(3) Special and promotional rates are offered to corporate travellers, traveling sales representatives, military personnel, airlines staff or other regular clients. Some times special rates are also offered along with an advertising campaign or to promote the hotel during lean periods.

(4) Package rates are offered to the public along with other services such as banquet or a ball, or recreational facilities or a special event. Such a package normally includes accommodation, tickets to the concerned event and transportation from hotel to the venue and back. Other popular packages offered by hotels are honeymoon, weekend, Christmas, New Year or any other sports activity. The package rate is normally lower than the combined component or rack rate.

A Case Study on Bentleys Hotel (Economy) and Hotel Godwin Hotel Bentleys, Colaba (Economy Hotel)

Bentley's is one of Mumbai's (formerly known as Bombay, India) best budget tourist hotels. It is highly rated in most Tourist/Traveller's Guides, including The Lonely Planet.

Ideally situated in South Mumbai, it is in the heart of the downtown area, close to the business, entertainment and shopping areas. The hotel has a clean, quiet, comfortable and homely atmosphere.

Victorian Ambiance

The hotel gets 95% of its customers as foreign tourists. The occupancy rate in this hostel is 110%. The rooms are occupied for the 365 days in this year. Demand is more than. Supply in this hotel. The customers are not provided with any food in this hotel. The hotel does not practice differential pricing for its customers. It charges single price for all of its customers irrespective of different nationality. Tourists generally would like to stay in this hotel for the wonderful service provided by the hotel. Generally the hotel gets repeated customers and the customer loyalty is very good over here. Marketing Strategies adopted by the hotel to attract more tourists:

- Reservation is done directly without the help of middleman like travel agents.
- Hotel provides prompt service to the enquiries of the customers mails. Usually the queries are answered within an hour.
- The services provided by the housekeepers are also very good. They are excellent in communication and they meet the customer demand promptly.
- Generally in this hotel, 80% of the customers are repeated which means there is customer loyalty to the maximum extent.
- Usually the hotels provide one room to one customer in a day. But Bentleys uses its perishable capacity 3 times a day for the purpose of maximizing the revenue.

Bibliography

Burkart, A and Medlik, S: *Management of Tourism,* The, London, Heinemann, 1975.

Chambers, Erve: *Native Tours: The Anthropology of Travel and Tourism,* Prospect Heights, Waveland Press, 2000.

Cukier, J. : *Tourism Employment in Bali: Trends and Implications,* London: Thompson, 1996.

Dann, Graham M S: *Language of Tourism,* The, Wallingford, CAB International, 1996.

Edensor, Tim: *Tourists at the Taj,* London, Retailed, 1998.

Edgell, David L: *International Tourism Policy, New York,* Van Nostrand and Reinhold, 1990.

Gamble, P. R: *The Educational challenge for Hospitality and Tourism Studies,* Tourism Management, 13, 1992.

Ghimire, Krishna: *The Native Tourist*: Mass Tourism within Developing Regions, London, Earthscan, 2001.

Ireland, Lewis: *Quality Management for Projects and Programs,* Upper Darby, PMI, 1991.

Judy A: *Tourism: Management of Facilities,* London, Pitman: M & E, 1993.

Kharbanda, O. and E. Stallworthy: *Waste Management Towards a Sustainable Society,* Auburn House, New York, 1990.

Kotler, Philip: *Marketing for Hospitality and Tourism*: New Jersey, Prentice-Hall, 1998.

Larkham, P J: *Building a New Heritage*: *Tourism, Culture & Identity in the New Europe,* London, Routledge,1994.

Lock, Dennis: *Project Management,* New York, Wiley, 1996.

Morrell, J. : *Employment in Tourism,* London: British Tourist Authority, 1985.

Nancy N.: *Choosing a Career in Hotels, Motels, and Resorts,* New York, Rosen Pub. Group, 1997.

Norman G.: *Hotel, Restaurant, and Travel Law: A Preventive Approach,* Albany, Delmar Publishers, 1993.

Pearce, Douglas: *Tourism Today: A Geographical Analysis,* Harlow, Longman, 1995.

Pearce, P L: *Social Psychology Of Tourist Behaviour,* The, Oxford, Pergamon, 1982.

Peters, M: *International Tourism,* London, Hutchinson, 1969.

Rocco, M.: *An Introduction to Hospitality Today,* Orlando, Educational Institute, 1998.

Rogers, H Anthea and Slinn, Judy A: *Tourism: Management of Facilities,* London, Pitman: M & E, 1993.

Rosemary, E.: *Managing Employee Relations in the Hotel and Catering Industry,* London, Cassell, 1995.

Rosenzweig, J. E.: *Organisation and Management,* New York, McGraw Hill International, 1963.

Schwaninger, M: *Trends in Leisure and Tourism for 2000 - 2010,* Prentice Hall, 1989.

Scottish Tourist Board: *Visitor Attractions: A Development Guide,* Edinburgh, Scottish Tourist Board, 1991.

Sharma Sunil : *Planning and Development of Tourism and Hospitality,* Rajat Pub, Delhi, 2007.

Smith, G. : *International Tourism and Hospitality Careers through Education and Training,* CHRIE Annual Conference, Washington DC, 1996.

Swarbrooke, J.: *Marketing Tourism, Hospitality and Leisure in Europe,* London, International Thomson Business Press, 1996.

Thomas, F.: *Introduction to Management in the Hospitality Industry,* New York, Wiley, 1995.

Timothy R.: *Cases in Hospitality Management: A Critical Incident Approach,* New York, Wiley, 1995.

Veal, A: *Leisure and Tourism*: Policy and Planning, Wallingford, CABI, 2001.

Wahab, S A: *Tourism Management,* Tourism International Press, 1975.

Index

❑❑❑